1992

Developing Resiliency
Through Children's Literature

Developing Resiliency Through Children's Literature

A Guide for Teachers and Librarians, K–8

by

Nancy L. Cecil

and

Patricia L. Roberts

McFarland & Company, Inc., Publishers
Jefferson, North Carolina, and London

British Library Cataloguing-in-Publication data are available

Library of Congress Cataloguing-in-Publication Data

Cecil, Nancy Lee.
    Developing resiliency through children's literature : a guide for
teachers and librarians, K–8 / by Nancy L. Cecil and Patricia
Roberts.
        p.   cm.
    Includes bibliographical references and index.
    ISBN 0-89950-707-7 (sewn softcover : 50# alk. paper) ∞
    1. Children's literature—Study and teaching.   2. Resilience
(Personality trait)—Study and teaching.   3. Children—Conduct of
life—Study and teaching.   4. Problem solving—Study and teaching.
I. Roberts, Patricia, 1936–   .   II. Title.
PN1008.8.C43   1992
809'.89282—dc20   91-51001
                                                                    CIP

Manufactured in the United States of America

McFarland & Company, Inc., Publishers
  Box 611, Jefferson, North Carolina 28640

Dedicated to
Anne Cunningham and Karen Mercante
and all the other teachers out there
who are interested in fostering resiliency.

Contents

Introduction

> *When I write a story for children it's not to make moral judgments, though the story may portray the observed human truth that behavior has consequences. I'm seeking to tell a story from my heart . . . with the hope that it will speak to another heart.* — Katherine Paterson, "Heart in Hiding," from *Worlds of Childhood,* edited by William Zinsser (Houghton Mifflin, 1990).

Researchers are seemingly obsessed with the subject of failure. "We pay too much attention to failure and not enough to success," observes V. Patricia Beyer, director of the Center for Effective Teaching at California State University, Los Angeles. Every conceivable area in which children could possibly fail—from failure at reading and other academic pursuits to failure at making satisfactory social and emotional adjustments—has been explored through a constellation of studies in the fields of education, sociology, and psychology. It might be better to focus attention on the "succeeders" to try to discover why they are succeeding; if those factors leading to success could be identified, perhaps that success could be made accessible to all children. For even in the most sordid of environments, some children succeed. Beset with distressing physical or intellectual handicaps, or under conditions of seemingly intolerable abuse, some children face the problems squarely and appear to become stable and healthy adults. Such children exhibit what current researchers have labeled "resilience," or the ability to recover from or adapt to misfortune or continual life stress (Werner, 1984).

A few researchers have started to look at these life survivors and have asked, "What is right (or resilient) about these children?" and, by implication for this book's focus, "Where are those traits of resiliency found in children's literature?"

Werner (1987) completed a longitudinal study of the development of 700 Hawaiian children from birth to age 30 and discovered that, in spite of extreme poverty, emotional and physical abuse, poor social conditions, alcoholic parents, and a host of other negative factors that would be expected to put the group at risk, one of every four studied thrived and became a stable and contributing member of society. Werner correlated the following abilities with the resilient quarter:

- gaining people's attention in a positive way;
- planning ahead and solving problems;
- developing a talent or hobby;
- having a feeling of autonomy;
- persisting in the face of failure;
- maintaining a positive vision of life;
- relating to a caring "other" person;
- developing a sense of humor;
- developing a sense of control over one's life.

One of these characteristics, persistence in the face of failure, surfaces again as a resilient factor in another study by Cecil (1989) who looked at a population of 18 academically successful adults who had once been severely disabled readers. All of the respondents in the study attributed their eventual success to their own perseverance and strong will to succeed. A significant number also cited the sincere praise and encouragement of caring adults as salient factors in their ability to overcome their reading difficulties.

Encouragement of caring adults was central in the findings of Gandara (1982) who studied 17 Mexican American women between the ages of 28 and 40 who came from lower socioeconomic backgrounds, yet succeeded in completing J.D., M.D., and Ph. D. degrees. Among the factors the researcher found to be most important for these women's academic success were the strong models their mothers provided, the emotional support of their families, and the fact that they had attended highly integrated high schools.

Rutter's study (1984) showed similar findings. Rutter followed into adult life 90 women who spent much of their childhood in institutions for a variety of reasons; some had been abandoned, while others had been taken from their parents because of abuse. Although as a group they fared not as well in adult life as a comparison group of women from the general population, approximately one-third became ordinary, well-functioning adults. Rutter noted that the survivors had good relationships with teachers, positive experiences at school (most reported nonacademic experiences such as success in sports or music), and social success.

For teachers, the research findings on resilient children have profound practical classroom implications. While once a teacher might have been able to expect a relatively homogeneous classroom filled with average middle-class children, he can now look forward to the challenge of a heterogeneous group of children with a diverse set of individual backgrounds. Each child will have a unique history and many will have sad stories to tell. If children's literature may affect resiliency of youngsters, teachers should determine what resilient models youngsters could be seeing and reading about. If pieces of quality literature, such as the Caldecott and Newbery books, are instructive vehicles, teachers should decide which contain resilient characters can be used to help foster resiliency.

The positive characteristics correlated with resilient children mentioned previously can be actively developed. Such traits need to be reinforced, when they are manifested, by a strong teacher-model who demonstrates her own conviction that life is good and worthwhile. Such a teacher can also foster so-called resilient behavior by introducing children to literature that has at its core main characters who are themselves in the process of overcoming adversity. Follow-up discussions of the literature can show children that there is more than one solution to problems and that they, like the literary characters, can become controllers of their own fate.

Retelling the same stories through dramatic play can thrust vulnerable, at-risk children into the roles of survivors and allow them, for a while, to be transformed into fictional characters that embody resilient behavior that they, too, will need to succeed.

One example from literature that could be selected is Jean Craighead George's *Julie of the Wolves*. This book features a strong female preadolescent who, lost in Antarctica without her parents, learns how to survive physically and emotionally by relying on only herself and by befriending some native wolves. A follow-up discussion to this book would underscore the range of alernatives open to Julie—some positive and others negative. A highly vulnerable, nonresilient child would likely perceive Julie's situation as terribly dreadful and stressful, whereas the same circumstance would probably be viewed more optimistically by the more stress-resilient child who could more easily relate to Julie's courage and adaptability. The teacher's role, then, would be to guide the less resilient children into seeing the situation in a more positive and challenging light. He would help the children brainstorm some possible paths Julie could have chosen when she found herself in a seemingly hopeless situation. She could, for example, have sat and frantically waited to be rescued, as some children may suggest. The teacher could then ask the children to speculate about the effect of such passivity. Finally, having those same children roleplay a strong character like Julie would allow them to "try on" resilient, invincible behavior, and perhaps over time, grow in their *own* resiliency.

Using children's literature to teach coping skills is not new. Bibliotherapy, the use of books to help children understand and cope with the problems of everyday life, is a practice dating back to the time of Aristotle, when the libraries of Ancient Greece carried inscriptions such as "The Medicine Chest for the Soul." There is little doubt that by empathizing with believable book characters, children may be able to understand themselves and others better. When children read about a character whose persistence in the face of failure causes her to succeed, as Julie did, they can reach into themselves to make adjustments in their own personalities. Obviously, the vicarious experiences of reading and dramatic play are less threatening to one's ego than the reality of everyday life. Moreover, they are reversible. The readers can reflect for weeks upon the action taken by main characters and continue to come up with a myriad of actions that might also have been taken. And in fiction, as opposed to real life, no one sits in judgment of the readers' decisions.

The use of books to help prevent the development of a problem (Thomas, 1967) or to help children solve, or at least better understand, their problems by interacting with literature has been documented through findings of studies related to the use of books and their effect on children (Zaccaria and Moses, 1968). Related to working with challenging populations in the schools, children's literature has affected coping behavior (Cianciolo, 1965), and has been useful with retarded readers (Kantrowitz, 1967), with the emotionally disturbed (Koon, 1970), and as an aid in preventing dropouts (Faust, 1969). Literature for children also has been a positive influence on the academic achievement of the educable mentally retarded (Limper, 1970), junior high underachievers (Waite, 1965), readers with emotional blocks (Bruell, 1966), and inner-city children (Brocki, 1969). Outside the schools, it has affected inmate students (Whipple, 1968), and adolescent girls in a correctional agency (Limper, 1970). Indeed, adolescents themselves have reported that they do respond positively to identification through literature (Koon, 1970).

Further, books have been aids in the general development of children's values, attitudes, and codes of conduct (Cooper, 1969; Bissett, 1969; Taba, 1950, 1955; Strickland, 1961; and Squire, 1968) as well as assisting in identification (Russell, 1949). Some books have been an influence on the child's mind and course of action and a help for a child needing to overcome conflicts. Related to overcoming conflicts, fiction has been a treatment to alter attitudes (Beardsley, 1980), to deal with school anxieties (Marrelli, 1965), and to solve personal problems (Appleberry, 1969). Other books have been a factor in changing attitudes toward minority groups, in diminishing fears, in helping students deal with death, and in developing moral maturity (Berstein, 1978).

Recent studies of resilient children support a conclusion that some children can and do develop healthy and happy personalities and can succeed academically, even under the most austere circumstances, with the support of caring adults, if they develop certain adaptive behaviors. A teacher who believes and models the notion that we are the masters of our own fate can encourage children to develop such resilient behavior. Additionally, carefully chosen children's literature, which has as its core those traits associated with overcoming adversity, can provide fictional dilemmas that allow children to exercise the problem-solving skills necessary for facing frustrating and difficult situations in real life. With a guided discussion of a range of alternative solutions, children can begin to see that they have the capacity to control their own lives. Also, by donning the role of fictitious survivors in children's literature through dramatic play, children further increase their repertoire of adaptive skills.

In the following sections, teachers will find some helpful tools that will allow them to use children's literature as a vehicle for fostering resilience. The first two sections contain short summaries of carefully selected children's books, each of which features main characters who are survivors. These characters have surmounted various trials while displaying one or a combination of traits—e.g., the ability to plan ahead and or solve problems—that have been found to be correlated with children who survive in real life. These summaries each identify the particular resiliency traits that are highlighted and also indicate the grade level(s) for which the book would be most appropriate. The book summaries are divided into two subsections: books suitable for young students (these are the picture story books, which are generally used with primary students; some, however, contain more sophisticated concepts and can be used with older children, as noted), and books suitable for older students (the multi-chaptered, nonpicture books that are generally targeted to intermediate grade children and often provide a more in-depth study of the character and her or his ordeal).

The two sections are then further subdivided by their literary genre. Each subsection includes examples of contemporary fiction (realistic and fanciful), folk literature, historical fiction or biography. Each book is followed by an identified trait and by a target activity that can be used to help children internalize the resiliency trait(s).

The final section in the book provides a wealth of ideas, activities, and discussion questions for a selected few of the children's literature titles summarized in the previous sections. Skilled teachers may use these examples of mini-units as models for adapting the book summaries to their classrooms as they see fit. Each mini-unit example contains bibliographical information, a brief summary, new vocabulary to be introduced, a list of needed materials, motivational activities, the purposes for reading or listening, retelling activities, discussion questions, extended activities, and interdisciplinary ideas.

This book is intended to be a starting point for caring teachers who find themselves challenged by the growing number of children living with a variety of traumas that cause them to be desperately in need of coping skills. While even the most committed teachers cannot change the home environments of all the children in their charge, they can provide positive role models. Furthermore, they can enhance the language curricula by molding quality children's literature into carefully crafted lessons that guide all children toward developing the coping skills necessary in today's world. This book is a step toward that end.

Notes

Appleberry, M. H. (1969). "A Study of the Effect of Bibliotherapy on Third Grade Children Using a Master List of Titles from Children's Literature." University of Houston. University microfilm 69-21, 746.

Beardsley, D. A. (1979). "The Effects of Using Fiction in Bibliotherapy to Alter Attitudes of Regular Third Grade Students Toward Their Handicapped Peers." Unpublished Ph. D. dissertation, University of Missouri–Columbia. University microfilm 80-07, 128.

Berstein, J. E. (1978). "Helping Young Children Cope with Separation: A Bibiliotherapeutic Approach." Paper presented at the third annual meeting of the Parents and Reading Conference, New York, New York, February, ED 170 695.

Bisset, D. J. (1969). "The Usefulness of Children's Books in the Reading Program." Paper presented at the International Reading Association, April 30–May 3, Kansas City, Missouri.

Bodart, J. (1980). "Bibliotherapy: The Right Book for the Right Person at the Right Time—and More." *Top of the News* (36), 183–88.

Brocki, A. C. (1969). "New Literature for Inner-City Students." *English Journal* (58), 1151–61

Bruell, E. (1966). "How to Block the Reading Blocks? Read." *Peabody Journal of Education* (44), 114–17.

Cecil, N. L. (1989). *We Have Overcome.* Dubuque, Iowa: Kendall/Hunt.

Cianciolo, P. J. (1965). "Children's Literature Can Affect Coping Behavior." *Personnel and Guidance Journal* (43), 897–903.

Cooper, B. (1969). "Using Children's Literature in the Elementary School." *Georgia English Counselor.* (17), 1–3.

Cornett, C. E., and C. R. Cornett (1980). "Bibliotherapy: The Right Book at the Right Time." Fastback 151. Bloomington, Ind.: Phi Delta Kappa Educational Foundation. ED 192 380.

Faust, H. R. (1969). "Books as an Aid in Preventing Dropouts." *Elementary English* (46), 191–98.

Gandara, P. (1982). "Passing Through the Eye of the Needle: High- Achieving Chicanos." *Hispanic Journal of Behavioral Sciences* (4), 169–180.

Garmezy, N., and A. Tellgren (1984). "Studies of Stress-Resistant Children: Methods, Variables and Preliminary Findings." In *Advances in Applied Developmental Psychological,* edited by F. Morrison, C. Lord, and D. Keating. New York: Academic Press.

Kantrowitz, V. (1967). "Bibliotherapy with Retarded Readers." *Journal of Reading* (11), 205–12.

Koon, J. F. (1970). "Cues for Teaching the Emotionally Disturbed: Turn On, Tune In, Drop Out." *The Clearing House*, (44), 497–500.

Limper, H. L., et al. (1970). "Library Services to Exceptional Children." *Top of the News* (26), 193–204.

Nigen, G. A. (1979). "Bibliotherapy for the Atypical Reader." *Wisconsin State Reading Journal*, (24), 12–16.

Russell, D. H. (1949). "Identification Through Literature." *Childhood Education* (25), 397–401.

Rutter, M. (1984). "Resilient Children." *Psychology Today*, (39), 57–65.

Schultheis, M., and R. Pavlik (1977). "Classroom Teachers' Manual for Bibliotherapy." Fort Wayne, Ind.: Benet Learning Center. ED 163 493.

Squire, J. R. (1968). *Response to Literature.* Champaign: National Council of Teachers of English.

Strickland, R. (1961). "What Thou Lovest Well Remains." *Elementary English* (38), 63–73.

Taba, H. (1950). *With Focus on Human Relations.* Washington, D. C.: American Council on Education, 1950.

————. (1955). *With Perspective on Human Relations: A Study of Peer Group Dynamics in an Eighth Grade.* Washington, D. C.: American Council of Education.

Thomas, V. (1967). "The Power of the Book." *The English Teacher* (12), 21–24.

Waite, D. D. (1965). "Therapy for Reading Ills." *Pennsylvania School Journal*, (114), 64–65.

Werner, E. E. (1984). "Resilient Children." *Young Children*, (40), 68–72.

————. (1987). "Vulnerability and Resiliency: A Longitudinal Study of Asian Americans from Birth to Age 30." Invited address at the ninth biennial meeting of the International Society of the Study of Behavioral Development, Tokyo, Japan, July.

Whipple, C. M. (1968). "The Effect of Short-term Classroom Bibliotherapy on the Personality and Academic Achievement of Reformatory Inmate Students." Ed. D. dissertation, University of Oklahoma.

Zaccaria, J. S. and H. A. Moses (1968). *Facilitating Human Development Through Reading: The Use of Bibliotherapy in Teaching and Counseling.* Champaign: Stipes.

I. Literature for Grades K–3

Contemporary Fiction

Realistic Fiction

1. **Alexander, Sally Hobart.** *Mom Can't See Me.* **Photographs by George Ancona. New York: Macmillan, 1990.**

   Traits: Perseverance; persistence; problem-solving.

   Blind author Alexander gives readers a picture of her life which is told from the view of her nine-year-old daughter. This shows how both mother and daughter have learned to cope with living with a disability. Alexander helps with cooking, cleaning, taking the children to lessons, and helping at school. She includes some of the frustrations of blindness (fear of children inheriting blindness) and her sadness in not seeing what her children are seeing. Through the narrative and the photographs, the child sees the ways that Sally Alexander copes with her blindness and solves her daily problems with the help of her young daughter. Black and white photographs. 2–3.

   Target Activity: "Use the News"

   Ask the students to find newspaper articles concerning a disabled group. Some articles will state the positions and points of view on issues, others will be stories about regional events, while still others will be about someone identified as a disabled American. With the students, discuss:

   1. What attitudes toward the disabled group were shown in the article?

   2. What types of news did you find that was useful for understanding more about the traits needed by a disabled peson?

   3. In what ways could you help a disabled person? In what situations would such a person need your help?

2. **Baylor, Byrd.** *Hawk, I'm Your Brother.* **Ill. by Peter Parnall. New York: Charles Scribner's Sons, 1976.**

   Trait: Sense of autonomy

   In the Santos Mountains, Rudy Soto wants to fly like a hawk and spends hours watching them, and he steals a baby redtail hawk from its nest. Seeing the wild hawks fly makes Rudy Soto yearn for the bird's sense of autonomy exemplified through their ability to fly. To Rudy, flying is a symbol of a sense of control over life. Seeing the hawk caged and resentful, Rudy releases the bird and watches it fly away and feels he is flying with the bird in spirit. They call to one another as one brother would call to another. 2–3.

Target Activity: "Feeling Close to Other Living Things"

In another Baylor book, *The Desert Is Theirs* (Charles Scribner's Sons, 1975), there is a relationship of humans and earth shown through the Papago Indian culture with an emphasis of sharing with the earth and not taking from it. With children, discuss the theme: it points out what humans can learn from the animals and plants that adapt to the sun and to scarce water supply in the desert. How does this theme (learning from nature) relate to the earlier Baylor story? Relate to the resiliency trait of sense of autonomy and sense of control over one's life.

3.   Blood, Charles. *The Goat in the Rug*. Ill. New York: Macmillan, 1980.

Traits: Positive vision of life; developing a hobby or talent.

Glenmae, with the assistance of her goat, Geraldine, creates a rug design that is unique. Using her talents, Glenmae finds she has a positive view of life. The story shows the tradition of Navajo weavers through hundreds of years. Pre–3.

Target Activity: "Letter to the Author: Help from Animals"

Ask children to talk about the way Geraldine, the goat, helped Glenmae create the rug design. What other animals seem to help humans? Invite the children to talk about their examples in the discussion. What have the children created with the help of a pet? Ask children to write a letter to the author telling him about their experience with a pet.

4.   Brown, Marcia. *Henry Fisherman*. Ill. by author. New York: Charles Scribner's Sons, 1949.

Traits: Perseverance and persistence in bravery; problem-solving.

Young Henry, who fetches water, washes clothes and goes to market with his mother, wants to be a fisherman like his father. When his father decides Henry is old enough to help on the family fishing boat, the *Araidne,* he gets the chance to prove his skills. When Henry is surprised by a shark, he manages to outswim it and reach safety. He shows his resiliency as he refuses to panic and perseveres as he outswims the dangerous shark. Returning to shore with the catch, Henry calls out their good fortune by blowing on a conch shell to tell others. There is some native dialect reflecting the setting on St. Thomas Island in the Caribbean. K–2.

Target Activity: "Henry and Armien"

Compare *Henry Fisherman* with Catherine Stock's book, *Armien's Fishing Trip* (Morrow, 1990). Armien stows away on Uncle Faried's boat, the *Rosie,* because he has "salt water in his veins." He is determined to prove himself old enough to go to sea like the other fishermen out of Kalk Bay off the African coast. When one of the crew is swept overboard by rough seas, Armien sounds the alarm which alerts Faried who rescues the crew member.

For both stories, discuss the problem in each and the resilient traits that each character uses to resolve the conflicts—their problems involving danger. Ask students to make a visual display (posters, chalkboard drawings, transparency sketches) that shows the traits of each character. Ask students to use the visual display as a resource. They should refer to it and write brief sentences in their literature journals about the characters.

5. Bunting, Eve. *The Wednesday Surprise.* Ill. by Donald Carrick. New York: Clarion, 1989.

Traits: Positive vision of life; perseverance; developing a talent.

Grandmother and Anna work together, secretly, on a present for Dad's birthday. It is a present that only the two of them can give to Dad. Anna and Grandmother are persistent and persevere as each day they work together and Grandmother develops a new skill. Anna teaches Grandmother to read. The concept of the importance of adult literacy supports a positive vision of life. Pre–3.

Target Activity: "Oral History of Learning to Read"

With children, discuss the idea of an oral history. They may interview an older person they know and report back to the class. In the interview, they may use such questions as:

1. How long have you lived here?
2. What was the town like when you first came?
3. Where did you live when you were a child?
4. What was school like?
5. How did you learn to read?

6. Carlstrom, Nancy White. *Blow Me a Kiss, Miss Lilly.* Ill. by Amy Schwartz. New York: Harper & Row, 1990.

Traits: Relationship with caring other person.

Sara, a young girl, responds to the death of her elderly friend, Miss Lilly. Miss Lilly lives across the street from Sara with Snug, her cat, and Sara is there often helping in the garden, in the kitchen, and talking to her friend. Each time Sara leaves, they both throw kisses to symbolize their friendship. When Miss Lilly becomes ill, Sara sends a get-well card with the message, "Blow me a kiss, Miss Lilly." Sara's sadness over her friend's death is eased somewhat by taking care of Snug and seeing the flowers blooming in the spring garden. Pre–2.

Target Activity: "Messages"

Invite children to try to explain Sara's real message when she wrote, "Blow me a kiss, Miss Lilly." What was Sara trying to say? Encourage children to design get-well cards for anyone they know who is ill and to dictate or write their messages for their friends, relatives, or family members.

Select and display books about friendships, and when possible, use them to read aloud. Discussion can focus on problems of getting along together. Some other titles to consider are Thomas Rockwell's *How to Eat Fried Worms* (Watts, 1973), *The Times They Used to Be* (Holt, 1974) by Lucille Clifton, and *Best Friends* (Macmillan, 1971) by Miriam Cohen.

7. **Carrick, Carol. *Dark and Full of Secrets*. Ill. by Donald Carrick. New York: Clarion Books, 1984.**

Trait: Sense of control over one's life.

Although Christopher likes the clear green ocean, he doesn't like the murky pond because he can't see what is in it. His father teases him about being afraid of sea monsters and teaches him to snorkel so that he can actually see what is in the pond. His dad returns to shore to read while Christopher happily continues snorkeling, but the boy's mask suddenly fills with water and he panics when his feet don't touch the bottom of the pond. He is even more frightened when something—the sea monster?—snatches his leg. It is the dog which helps tow him in to shore. That night, when the family goes for a canoe ride, Christopher looks at the dark surface of the water and realizes his fear is gone because he knows what is underneath the surface of the pond. By seeing what is in the pond and then facing his worst fears about its contents, Christopher learns that he can conquer fear by confronting it. Conquering fear by confronting it gives Christopher control over this part of his life. 2–3.

Target Activity: "Grab Bag"

Bring into the classroom several containers filled with various ingredients such as cooked spaghetti, jello, or yogurt. Blindfold several class members and have them put their hands in each of the containers. Take note of any reluctance and or hesitation. Ask for volunteers among unblindfolded class members to put their hands in the containers.

Discuss differences in eagerness to participate of those who know what is in the container as compared with those who do not. Ask children why they think what is known is less frightening than the unknown. Let them offer additional examples of this phenomenon from their own lives.

8. **Caudill, Rebecca. *Pocketful of Cricket*. Ill. by Evaline Ness. New York: Holt, Rinehart & Winston, 1964.**

Trait: Relationship with significant other.

On an August afternoon, six-year-old Jay carries a cricket home as a pet. The cricket lives in a wire-screen cage in his bedroom. In September, Jay takes the cricket to school in his pocket because he is reluctant to leave it behind. Jay's understanding teacher asks him to show his chirping pet to the class. An intimate relationship between a child and his pet develops and is supported by Jay's relationship with his understanding teacher. The teacher is sympathetic for the small boy's need for something familiar near him on the first day of school. K–2.

Target Activity: "Jay's Record"

Jay did not want to be away from his pet cricket. So Jay decided to write with pictures and words (a rebus record) and tell about some of the happenings with his pet—things like the cricket living in a wire-screen cage, his surroundings in the bedroom, his journey to school in Jay's pocket, and his debut as a chirping cricket in the classroom. Draw some of the pictures for a rebus record that Jay might have drawn. Share your pictures with others.

9.　Clark, Ann Nolan. *In My Mother's House.* **Ill. by Velina Herrera. New York: Viking, 1941.**

Trait: Relationship with significant other.

Though out of print, the book may be found in some branch libraries and shows the view of a young boy's life as a Pueblo Indian: "I string them together/ Like beads./ They make a chain,/ A strong chain,/ To hold me close/ To home,/ Where I live in my Mother's house." Illustrations and text have details from the world of Pueblos about the council, fire, home, mountains, pasture, pipeline, people, and wild plants. 1–3.

Target Activity: "A Strong Chain to Home"

Discuss with the children the things in their lives that link them to their families and their homes. Invite the children to draw their own large links in a chain to show a visual display of an enlarged chain. Ask the children to write one fact inside each link. Each fact is to tell about something in their lives that ties them to their families and their homes (the friendship, the family jokes, the pets, the good cooking, the atmosphere, the care when they are hurt and so on). Display the "Strong Chains to Home" in the classroom.

10.　Cleary, Beverly. *Ramona and Her Father.* **Ill. by Alan Tiegreen. New York: Morrow, 1977.**

Traits: Problem-solving; humor.

Father loses his job when Ramona is in second grade and there is less money for the family. Mother begins to work full-time and Father, worried and irritable, looks after Ramona after school. Worried about their father smoking, Ramona and Beezus begin an anti-smoking campaign. Christmas brings happier times with Beezus cast as Mary in the Christmas pageant at church and Ramona as a sheep. Further, Father announces a new job that starts January 2. The reader finds the problems are dealt with in a realistic and reassuring manner. 2–3.

Target Activity: "Ramona's Anti-smoking Campaign"

Invite the students to design posters for Ramona's anti-smoking campaign.

11.   Fradin, Dennis B. *Bad Luck Tony*. Ill. by Joanne Scribner. Englewood Cliffs, NJ: Prentice-Hall, 1978.

Traits: Persistence in the face of failure; relationship with a caring other person.

Tony is looking forward to a visit by his eccentric grandfather who lives in a motor home and doesn't like to stay in one place for too long. He is eager to develop a relationship with his grandfather, although he has not seen him since he was a baby. At the same time, Tony finds a stray pregnant dog and is trying to find a warm, safe place in which the animal can have her puppies. He goes all over town looking for a home for the dog, with no luck. Finally, he convinces his grandfather that he should stay with him and his mother until Christmas and wait for the dog to have her puppies. Christmas morning, the dog has her puppies in the driver's seat of the grandfather's motor home. The grandfather decides to take the dog and puppies with him on his next journey. He also agrees to visit Tony more frequently in the future. Tony is clearly not a quitter, and his strong determination leads to a positive solution to his concern about the dog and also leads to a burgeoning relationship with his grandfather. 2–3.

Target Activity: "Find Me a Home"

Invite a representative from the local SPCA to speak to the class. Discuss with her or him what can be done to find homes for stray animals. Divide the students into three groups to explore the following topics:

    1. What information should people have about the responsibility of owning a dog before acquiring a puppy?

    2. How could people who would like a dog find out about animals that might be available at the SPCA?

    3. What could you do if you found a stray animal roaming the streets?

    4. What traits of resiliency (persistence, problem-solving, and so on) do you think you need to take care of a pet?

12.   Gray, Nigel. *A Country Far Away*. Ill. by Philippe Dupasquier. New York: Watts/Orchard Books, 1989.

Trait: Positive vision of life.

The book shows an African boy in the illustration, and below, a Western boy. With the words, "Today was an ordinary day. I stayed home," a reader sees the African boy's village home with him tending goats. The Western boy is washing the car with his father. Differences and similarities in the two cultures can be discussed and the reader can review cultures different from his own. Their positive visions show through their acceptance and seeming contentment with their lifestyles. 1–3.

Target Activity: "Your Positive Outlook on Life"

Ask children to begin creative writing with the words, "Today was my lucky day because..." When finished, each child should read his essay to a reading partner. They should discuss it and make any revisions the writer wants to make.

13. Heide, Florence Parry & Judith Heide Gilliland. *The Day of Ahmed's Secret.* **Ill. by Ted Lewin. New York: Lothrop, 1990.**

Trait: Persistence and perseverance.

Ahmed, a *butagaz* boy who delivers cooking gas to customers in Cairo, has news for his family. After his rounds with his donkey cart, he goes home where he shows his family that he can write his name in Arabic. Ahmed has been persistent and has persevered as he learned. K–3.

Target Activity: "Drama with Ahmed's Secret"

With the children, discuss some of the accomplishments they have made and the feelings they had when they did those things.

In teams of two, the children should create a scene where Ahmed and his donkey deliver cooking gas to a customer in Cairo. Ask the students to change roles and play the scene again. Then joining with other groups, they will dramatize the loving family gathered around and watching Ahmed as he shows them he can proudly write his name. Invite each student to write the name, Ahmed, on the writing board and to pantomime or show the excitement by dramatizing the boy's feelings about this accomplishment.

14. Isadora, Rachel. *Ben's Trumpet.* **Ill. by the author. New York: Greenwillow, 1979.**

Traits: Persistence and perseverance; developing a hobby or talent.

Ben, a young black child in the inner city, sits on the fire escape and plays his invisible trumpet to the beat of the music from the nearby Zig Zag Jazz Club (his favorite thing to do). Ben suffers the ridicule of his peers and the lack of interest of his family. Despite these negative influences, Ben perseveres. When the trumpeter of the club recognizes his potential, he has the chance to try out a real trumpet. K–2.

Target Activity: "To the Beat of the Music"

With children, discuss some of their musical ambitions and interests. With a record player, tape recorder, or a radio, play some music for the members of the class and ask them to observe and watch one another as they all listen. What do the students do when they want to keep time to the music? Each student should make a list of what other listeners do to keep the beat. Discuss: Which ways seemed to work best? Why do you think so? Did anyone persevere and keep the beat all the way though the song? Who? Invite that student to tell the class what made her or him persistent in this activity.

15. Keats, Ezra Jack. *Goggles!* Ill. by the author. New York: Macmillan, 1969.

Traits: Perseverance; problem-solving.

Two young black boys, Peter and Archie, live in the inner city. They find a pair of motorcycle goggles near their hideout in a deserted lot. They have to stand up to three older bullies who also want the goggles. Willie, the dog, grabs the goggles, and runs off with them as the boys head for their hideout.

The boys trick the bullies into heading off in another direction and the two young boys and Willie run back to Archie's house to savor their escape and their find. Their persistence has paid off. Pre-1.

Target Activity: "Peephole Drawings"

The actions and feelings of the boys will seem close to home for young readers. Archie peers through the hole in a board in the fence to secretly observe the big boys chasing him. There is some security in being hidden behind the board of the fence. Ask the children to name some things that frighten them and then draw the frightening things to show what they would look like when seen through a peephole of a fence. Encourage the girls and boys to make their own drawings to gain insight into Archie's feelings as he hides from the chasing boys.

16. Lyon, George Ella. *Come a Tide*. Ill. by Stephen Gammell. New York: Orchard Book/Watts, 1990.

Traits: Persistence; humor.

In March, in the hills, it rains and snows for four days and nights. Grandma says "It'll come a tide" and it does. Four families cope with the flood, gather family members, find a boat, and ride to higher ground. The rains wash away chickens, gardens, pigs, and porches. These families persist in spite of the flooding waters and they cope with the trouble it causes. When the flood stops, they return to "make friends with a shovel." Pre–2.

Target Activity: "Survivors in the Daily News"

Talk about the characters in the story, Grandma's prediction, family and neighbor cooperation, and the escape from danger by working together. Discuss the meaning of "making friends with a shovel."

By looking through as many newspapers as they can, students cut out all articles they find that remind them of the characters, events, or idea of cooperation in *Come a Tide*. Articles may include reports on rescues, stories of survival during natural disasters, and stories of cooperation for a bulletin board display or a class album. Students link experiences in the book to experiences in real life by dictating or writing one or two sentences linking the news article to a similar character or event from the book and placing the sentences next to the article on a page in the album or on the display.

17. Maury, Inez. *My Mother the Mail Carrier—Mi Mama la Cartera*. **New York: Feminist Press, 1976.**

Trait: Positive vision of life.

In this bilingual book, Lupita's mother is brave, strong, and a good cook. She loves outings and likes her work, carrying mail. Lupita wants to be a jockey when she grows up. Lupita sees a positive vision of life through her mother's abilities at home and at work. She yearns for a nonstereotypical occupation and, like her mother who likes her work, knows she will like her work too! Well-designed. Pre–3.

Target Activity: "Tough Jobs People Do"

Look in the newspaper for articles about jobs people do. Discuss the character traits you think the person needs to do her job. Relate those character traits to traits of resiliency. What worker would need perseverance? to overcome obstacles? to solve problems? to maintain a positive vision of life?

18. Mendez, Phil. *The Black Snowman*. **Ill. by Carole Byard. New York: Scholastic, 1989.**

Trait: Positive vision of life.

Young Jacob Miller wakes up on a snowy Saturday angry at being poor and black. "I hate being black," he tells his mother. Try as she may to humor him, he sulks. Then his brother cajoles him into making a snowman, which is black from dirty snow. Among the scraps they use to dress the snowman is a kente cloth, the brightly colored material that brought magic to the Ashanti people before they were sold into slavery. This bit of kente was sold, too. Though in tatters, it has kept its power. How that power is used makes this story a richly woven original folk tale. With this material as a symbol that life has meaning, Jacob can reassess his anger at being black and can look toward a more positive vision of life. Full page watercolors by Carole Byard add depth to this story. 1–3.

Target Activity: "Drama with a Kente Cloth"

With the children, discuss the Kente cloth and its power in the story. Discuss ways you and others can dramatize scenes from the story to show traits of resiliency—having perseverance, overcoming obstacles, and keeping a positive vision of life.

To emphasize some of these resilient traits dramatize the scene between Jacob and his brother talking him into making a snowman, and interview young Jacob Miller as he explains the power of the Kente cloth.

19.   Miles, Miska. *Annie and the Old One*. **Ill. by Peter Parnall. Boston: Little, Brown, 1971.**

Trait: Relationship with a significant other.

Annie lives on the Navajo Indian reservation with her grandmother, called the "Old One," her father, her mother, and a herd of sheep. She helps tend the sheep and garden and goes to school. She lives a happy life until she learns from her grandmother that when the new rug being woven by her mother is completed, her grandmother will go back to mother earth. Since her grandmother means so much to her, Annie feels she must do something to prevent this from happening. She attempts to keep her mother from weaving the rug by misbehaving at school and letting the sheep out of the corral at night so as to distract her mother. Both these ploys fail, as her mother is merely amused by Annie's antics, and the sheep do not wander far. Annie then resorts to stealthily unweaving the rug at night, and is caught in the act by the Old One. The Old One then takes Annie aside, out into the mesa, and points out the natural evolution of seasons, time, and destiny. With this, Annie realizes that "she was a part of the earth and the things on it. She would always be a part of the earth, just as her grandmother had always been, just as her grandmother would always be, always and forever." Annie gains a deep, unspoken realization of the inevitability of the earth's natural order and accepts this way of life. The next morning, Annie starts weaving the rug. 3.

Target Activity: "Annie Grows Up"

Discuss what students have learned about Annie. Write descriptive traits on the board. Brainstorm some ideas about how Annie will be feeling when the rug is finished; several years later, when Annie is grown up and has children; or when Annie is an "Old One." Determine what values Annie has learned from the Old One and how she would carry them into later life. Ask children to choose one of Annie's later stages and write several sentences about what her life will be like at that time.

20.   Paustovsky, Konstantin. *The Magic Ringlet*. **Ill. by Leonard Weisgard. Reading, MA: Young Scott Books, 1971.**

Trait: Positive vision of life.

An old soldier gives a magic ring to little Varyusha, telling her it has the power to bring happiness to her and health to her sick grandfather. As she is returning home through the woods, the ring slips off her finger and falls into the deep snow. However much she digs, she cannot find it. Each day, as the winter winds blow more fiercely and her grandfather's cough grows worse, she blames herself for being so careless. One spring day when the snow has melted, she finds the ring. As she waits for the "enormous happiness" to happen, she realizes the happiness dwells within her. Varyusha learns that she must open her eyes and appreciate all the simple beauty of her own environment—spring in the woods, the birds, the flowers and the clear sky. She realizes that how she views what she has will cause happiness. She decides not to put the ringlet on her index finger, because her happiness is within her. 1–3.

Target Activity: "My World"

Discuss with children the idea that sometimes we are so close to our own home, city, and surroundings that we fail to appreciate the good things that we have. Ask children to pretend that they are about to go on a journey to Russia, where Varyusha lives. Ask them to take two or three minutes to think about what they would like to tell Varyusha of the beauty in their surroundings. Tell them to visualize a favorite tree, a stream or lake, flowers in their yard, birds that they have heard, or other features of their environment of which they are fond. Then ask them to turn to a neighbor. Have the neighbor pretent to be Varyusha while the other child tells what makes him happy about his world. When they finish, let the children reverse roles.

21. Peavy, Linda. *Allison's Grandfather.* **Ill. by Ronald Himler. New York: Charles Scribner's Sons, 1981.**

Trait: Relationship with a caring other person.

Allison's grandfather is in the hospital dying. Erica, Allison's friend, thinks back on the wonderful times she has had visiting Allison and her grandfather on his ranch and listening to the tales of when he was a cowboy. Erica wants to ask about dying, but cannot bring herself to accept the death of this strong and lively man. Erica expresses how much she cared for Allison's grandfather, but she faces her first encounter with death. She overcomes her fear, with her mother's help, and begins to understand death as a peaceful and natural life process. The book concerns Erica's full range of emotions about Allison's grandfather and his impending death. 2–3.

Target Activity: "Living History"

What Erica recalls most about Allison's grandfather is his colorful stories about his days as a young man in the rodeo circuit. Allison's grandfather had enjoyed telling his stories and they were a way to share his past history with his granddaughter and her friend, drawing them all closer.

Similarly, many children have close relationships with their grandparents and miss their stories of "the way it was in the old days" when they die. Discuss the value of the recollections of the elderly with the class.

Ask each child to select an elderly grandparent, aunt, uncle, or friend, etc., whom they care about and who lives close enough to speak to (the telephone can be used for this purpose). Write a list of possible questions on the chalkboard:

What was life like when you were my age?

What things were very different from now?

What were your favorite things to do?

How did you make a living?

How did you meet your wife/husband?

What do you miss most about those days?

Ask children to tape-record the answers or take careful notes. Encourage them to share their "living history" with the class. Ask the students to tell what was the most interesting thing they learned, and how the activity has changed their relationship with the elderly person to whom they spoke.

22. Peters, Lisa Westberg. *Good Morning, River!* Ill. by Deborah Kogan Ray. New York: Arcade, 1990.

Trait: Relationship with significant other.

Through the seasons, Katherine has a special relationship with her elderly neighbor, Carl, as she looks forward to hearing him yell at the river in a booming voice each morning; it seems that the river always answers him softly. When Carl's illness forces him to move away, all is quiet at the river. When he returns, and is able to talk only in whispers, Katherine is the one to make the river talk again as the special relationship continues to grow. K–3.

Target Activity: "Drama with *Good Morning, River!*"

Ask the students to dramatize Katherine's early morning meeting with Carl as he yells at the river to say "Good Morning." How will you show that Katherine has a positive friendly relationship with Carl? Discuss the story and some of the actions that show traits of resiliency. What would show that one of the characters has perseverance? has a positive vision of life? can overcome obstacles? In role playing, create a dramatic play scene where Katherine learns water activities from Carl. For more role-playing, interview Katherine. How does she describe what she had to do to get the river to answer her?

23. Pomerantz, Charlotte. *The Chalk Doll.* Ill. by Fran Lessac. New York: Lippincott, 1989.

Trait: Relationship with significant other.

Mother tells Rose stories of her childhood and her wish for a store-bought chalk doll. Rose compares her own life with the fun of her mother's—having a rag doll, drinking milk from a can, and special parties. To extend her significant relationship with her mother, and sample another part of her mother's childhood, Rose wants Mother to make her a rag doll. She gathers scraps of materials and together Mother and Rose make the doll. The book contains watercolors of colorful Jamaican countryside with bright foliage and painted buildings. They show the daily life—chickens at the front door, lizards on the walk, cows grazing, and donkeys used for transportation. 3 & up.

Target Activity: "Family Memories"

Read excerpts from your favorite book of poems or from *Childtimes* (Crowell, 1979), a book of memories of three generations written by Eloise Greenfield and her mother, Lessie Jones Little. The social concerns of the family is a theme of the text. After listening to some selected verses, encourage children to tell a memory they have had with a family member.

24.   Robinet, Harriette Gillem. *Ride the Red Cycle*. Ill. by David Brown. Boston: Houghton Mifflin, 1980.

Traits: Persistence in the face of failure; will to succeed; sense of control over one's life.

A viral infection in the brain left damage that affected Jerome Johnson's whole body. When he got better he had to learn to support his head and crawl all over again, but his legs remained crippled and he was confined to a wheelchair. He had a dream, however; he wanted to learn to ride a tricycle. When his father buys him one, the whole family is disappointed when he cannot even move the pedals. Secretly, he painstakingly learns to ride it—and to take his first steps. His courage and pride take him further than his parents or the host of specialists that treat him ever expected. Jerome holds on to his dream in the face of humiliating defeat and works to show others and himself that he can succeed. He learns to walk by himself, through his own persistence. 2–4.

Target Activity: "Obstacle Walk"

That Jerome Johnson persisted and took great pride in finally learning how to ride a tricycle is a concept that is lost on many able-bodied youngsters, but they are better able to appreciate their own accomplishments if they can empathize with Jerome's success. To help children understand life with a handicap, set up an obstacle course in the classroom with desks and chairs. Using a watch with a second hand, time a child's walk through the obstacle course. Then blindfold the same child and time him again. Have the child make successive trials in an attempt to match the original time that was achieved without the blindfold. Let all in the class participate in the obstacle path walk, both sighted and blindfolded, until they can reach their sighted time when blindfolded. Ask them which success they feel proudest of—with or without the blindfold? Finally, ask them to write a letter to Jerome Johnson telling him what they have learned about perseverance.

25.   Rylant, Cynthia. *Miss Maggie*. Ill. by Thomas de Dirazia. New York: E. P. Dutton, 1983.
    Trait: Relationship with a caring other person.
    A young boy, Nat, has heard stories about the reclusive elderly lady who lives in the log hut on his family's property; a big black snake, among other scary things, is reputed to live with her. Nat, initially fearing Miss Maggie, looks in her window, then runs away. One day he overcomes his fears when he finds her in trouble: in the heart of winter she is without heat. He finds her sitting on the floor of her cabin clutching a dead starling. He runs to get help for her. His family begins taking care of her and taking her with them on outings. Nat establishes a special, caring relationship with Miss Maggie. 2–4.
    Target Activity: "A Letter to Miss Maggie"
    Begin the activity with a discussion about rumors. Ask children if they have ever heard many people making the same unkind statements about someone and then later, although several people had said the same thing, they found the statements were untrue. Recount the rumors that were circulating about Miss Maggie. Discuss which were true and which were untrue and where such rumors may have originated. Instruct children to write a letter to Miss Maggie as if they were Nat. Ask them to include in the letter why they used to peer in her windows and be frightened of her, what they learned about her from their own experience, and how much they care about her now.

26.   Schick, Eleanor. *Joey on His Own*. Ill. New York: Dial Press, 1982.
    Trait: Problem-solving.
    Joey has never gone shopping by himself. His mother asks him to go to the store and buy some bread for lunch, so he reluctantly starts off. He is frightened and the buildings seem taller than he remembers, the traffic noisier, and the neighborhood bullies meaner. When he gets to the store, he doesn't know which bread to choose; he is overwhelmed. When he brings the bread home, his mother tells him he has done a fine job, and he is proud of himself. Joey's mundane adventure is a good example of how fear of the unknown is reduced by experience with it. Joey panics when given a task he has never been asked to do before, but feels triumphant when he completes it successfully. 1–2.
    Target Activity: "A Special Shopping Trip"

After reading *Joey on His Own* with children, tell them they are going on a pretend shopping trip. Have them close their eyes. Lead them through the following visualization activity:

"Your mother has asked you to go and buy her a loaf of bread from the store. You have gone to the store many times with your mother, but you have never gone to the store by yourself. She gives you one dollar and kisses you goodbye. You walk out the door and down the street. Trucks and cars whiz by you and you are a bit scared. You look both ways and, when there are no cars, you run across the street. There is the supermarket! You walk up and down the aisles looking for the bread. Finally, on the other side of the store you find the bread, but you can't remember what kind your mother wanted. Will she be angry if you buy the wrong kind? Way in the back of the shelf you see some bread in a red wrapper. Yes, you're *sure* that is the kind of bread you usually eat. You pick up the loaf and hand the dollar to the woman at the check-out counter. The woman says, 'Will that be all today?' and you answer, 'Yes, thank you.' She gives you three pennies in change, puts the bread in a paper sack, hands it to you and you walk out the door. You skip home and give your mother the bread and the three pennies. She smiles and thanks you."

Tell children to open their eyes. Write two columns on the chalkboard, one titled "before" and the other "after." Ask them to share their feelings before and after buying the bread. Discuss the differences in the feelings and why we feel pride when we have accomplished something we were afraid to do. Ask children to share any experiences they had where they were afraid to do something, but proud when they accomplished it successfully.

27. Seed, Jenny. *Ntombi's Song*. Ill. by Anno Berry. Boston: Beacon Press, 1989.

Traits: Persistence; positive vision of life.

In South Africa in a rural Zulu life setting, six-year-old Ntombi takes her first journey to the village store to buy sugar for her mother. Told by other women that a monster lives in the forest, she is frightened by a passing bus, and spills the sugar onto the sand. Deciding to earn the money to replace the sugar, she perseveres, dancing for tourists and singing a song her mother created for her when she was a baby. She receives a coin and uses it to buy sugar. Watercolor illustrations are included. 2–3.

Target Activity: "Mishaps Happen"

Look at the illustrations again so the students get a close-up view of the mishap that happened to Ntombi. Encourage them to relate a mishap that has happened to them in their lives and to talk about solving problems. Discuss the way each solved or could solve the problem if it happened to them again. Invite them to draw a picture of what they would have done to help Ntombi if they had been there when she spilled the sugar on the ground.

28.   Schertle, Alice. *William and Grandpa*. Ill. by Lydia Dabco-vich. New York: Lothrop, Lee & Shepard, 1989.
   Trait: Relationship with significant other.
   William rides the bus by himself to visit his Grandpa who meets him at the station. They sing and jump, Grandpa makes chili, and William uses shaving lather to make a white mustache. After supper, they share a story, look at the stars in the night, and drink hot chocolate. This book shows continuity of generations and a warm relationship between a child and a grandparent as they enjoy some of the activities of any ordinary day. Pre–1.
   Target Activity: "True Stories"
   Invite children to share a memory that they remember with fondness involving an older person. They may ask an adult at home to tell them a story from his own family history that the adult remembers with fond-ness. If desired, each may tell a brief part of the history to a learning part-ner or to a small group. To record the story for part of a family's history, engage the students in writing the stories on small poster boards, prepar-ing a decorative frame or border around each written history, and insert-ing colorful yarn so the history can be hung somewhere in the home. The children can present their histories to someone in the family.

29.   Stanek, Muriel. *I Speak English for My Mom*. Ill. Chicago: Whitman, 1988.
   Traits: Persistence and perseverance.
   Lupe Gomez helps her mother who speaks and reads only Spanish. Lupe helps her with trips to the dentist and with shopping, even though Lupe acknowledges she would rather play. Pre–3.
   Target Activity: "Persevere and Speak Another Language with *A Show of Hands*"
   Learn to speak another language and use the *A Show of Hands: Say It in Sign Language* (Harper & Row, 1980) by Mary Beth Sullivan and Linda Bourke. Many people communicate by reading lips and using sign language—a language made up of hand shapes and movements. This language is expressive, beautiful when seen by others, and fun! Practice making the hand and finger signs for some of the letters. Practice spelling your name and then practice sending a message to a learning buddy. Do you have the perseverance to learn all of the signs for all of the letters of the alphabet? Show others evidence of your perseverance by signing as many of the letters as you can. Help translate for another student who is using only sign language.

30. Steig, William. *Brave Irene*. **Ill. by the author. New York: Farrar, Straus & Giroux, 1986.**

Trait: Perseverance.

Irene's mother, a dressmaker, is ill and cannot deliver a ball gown that she has sewn for the duchess to wear that evening. Irene volunteers to bring it to the duchess, despite a fierce snowstorm. A series of obstacles—the box is blown from her arms, the dress blows away, and she is nearly buried alive when she falls off a cliff—almost prevents Irene from fulfilling her mission. But Irene perseveres and the gown is delivered to a very grateful duchess. 1–3.

Target Activity: "Guess What Happened, Mother?"

Tell students that Irene's mother cannot fully appreciate the errand that Irene successfully completed unless she hears every detail of that very difficult mission. Divide the students into pairs. Ask one child to play the part of Irene's mother. Encourage the child playing the part of Irene to recount the many misadventures she had delivering the dress, sharing her feelings of frustration along the way as well as her feeling of jubilation when she arrives at the house of the duchess. Allow the child playing the part of the mother to ad-lib some reaction that the proud mother might have had. Have children reverse roles. Several pairs may volunteer to share their role plays for the whole class.

31. Stock, Catherine. *Armien's Fishing Trip*. **Ill. by the author. New York: Morrow, 1990.**

Traits: Persistence; problem-solving.

While visiting his aunt and uncle one weekend, Armien stows away on Uncle Faried's boat, the *Rosie*, because he has "salt water in his veins." He is determined to prove himself old enough to go to sea like the other fishermen out of Kalk Bay off the African coast. When one of the crew is swept overboard by rough seas, Armien solves the problem about how to call for help and sounds the alarm which alerts Faried who rescues the crew member. K–3.

Target Activity: "Rescue at Sea: Front Page News Story"

Invite children to look in the newspapers for articles about current rescues. Discuss the articles and talk about some of the traits the rescuers had to have to accomplish what they did. Relate the traits to some of the traits of resiliency: perseverance, overcoming obstacles, and problem solving. Ask children to write a story that would fit the headline: "Rescue at Sea." Read the dictated story together and discuss. Talk about ways the children's story relates to the incident in *Armien's Fishing Trip*.

32. Williams, Karen Lynn. *Galimoto*. **Ill. by Catherine Stock. New York: Lothrop, Lee & Shepard, 1990.**

Traits: Persistence; perseverance.

In a small African village, seven-year-old Kondi decides to make a push toy—a galimoto. When his older brother tells him that he does not have enough wire to make a toy, Kondi goes on a search to get wire from other children and adults with his persuasion and know-how. He shows he is resourceful and gets the wire he needs. He coaxes a girl to trade her wire. He swaps his knife with a friend for more. He rummages for wire at a junkyard. When the moon and his friends ask him out to play, he would rather play with the galimoto. His persistence is rewarded and his goal is reached. 1–3.

Target Activity: "Building Toys"

Before the book: Talk about building toys of all kinds. Ask students to describe the different shapes, sizes, and types of toys they have used. Have students draw some of the shapes of toys on the writing board and suggest some geometrical descriptions—find shapes or circles, squares, and triangles. Ask what sorts of things the students like to build (or toys they repair). Next, tell students that they will hear a story that involves making a push toy. Ask students to listen for ways the boy solves his problem to find wire to make the toy.

After the book: Invite students to retell the action in the story with questions that focus on the details in the story:

1. What were some of the problems that Kondi had in his search for wire to make the toy?

2. How did Kondi deal with each situation to find wire?

3. Have students suggest other items that could have been built with the wire.

4. Have students make a list of other things made from wire.

Extending the story: To encourage divergence in thinking, tell students that a pipecleaner is like the wire that Kondi had; the more you change it (twist it, bend it, reshape it), the more things the pipecleaner can become. Ask students to sit together in a circle on the floor. Pass a pipecleaner from student to student. Ask each one to use the pipecleaner to tell something about himself or herself. For an example, hold the pipecleaner up like a baseball bat, and say, "I like to play baseball. This is what I use to hit the ball and make a home run." According to the divergence of each student, the pipecleaner becomes a magic wand, a musician's baton, a bow tie, a weight to lift, antlers.

Continue passing the pipecleaner around until all have had one time to bend it into something different. Then, give each student a pipecleaner and ask each one to think of a problem and then solve the problem by bending the pipecleaner into an object that represents the solution to the problem. Those who "can't think of anything" could decide to take on Kondi's problem and make a small push toy.

Ask each student to talk about the problem that he or she selected and show the pipecleaner object that "solves" the problem. Example, "I like to play baseball but I do not have a bat so I made a pipecleaner bat."

Option: "Inventory of a Problem"

Ask children to give as many examples as they can from the story in which they think Kondi's first difficulties were the result of his being:

1. a small seven-year-old boy   _____
2. a boy who lives in a village   _____
3. too young for such a difficult task of making a wire toy _____
4. the younger brother   _____

With the children, discuss the view that problems often have more than one beginning or cause. Invite children to tell of similar experiences and discuss one trait of resiliency, that of solving problems.

33. Yashima, Taro. *Crow Boy*. Ill. by the author. New York: Viking, 1955.

Traits: Perseverance; developing a hobby or talent.

A small Asian boy, Chibi, is an isolate at school and spends the time looking at the ceiling, his desk, or out the window. Every day he walks miles to school and notices what is around him. He has six years of perfect attendance and receives attention from a new teacher, Mr. Isobe, who recognizes Chibi's knowledge of nature and discovers that Chibi can imitate the voices of crows—and does so with the others in the school talent show. With this, he earns respect of others and himself and is nicknamed "Crow Boy." K–2.

Target Activity: "Looking for Evidence in Print and Pictures"

To collect evidence of the resiliency of the main character, Crow Boy, review the story again and look at the illustrations closely. Talk about these questions with the students: What evidence can be found that Crow Boy had perseverance? could overcome obstacles? could develop a talent? Invite the students to draw a picture of Crow Boy showing he could do some of these things. After the drawings are completed, the students team up in pairs and talk about what they drew. Display the illustrations in the classroom.

34. Zemach, Margot. *To Hilda for Helping*. Ill. New York: Farrar, Straus & Giroux, 1977.

Trait: Positive vision of life.

Hilda, a cooperative and helpful little girl, receives a tin-can top medal from her father for helping set the table at night. Her sisters, Rose and Gladys, never help, but Gladys becomes extremely jealous of Hilda's medal. Gladys makes up a prediction of doom about what will happen to the medal—it will get dirty or rust, or Hilda will lose it. Maybe (Gladys fantasizes), it will be buried under a tree. But Hilda, strong within herself, recognizes Gladys's jealousy and offers her own happy version of the medal's future; it will be buried and grow a tree with medals on it. 1–3.

Target Activity: "We Are Special"

Discuss with children the fact that each is special in a unique way. List on the chalkboard all the ways in which they have at one time or another helped their families, helped in the classroom or helped a friend. Collect tin-can tops to make medals for each child similar to Hilda's, which will say, "To _____ for Helping with _____" Use construction paper for the letters and glue them on. Have each child select a task with which they have helped recently.

Fanciful Fiction

35.   Bach, Alice. *Millicent the Magnificent.* **Ill. by Steven Kellogg. New York: Harper & Row, 1978.**

Trait: Ability to gain people's attention in a positive way.

Oliver greatly admires his new friend Millicent, who is a circus bear and knows how to do lots of acrobatic tricks. She teaches her tricks to Oliver, but Oliver's brother Ronald is put off by Millicent's bragging and decides to secretly teach himself the same tricks by reading a book and practicing in his room. He becomes very grumpy when he finds he is not progressing nearly as quickly as his brother, who is ready to perform with Millicent in an upcoming show. His father senses his frustration and suggests that he use his own talents to become the ringmaster for the show. Ronald realizes he may not have the same talents, but that he does have other talents that allow him to stand out. Ronald, as well as Millicent and Oliver, is very pleased with this solution. 1–3.

Target Activity: "Guess What I Can Do?"

Have a general discussion with children about their many talents. Write the results of their discussions under the heading, "Things we can do," on the chalkboard. For those who insist that they have no talent, allow them to see "talent" more broadly. Include riding a bike, roller skating, telling jokes, etc. Have each child choose a talent that (s)he possesses and act it out. Allow others to guess the talent.

36.   Coombs, Patricia. *Lisa and the Grompet.* **Ill. New York: Lothrop, Lee & Shepard, 1970.**

Traits: Problem-solving; feeling of autonomy.

Lisa is constantly being told what to do by her mother, father, and big sister. She is beginning to resent it. When she goes outside to mull this over, she comes upon (or imagines), a grompet who tells her *his* sad tales:

because no one ever disciplined him as a child he has shrunk to almost nothing. Lisa takes the grompet home with her and gives it orders ("Wash your wings and face, Grompet") as she is given orders; this makes the grompet very happy, and Lisa becomes more agreeable about doing what she is told. K–3.

Target Activity: "Daily Reminder"

Assign children to make note of all the things they have been reminded to do during the week. Have them write these items down in list form with spaces next to each. Ask them to use the list for one week to try to help themselves remember to do these activities. If they remember to do it without being told, tell them to check the items for that day. After the week is up, have the children bring in their lists and discuss how they were helped by this reminder.

37. Hoban, Lillian. *Arthur's Funny Money.* **Ill. by the author. New York: Harper & Row, 1981.**

Trait: Problem-solving.

Arthur needs money for a "Far Out Frisbee" T-shirt, but he doesn't have enough in his piggy bank. His sister Violet suggests that he wash bicycles to earn some money. He faces many of the problems of a real-life entrepreneur: What does he charge for a trike? What does he do when the dog eats the soap? How can he advertise? How about a special price for a group of vehicles? Finally, on his way to the store to buy more soap, Arthur sees a "Far Out Frisbee" T-shirt in the window of a store, reduced because it is a window sample. He calculates that he has just enough money to buy this shirt—with a bit left over for licorice twists for himself and Violet. 1–2.

Target Activity: "Create a Business"

Discuss with children how Arthur managed to earn the money to buy the T-shirt that he wanted. Divide children into pairs and explain to them that they are going to develop a little business like Arthur's. Like Arthur, they have to find the answers to the following concerns:

1. What service will you offer your customers?
2. What will you charge?
3. How will you let people know about your service?

Let the children in each group draw pictures of the customer before the service and after the service.

38. Hoff, Syd. *Who Will Be My Friends?* **Ill. by the author. New York: Harper & Row, 1960.**

Traits: Problem-solving; ability to attract attention in a positive way.

Freddy has just moved to a new house in a new neighborhood. He needs someone other than his pets to play with. He plays ball with his dog and cat but they don't return it. He makes friends with the policeman and the postman, but they are too busy to play. He goes to a park where children are playing ball, but they ignore him. He starts playing by himself with his ball, throwing it increasingly higher and higher into the air and catching it. The other children notice his talent and ask him to play with them. K–2.

Target Activity: "New Kid on the Block"

Ask children if they have ever moved to a new neighborhood and been the "new kid on the block," like Freddy. Have children pick a partner and take the role of either a child who has just moved into a neighborhood, or one who has lived there for a long time. Have each pair engage in a conversation. The neighborhood "resident" should try to make the new child feel welcome in the neighborhood. When each pair has finished, ask them to reverse roles.

39.   Hogrogian, Nonny. *Billy Goat and His Well-Fed Friends*. Ill. New York: Harper & Row, 1972.

Traits: Problem-solving; relationship with caring others.

Billy Goat is playing less and eating more. One day he overhears the farmer saying to his wife that he would soon be ready to eat. Billy Goat runs away. On the way he encounters a chubby pig. He encourages the pig to come with him, telling him the farmer would like to eat him, too. Likewise, when he meets a plump goose, a lazy lamb, and a round rooster, he befriends them and persuades them to join them in running away, lest they should be soon eaten. The friends build a house and begin living happily together. When a wolf tries to attack them they all gang up on him and he runs off. K–3.

Target Activity: "Chase Away the Wolf"

Discuss the fact with children, that when all the five friends ganged up on the wolf, they drove him away. Ask children what might have happened if the Billy Goat had been living by himself when the wolf came. Put children in "teams" of six. Select one child to be the wolf. Assign the others the roles of pig, rooster, goose, billy goat, or lamb. Explain to them that, as a team effort, they must try to scare the wolf away; however, they may not use force, only words. Let each team of five friends plan their strategy and then act it out, one group at a time, for the rest of the class.

40.   Lagercrantz, Rose and Samuel Lagercrantz. *Brave Little Pete of Geranium Street*. Ill. New York: Greenwillow, 1984.

Trait: Overcoming fear.

Pete wishes he were big and strong, but he is four years old and weak, and scared of the bullies who live nearby who delight in frightening him.

He dreams of standing up to the bullies of Geranium Street. Pete is convinced that "a magic cake" would make him strong and brave. When his grandma finally brings him one, he takes one bite and then runs after the bullies. Impressed by his bravery, the bullies become friends with Pete and never chase or tease him again. He later tells his own children about "when he was strong," allowing them to see the importance of at least putting on a brave front. 1–3.

Target Activity: "Putting on a Brave Face"

Bring in one of the following items: a rabbit's foot, a four-leaf clover, or another similar talisman. Ask children if they know what it is for. When they respond that it brings good luck, ask them if this is really so. Ask them if Pete's "magic cake" is what kept him from being beaten up. Discuss how differently Pete behaved after eating the magic cake. Have children stand up and pantomime how Pete looked, talked, and walked before he ate the magic cake. Then have them pantomime the same behaviors after he had eaten the cake. Ask them which one looks brave and which one looks afraid. Finally, have children draw a picture of Pete with a "brave face," making friends with the bullies. Ask them to share their pictures with the class, explaining why Pete no longer has to be afraid.

41.   Lionni, Leo. *Six Crows*. Ill. by the author. New York: Knopf, 1988.

Trait: Problem-solving.

In a wheat field, a farmer puts up a scarecrow to rid the field of the nearby crows. In return, the crows try to scare the scarecrow away with a kite. The kite frightens the farmer. The farmer-scarecrow-kite situation escalates until the owl is called to act as a mediator and negotiator. Owl convinces them all to talk over the situation. K–3.

Target Activity: "Suppose You Were the Farmer?"

Suppose you were the farmer and you wanted to build a scarecrow. Use as many lines as you wish on a sheet of paper, add the colors you want, and write down the reasons why you think your scarecrow would frighten the birds away from your crop in the field. Jot down your ideas about your drawing. Describe your scarecrow and explain how it works to do what you want it to do.

Option: Other point of view. Suppose you were the crows and you wanted to frighten a scarecrow away. Use as many lines as you wish on a sheet of paper, add the colors you want, and write down the reasons why you think your imaginative idea would frighten the scarecrow away from the food you wanted to eat in the field.

42.   Lobel, Arnold. *Frog and Toad Are Friends*. Ill. by the author. New York: Harper & Row, 1970.

Trait: Relationship with significant other.

In this book, there are five short stories about these friends. In one story, Frog entices Toad out of his home so he can enjoy the spring day. Children enjoy Toad's reactions when Frog knocks on the door: "Toad, Toad," shouts Frog. "Wake up, it is spring!" "Blah," says a voice from inside the house. In another story, Frog finds Toad looking very sad and asks him what is wrong and Toad replies: "This is my sad time of day. It is the time when I wait for the mail to come. It always makes me very unhappy." "Why is that?" asks Frog. "Because I never get any mail," says Toad. Children enjoy the brief stories for each chapter. Children can read them separately, or listen to them read aloud, and smile at the humor in the author's writing. When animals pose as people in stories, an animal can develop a significant caring "other," just as a child can. There is friendship between the two characters, Frog and Toad, in this book and caring shown when Frog finds Toad is sad. K–3.

Target Activity: "Friends Check List"

Read other stories of friendship in *Frog and Toad All Year* (Harper & Row, 1976) or in *Frog and Toad Together* (Harper & Row, 1972). Make a list of traits such as the following: helpful, friendly, kind, bossy, understanding. Ask the students to select a different colored crayon for the two characters (such as green for Frog and brown for Toad). With the Frog crayon, have each child put a check on the line where they believe Frog has that trait. After the students have rated Frog on the traits, then ask them to check the traits for Toad. Engage children in showing others in the class how to "read" the check list and get information from it.

43.   Pollock, Penny. *Ants Don't Get Sunday Off*. Ill. by Lorinda Bryan Cauley. New York: G. P. Putnam's Sons, 1978.

Traits: Problem-solving; courage.

Anya is a brave, hardworking ant who is getting tired of working so hard and longs for an "adventure." One day there is a heavy rainstorm that washes away her nest and Anya gets more adventure than she bargained for. Anya becomes a heroine as she courageously saves the queen's life, goes back for the baby ants and finally does a daring rescue of three lost eggs. By this time she has lost her nest mates and the rest of the story outlines her harrowing search for her home. When she finally makes it home and the other ants immediately tell her of all the work that is to be done, Anya realizes that work is exactly what she wants to do. 1–2.

Target Activity: "The Flood"

Show children the "Map of Anya's Trip" on page 46 of the text. Discuss Anya's trials and tribulations trying to find her way back to her ant colony. Ask children to imagine they have been in a huge flood and have traveled in a turbulent stream far away from their homes. Have them chart, using construction paper and magic markers, their voyage home. Allow children to share their illustrations with the class when they are finished and describe their journeys.

44. Sharmet, Marjorie Weinman. *Grumley the Grouch.* **Ill. by Kay Chorao. New York: Holiday House, 1980.**
     Trait: Positive vision of life.
     J. Grumley Badger doesn't like anything; either the sun is too hot, or the rain is too wet, or the sky is too high. When his house gets flooded, he stays at Hank Muskrat's house, but Hank gets tired of his complaints. Next he stays with Nero Pig, but Nero gets tired of this grouchy nature, too. Finally, he stays with Brunhilda Badger, who has a similar mean disposition. As they get to know one another and begin to care for one another, they begin to find that they actually like one another. At first Grumley doesn't realize that his negative views of everything are making him, and everyone who meets him, unhappy. When he meets someone with an equally negative disposition, each can see how ludicrous the other's complaints are. As they grow in their relationship, their vision of life becomes much more positive. 1–2.
     Target Activity: "Positive Responses"
     Have children recount all of Grumley's complaints from the text as you list them on the chalkboard. Divide children into groups of three and assign them two of Grumley's complaints. Let one child in each group play the role of Grumley and voice one of the complaints while the other two children in the group offer an alternative way of looking at the situation. For example, Grumley says, "The sun is too hot," and one of the other two children might reply, "Yes, it's a perfect day to go swimming!" The third child might respond, "It's lovely and cool in the shade!" Let each child in the group take a turn playing the part of Grumley.

45. Stevenson, James. *Howard.* **Ill. by author. New York: Greenwillow, 1980.**
     Traits: Problem-solving; forming relationships with others.
     It is time to go south for the winter, but Howard is lagging behind and so the other ducks go without him. He tries to find his group, but doesn't succeed. He spends the winter in New York City with assorted creatures who show him how to survive as a "homeless duck" on the street. He adjusts to this lifestyle and when, one morning, he hears ducks overhead, he decides to stay with his new friends. 1–2.
     Target Activity: "Duck Diorama"
     Ask children if they have ever missed someone when they went away. Discuss the feelings associated with missing someone. Bring out the fact that when new friendships are made they need not replace other ones, but

that we can have new friends and still care about the old ones. Show children how to make a diorama of Howard and some of his old or new friends, using a shoe box, pipe cleaners, crepe paper and paste. Ask them to pick a scene in the book that shows how Howard made new friends and make the scene into a diorama. Allow children to share with the class their selected scenes and why they chose them.

46.   Uhl, Melvin. *Dexter, a Discontented Dog*. Ill. by Madalene Olteson. San Carlos, CA: Golden Gate Junior Books, 1963.

Trait: Positive vision of life.

Dexter looks at himself in the mirror and decides he doesn't like what he sees. He is a fat, pudgy bulldog but he tries to imagine himself looking more like his other canine friends that he meets on a walk down the street. He is envious of the poodle's curly coat, the dalmation's spots, the wiry whiskers of the terrier, the silky ears of the cocker spaniel, the pointed nose of the collie, and the long body of the dachshund. One night he has a dream that he acquires all of the other dogs' features, becoming truly strange-looking. When he wakes up and looks in the mirror, he sees he is still the same fat, pudgy bulldog. Now, however, Dexter is contented to look just as he does. K–3.

Target Activity: "Life-Size Portraits"

Have each child select a partner and trace the outline of the other child's body on a piece of butcher paper. Then have each child in the pair fill in the other child's features using crayons. Next ask each child to consider one "true" and "good" feature that they like about the other child. Finally, have children, one by one, share one positive phrase about their partner (e.g., "I like Jose's black hair" or "I like Leroy's long legs").

47.   Yolen, Jan. *Commander Toad in Space*. Ill. by Bruce Degen. New York: Coward-McCann, 1980.

Traits: Problem-solving; courage; sense of humor.

Commander Toad is the captain of the Star Warts, whose mission is to go where no spaceship has ever gone before. Though Toad is the bravest of them all, he is aided by his crew—deep-thinking Mr. Hop, the copilot; Jake Skyjumper, the navigator; and Lieutenant Lily, the mechanic. When they are about to land on a planet in an alien galaxy, all kinds of problems ensue. First, the planet is made of water and there is no place to land, so they devise a rubber lily pad. Then, when they land, they are approached by a huge and horrible monster, Deer Wader, who says the planet belongs to him and threatens to eat them. They escape by heating up the rubber lily pad and turning it into a hot air balloon. 1–3.

Target Activity: "What Do You Say to a Monster?"

Have children close their eyes and prepare to take an imaginary trip to the stars. Lead them through the galaxy, past the Milky Way, around Mars, to the little known planet of Uranus. Tell them to land their space ship and step onto barren land. As they trek over the closest mountain, they see a ferocious looking monster. Ask them the following questions:

1. What does the monster look like?
2. What does the monster say to you?
3. Is the monster friendly or mean?
4. Think about how you can convince the monster that you come in peace.

Allow children to share their visualizations orally with the class.

48. Young, Miriam. *Miss Suzy's Birthday*. Ill. by Arnold Lobel. New York: Parent's Magazine Press, 1974.

Trait: Problem-solving.

Miss Suzy is about to have a birthday and all her friends are trying to figure out what present she would like. They decide to have a formal meeting to determine what the best present would be. They invite Miss Suzy's four adopted children to help in the decision making. At the meeting it seems that everyone has a different idea and it is more confusing than ever, until Stevie, one of Miss Suzy's adopted children, comes up with a solution that consolidates everyone's ideas. K–3.

Target Activity: "The Perfect Gift"

Ask children if they have ever had problems thinking of the right gift to give a special person in their lives. Have children make suggestions as to what a person should know about another person in order to buy them "a perfect gift." Then have children ask those same questions of a partner. With information, let each child copy the phrase, "If I were buying a present for you, I would buy _____." Have each child then explain her/his selection to the class, based upon how the other child's questions were answered.

Folk Literature

49.   Aardema, Verna. *Bringing the Rain to Kapiti Plain: A Nandi Tale*. Ill. by Beatriz Vidal. New York: Dial, 1981.

Trait: Persistence.

This is an accumulating tale from Kenya and tells of Ki-Pat, a herdsman, who pierces a cloud with his eagle-feathered arrow to bring rain. On a barren, parched, dry African plain, hungry cattle wait for a huge dark cloud mass and rain to make the plain green with grass. An appended note mentions the origin in terms of the country, a sign of sensitivity on the author's part. Search for this title in UNICEF Curriculum Guide: *African Folktales*. 3.

Target Activity: "Herdsman and Hero"

Explore what this hero from the African culture has in common with some of the heroes in the culture of the United States. What traits of resiliency will the students discuss? To show similarities and differences of traits of resiliency between the two, draw two overlapping circles (Venn diagrams) and in one circle place the word, herdsman, and in the other, the name of their hero. In the appropriate circles, write down the traits the herdsman has (perseverance, ability to overcome obstacles, solving problems) and the hero has. If there are traits that the two have in common, write those traits in the overlapping area of the circles. Discuss the traits as they are written in the circles.

50.   Carreno, Mada, reteller. *El Viaje del Joven Matsua (The Travels of the Youth Matsua)*. Ill. by Gerado Suzan. Mexico City: Trillas, 1987.

Traits: Overcoming obstacles; problem-solving.

When Matsua and his family leave their land because there is no longer water, they travel to another place and wonder if the Tarahumara will receive them well. As they grow closer, Matsua discovers a young Tarahumara trapped on a cliff threatened by a large vulture. Matsua shows courage and overcomes the obstacles of scaling a dangerous cliff and warding off a large vulture to save the young Tarahumara. Matsua's family is welcomed by the family of the boy Matsua has rescued. 1–3.

Target Activity: "Similarities"

With the children, compare the main character in this story to the herdsman in *Bringing the Rain to Kapiti Plain: A Nandi Tale*. What traits of resiliency do they have in common? Ask children to outline the shapes of their right and left hands on paper. In the outline of one hand, write the word "herdsman," and in the outline of the other, write "Matsua." Under each name, place key words that identify the traits of each. Discuss each as the traits are identified and written. Have children trade papers with study partners and discuss what was written.

51.   Chan, Chin-Yi. *Good Luck Horse.* **Ill. by Platon Chan. London: Whittlesey, 1943.**

Trait: Positive vision of life.

Out of print but still available in some library collections, this pre–Hsia Dynasty Chinese legend is told by Chin-Yi Chan because it is a favorite one of her son, Plato. The tale is of Wah-Toong, the only son of a rich merchant, who cuts himself a horse from paper which becomes a live horse when wind snatches it and drops it in a magician's garden. The Good Luck horse damages a garden, scares other horses and is known as a bad-luck horse. Running away, he meets a beautiful mare and returns with Good-Luck Wife to Wah Toong. When war breaks out, the horse talks with the enemies' horses who all plan to mingle with the opposition so that no battle can take place and peace is achieved without fighting. When peace is achieved without fighting, all realize that there is no difference between good and bad luck. "There is only luck! Every day must be lived so that a man always does his best." 1–2.

Target Activity: "Class Interview"

Ask the students questions designed to get to the meaning that certain things have for them, what the girls and boys are familiar with, or to get descriptions of experiences they have had which can be used by the teacher to interpret their background and their feelings or their understanding of concepts of "luck." For this story, ask the students to describe what a good-luck horse might do. Accept the collection of notions from the children, even the ones the teacher suspects come from watching television.

1. What happens to turn the paper horse into a live one?

2. Who damages a garden? What would we expect to see in a damaged garden?

3. How are the other horses frightened? What name was the horse given then?

4. How does the horse achieve peace without fighting? From this, what can we learn about achieving peace without fighting?

52.   Cohen, Caron Lee. *The Mud Pony*. Ill. by Shonto Begay. New York: Scholastic, 1988.

Traits: Perseverance; problem-solving; positive vision of life.

A poor boy in an Indian camp shapes a pony of mud and cares for it. When he is separated from his people, the white-faced mud pony comforts him in a dream, and then comes to life, a gift from Mother Earth. The pony guides him to his parents and directs him in becoming a great warrior, hunter, and chief. When it is time for the pony to return to the earth, the chief removes the blanket which has always covered her, and she disappears in shrill winds and rushing rain leaving a patch of white clay on the wet ground. This ancient boy-hero story of the Pawnee Indians is illustrated by a Navajo artist and tells of a mud pony who comes to life and helps a young boy persevere, assist his people, and defeat their enemies. 1–3.

Target Activity: "Discussion of *The Mud Pony*"

1. What can you tell about different animals who seem to help people?

2. Why do you think there was a need for warriors and chiefs in this story? What traits of resiliency can you find about the boy-hero in this story?

Ask a student to retell the action in this story. The teacher also guides the students through the events: 1) the white-faced mud pony comes to life; 2) it guides the boy to his parents; 3) it directs him in becoming a great warrior, hunter, and chief; and 4) it returns to the earth.

Suggest to the girls and boys that they imagine the conversation that might have taken place at these times: 1) when the pony comes to life and the boy first talks to the pony; 2) when the boy reaches his parents; 3) what the pony says to guide the boy in becoming a chief; and 4) the boy's farewell to the pony when it returns to earth.

Use separate sheets of butcher paper or separate sides of the writing board to show the dialogue between the boy and the pony. Introduce the use of quotation marks. Assign a student to each line of back-and-forth dialogue to say the words between the two conversationalists. Assign a student to each line of dialogue to copy and to illustrate. When finished, the students get in pairs and read their lines to one another and talk about their drawings.

53.   Davis, Deborah. *The Secret of the Seal*. Ill. by Judy Labrasca. New York: Crown, 1989.

Traits: Overcoming obstacles; problem-solving.

Using initiative and resourcefulness, Kyo, a young Eskimo boy, protects his playmate—a seal pup—from his uncle, the hunter. Young Kyo goes out to kill his first seal and finds a bond between himself and the female seal that he names Tooky—originally his quarry. Kyo tries to prevent the capture of his new animal friend which brings a clash between traditional and modern values and a conflict in loyalties. 2–3.

Target Activity: "Kyo's Solution"

Encourage children to discuss the ways Kyo solved his problem about his seal pup playmate. How will the children try to explain the clash between traditional and modern values that occurred in the story? What are some of the main reasons that the children believe Kyo got into a conflict of loyalties? Invite children to relate experiences from their lives to the story.

54. de Paola, Tomie. *The Legend of the Bluebonnet.* **Ill. by the author. New York: Scholastic, 1983.**

Trait: Positive vision of life.

In this retold Comanche legend, a drought and famine have killed the mother, father and grandparents of She-Who-Is-Alone, a small girl. All she has left is a warrior doll that her mother once made for her. One evening, the shaman of the camp tells his people that the famine is the result of the people becoming selfish. They must make a sacrifice of the most valued possession among them and life will be restored. No one volunteers a valued possession except She-Who-Is-Alone, who offers her warrior doll. Deep in the night she makes a burnt offering of the doll, and then scatters its ashes over the fields below. Where the ashes have fallen, the ground becomes covered with bluebonnets. The Comanche people take the flowers as a sign of forgiveness from the Great Spirits. From that day on, the little girl is known as One-Who-Dearly-Loved-Her-People. The small girl gives up the thing she loves best in all the world for her people. She spends a frightening night alone on a hill offering her doll as a burnt offering to the Great Spirits, clearly a courageous act of self-sacrifice and unselfishness. 2–3.

Target Activity: "Stories of Precious Possessions"

Bring to students' minds other stories they have read or heard where the main character has a most precious possession, e.g., Tera and her pig, Wilbur in *Charlotte's Web* by E. B. White; Sarah and her unicorn in *Sarah's Unicorn* by Bruce and Katherine Coville; the child and his carrot plant in *The Carrot Seed* by Ruth Kraus; Dick and his cat in *Dick Whittington and His Cat* by Kathleen Lines. Have children rewrite *The Legend of the Bluebonnet*, superimposing the new character and her/his prized possessions in a famine of modern times. Tell students to describe the famine. "Tell what your character says when (s)he offers his/her prized possession as a sacrifice to end the famine. How does your character feel? Describe the night on the mountain. What happens as a result of your character's sacrifice? How does your character feel about saving his/her people? What has your character learned from the experience?"

55.   de Paola, Tomie, reteller. *The Legend of the Indian Paint-brush*. Ill. by the reteller. New York: Putnam Group, 1988.

Trait: Perseverance.

This is the story of Little Gopher, who cannot be like other children, but who, through his art, has a special gift for his people. Little Gopher finds his place among his people by painting their deeds so that they will always be remembered. He is lonely, but faithful and true. He is rewarded with magical brushes left for him on a hillside. They hold colors and allow him to paint his vision of the evening sky. Discarded, they take root and multiply and bloom in colors of red, orange, and yellow. K–2.

Target Activity: "Colors for Paintbrushes"

Invite children to see the ways primary colors turn into other colors with the overhead, a clear glass or plastic container, water, and drops of food coloring. Drops of red and yellow food coloring in the water in the container are swirled and the overhead projects the mingling as the colors turn into orange. Encourage children to use the colors of red, orange, and yellow, and other shades to create their own visions of the evening sky or of other deeds of people to show in their drawings that no matter how small or young we are, our visions are important ones.

56.   Esbensen, Barbara Juster. *The Star Maiden*. Ill. by Helen K. Davie. Boston: Little, Brown, 1988.

Trait: Positive vision of life.

This is an explanatory tale that tells the origin of a flower that originated with the Ojibway (Chippewa) in the north lake country. A star maiden watches the earth and wants to make her home with the tribe who prepare to welcome her. The rose on the hillside where she first comes to rest is too far from the village and a flower on the prairie is too near the trampling feet of buffalo. Finally, she finds the peaceful surface of a lake and calls her sisters down to live with her where they can be seen today as water lilies. 1–3.

Target Activity: "Pattern in Ojibway (Chippewa) Tales"

To continue a study on Ojibway Indian legends, discuss the poetic use of words in this story and the illustrations that are framed on three sides with the patterns authentic to the tribe. Read another legend about a positive vision of life, Esbensen's *The Ladder in the Sky* (Little, Brown, 1989).

57.   Goble, Paul, reteller. *Her Seven Brothers.* **Ill. by the reteller. New York: Bradbury Press, 1988.**

Trait: Perseverance.

A lonely Indian girl makes clothing decorated with porcupine quills for seven brothers she has never seen, and after many months, she travels north with her mother to find the seven brothers. When she finds the trail she wants, the girl says goodbye to her mother with the words, "Soon you will see me again with my brothers; everyone will know and love us!" In the land of pines, she finds the tipi of the brothers, gives them their clothing, and is looked after well by the brothers. One day, the chief of the Buffalo nation wants the sister, and when the brothers refuse to let her go, the chief threatens to return with the whole Buffalo nation and kill them. Later, a shaking of the earth announced the rumbling of the Buffalo people stampeding toward the tipi. When the youngest brother shoots an arrow up into the air, a pine tree appears and grows upward as fast as the flight of the arrow. The girl and the brothers climb up just as the chief of the Buffalo strikes the tree a mighty blow and the tree starts to topple over. The youngest brother shoots arrow after arrow into the sky and the tree continues to grow taller and taller until they were all far away up among the stars. There, they jump down from the branches on to the prairies of the world above the Earth. The girl and her brothers are still there and can be seen as the Big Dipper. If one looks quite closely, one of the stars is near a tiny star that is the little boy walking with his sister who is never lonely now.

Target Activity: "Meaning in Cheyenne Designs"

In the Cheyenne designs (circa 1900), one sees animals, birds, butterflies, and flowers. Since these living creatures share the Earth with humans, the creatures are included in the designs. Sometimes two of each are drawn, or to show abundance, many are drawn. What design would you make for a tipi? Would your design include the members of the Buffalo nation, the faithful dogs, the nearby deer, the porcupine "who climbs trees closest to Sun himself?" Draw a sketch of your design and show it to others. Discuss your design with someone and explain your reasons for drawing what you did. What meaning does your design have?

58.   Goble, Paul, reteller. *Iktomi and the Bolder: A Plains Indian Story.* **Ill. by the reteller. New York: Orchard Books/Watts, 1988.**

Trait: Humor.

The vain Iktomi (eek-toe-me), the Plains Indian who gets into the worst kind of trouble, has overdressed for his journey. When he grows too warm, he offers his blanket as a gift to a boulder. When it begins to rain, Iktomi pretends the gift was only a loan. While Iktomi is congratulating himself on his foresight to bring the blanket, the boulder comes to reclaim the gift. Iktomi tries to elude the boulder, but it pins his legs. As the moon rises, bats appear and Iktomi tricks them into attacking the boulder. The bats break it into small stones. This is why bats have flat faces and there are rocks scattered over the Great Plains. Ink and watercolor illustration show movement. A boulder is chasing him and won't let him go. Young children enjoy the humor in this trickster tale. K–3.

Target Activity: "Indian Trickster Characters"

Discuss the background information in the foreward about Indian trickster characters and Iktomi. Point out that the book has large type and an informal, narrative voice with asides from the storyteller and the character, Iktomi. Dark print tells children what happens; light print gives the asides for the teller, e.g., *That's not true, is it?* and invites comments from the audience. Invite children to tell about other trickster characters they know about from other stories. Build a chart of information to show what they know about this type of character in literature.

Continue the focus on Indian trickster tales with Goble's *Iktomi and the Berries: A Plains Indian Story* (Orchard, 1989). In *Berries* the Lakota trickster is dressed inappropriately in full ceremonial clothing to set out to hunt prairie dogs. He plans a feast to impress his relatives. After several failures, the silly Iktomi sees buffalo berries in the water, dives for them, and is unaware that they are a reflection. He ties a rock to his neck with a long rope to stay below surface to find the berries and barely escapes. He beats the berry bushes with his bow in anger and this is the way the berries are still harvested today in the plains. Italic text asks for comments as in the Lakota tradition.

59.   Grimm Brothers. *Rumpelstiltskin*. Ill. by Paul O. Zelinsky. New York: Dutton, 1986.

Trait: Problem-solving.

Parents boast that their daughter has an ability to spin and are told that she must spin straw into gold or lose her head. Crying, the girl notices a creature who offers to do the spinning for her. In return, she will give him her firstborn child when she marries the king. When he comes to claim the child, he returns three times to give her three chances to guess his name. If at the end of the third time, she hasn't guessed his name, the child will be his. Each time she tries to solve her problem by bargaining and by guessing the creature's name. Before the last day of the bargaining time, a maid follows the creature and hears him singing his name. She returns and tells the queen.

Target Activity: "Do We Know the Name?"

Compare this book with *Duffy and the Devil* (Farrar, Straus, 1973) by Harve Zemach in which an inefficient maid, Duffy, misleads her employer about her ability to spin and makes an agreement with the devil who promises to do her knitting for three years. At that time, Duffy must know his name or go away with him. When the time arrives, the squire tells Duffy what he has overheard while out hunting. The creature sings a verse that children can repeat:

> Tomorrow! Tomorrow! Tomorrow's the day!
> I'll take her! I'll take her! I'll take her away!
> Let her weep, let her cry,
> Let her beg, let her pray—
> She'll never guess my name is . . . Tarraway!

60. Louie, Ai-Lang. *Yeh Shen: A Cinderella Story from China.* **Ill. by Ed Young. New York: Philomel, 1982.**

Traits: Formation of close, trusting relationships; persistence in the face of failure.

Versions of Cinderella from other cultures have many similarities to this ancient tale (A.D. 618–907). It appears in *The Miscellaneous Record of Yu Yang* and is authored by Tuan Ch'eng-Shih. It predates European versions. A beautiful girl is treated badly by her stepmother, and when a festival approaches, Yeh Shen is left weeping at home to do the heaviest and dirtiest of chores while Stepmother and Stepsister go off dancing. Her wish to go to the festival is granted by an old man through the power of magic fish bones. Her slippers are woven of golden threads in a pattern similar to the scales of a fish, her gown is azure, and she has a beautiful blue feathered cloak. When her foot fits into the beautiful slipper she loses at the festival, she marries the king who refuses to let the stepmother and stepsister come to the palace to live. 2–4.

Target Activity: "Resilient Yeh Shen"

Return to the book and look for traits of resiliency in Yeh Shen. Did she have a relationship with a significant other? Did she persevere? Did she overcome obstacles? Did she solve problems? Ask the students to compare this version with another version of this story and look for traits of resiliency there, too. Make a comparison chart to show the similarities and the differences.

Resilient Cinderellas

Titles of Books	Character	Setting	Magic	Problem	Resolution
1.					
2.					

Some of the versions of Cinderella you may want to consider are:

Mbane, Phumla. *Nomi and the Magic Fish*. Ill. by Carole Byard. New York: Doubleday, 1972. (Africa)

Nygren, Tord. *Fiddler and His Brothers*. Ill. by the author. New York: Morrow, 1987. (male Cinderella)

Perrault, Charles. *Cinderella*. Ill. by Marcia Brown. New York: Scribner's 1954. (France)

Steel, Flora Annie. *Tattercoats*. Ill. by Diane Goode. New York: Bradbury, 1978. (England)

Steptoe, John. *Mufaro's Beautiful Daughters: An African Tale*. Ill. by the reteller. New York: Lothrop, Lee & Shepard, 1987.

Whitney, Thomas P., translator. *Vasilisa the Beautiful*. Ill. by Nonny Hogrogian. New York: Macmillan, 1970. (Russia)

61. Lottridge, Celia Barker, reteller. *The Name of the Tree*. Ill. by Ian Wallace. New York: McElderry Books/Macmillan, 1990.
Trait: Problem-solving.

When a drought settles on an African plain, animals search for food and find a tree with every fruit imaginable. This Bantu folktale tells that the animals must learn the name of the tree before it will surrender its bounty. Faced with this problem, the animals persevere. Muted gray and green illustrations show the dry land and hot African sun. Recommended storytelling. K–3.

Target Activity: "Problem-solving: the Importance of Water"

Explore what the Nandi and Bantu cultures in Africa have in common with our own, the reliance on water, the resiliency of people (or animals posing as people in stories) when they are faced with a problem. Compare the solution in this story to the one in *Bringing the Rain to Kapiti Plain: A Nandi Tale* and identify the importance of water to all people.

62. McDermott, Gerald. *Anansi the Spider: A Tale from the Ashanti*. Adapted and ill. by Gerald McDermott. New York: Holt, Rinehart & Winston, 1972.
Traits: Overcoming obstacles; problem-solving.

Six wondrous deeds are performed by the sons of Anansi, the spider-hero. Each of the sons is an expert in some way. Their names relate their expertise that is useful in solving problems. Their names are See Trouble, Road Builder, River Drinker, Game Skinner, Stone Thrower, and Cushion. They save their father from a terrible danger. 2–3.

Target Activity: "Movements for the Characters"

Before the story is reread, the children decide on motions and movements for the characters for an audience participation story. The names of the sons will lead the young children quickly into ideas for movements. When a character's name is mentioned in the rereading, the teacher pauses and gives the audience time to respond with the movements that identify the character.

63.   McDermott, Gerald. *Arrow to the Sun: A Pueblo Indian Tale*. **Ill. by the adapter. New York: Viking, 1974.**
  Traits: Overcoming obstacles; problem-solving.
  This is the desert world where humans, nature, and spiritual forces are intertwined (e.g., the yellow sun is the people's god, worshipped in the circular ceremonial chamber, the kiva). A spark of life from the sun becomes the sun god's son on earth. He decides to search for his father, and during his quest, he meets Corn Planter who silently tends his crops, Pot Maker who silently makes clay pots, and Arrow Maker who silently creates a special arrow into whose shape the boy changes. The Arrow Maker then fits the arrow into a bow to shoot it into the heavens to the sun. The boy proves he is the son of the sun god by passing through four chambers of ceremony—he fights the Kiva of Lions, the Kiva of Serpents, the Kiva of Bees, and the Kiva of Lightning—and takes on the sun's power. He returns to earth as an arrow returning with all the colors of the rainbow. The people celebrate with the dance of life. Motif of transformation as the boy becomes an arrow in the search for his father. 2–3.
  Target Activity: "Proving Myself"
  With the children, discuss a time in their lives when they had to "prove" themselves. Discuss how one (some) of the traits of resiliency would help people "prove" themselves against adversity. Invite the girls and boys to complete a sentence that begins: "One day to prove myself, I . . . ." Encourage the children to create original drawings to illustrate their sentences. Ask the children to read their sentences and discuss their drawings with others in the room. When completed, collect the pages and staple them together with a cover titled "Proving Myself." Place the children's book in the classroom book corner for future reading and browsing.

64.   Mahy, Margaret, reteller. *The Seven Chinese Brothers*. **Ill. by Jean and Mou-sien Tseng. New York: Scholastic, 1990.**
  Trait: Developing a special hobby or talent.
  Seven brothers walk, talk, and look alike. Each has a special power which assists him in overcoming obstacles and solving problems. When the third brother is sentenced to be beheaded by the emperor, the fourth brother (who has bones of iron) takes his place. When sentenced to drowning and burning, he is replaced by a different brother who survives. Rich watercolors show the ceremonial robes of court. The positive outcome of story is foretold by the book's cover, a flash-forward into the story's ending, showing the smiling brothers towering over a cowering emperor. Recommended storytelling. K–3.

Target Activity: "Special Talents"

Discuss the special talents of the brothers in the story and ask children to contribute additional information about other talents of characters they know about from folk literature. (See Gerald McDermott's *Anansi the Spider: A Tale from the Ashanti* [Holt, Rinehart & Winston, 1972].) In McDermott's retelling, the brothers' names are See Trouble, Road Builder, River Drinker, Game Skinner, Stone Thrower, and Cushion. Begin a word map about special talents of brothers in folk tales to record the information the children contribute. Display the map so additional facts can be added during the week.

65. Mosel, Arlene. *The Funny Little Woman*. Ill. by Blair Lent. New York: Dutton, 1972.

Trait: Humor.

In this Japanese tale, a little woman pursues a rice dumpling and is captured by the wicked Oni (green underground creatures who live in dark caverns). A captive, the woman must cook for them with a magic paddle that makes grains of rice. Trying to escape, she leaves in a boat floating on an underground river. To recapture her, the Oni suck the river water into their mouths and leave the woman's boat in the river's waterless bed. The funny little woman has a contagious laugh and it makes the Oni laugh, too. Laughing, they spill all the water back into the river bed. She floats back to her home and becomes the richest woman in Japan by making rice cakes with her magic paddle. 1–3.

Target Activity: "Humorous Poems"

Share poems about being humorous to show another way of being resilient. Several traits of resiliency are discussed in humorous ways in the verses of J. Prelutsky's *Something Big Has Been Here*. For example, in "The Turkey Shot Out of the Oven," the unknown narrator promises to plan ahead the next time he/she stuffs a turkey and promises "never again to stuff a turkey with popcorn that hadn't been popped."

Trait	*Titles of Poems*
ability to gain attention in a positive way	"I Am Growing a Glorious Garden"
ability to plan ahead and solve problems	"The Turkey Shot Out of the Oven"
development of a hobby or talent	"I Am Wunk"
feeling of autonomy	"Kevin the King of the Jungle"
persistence in the face of failure	"A Remarkable Adventure"

positive vision of life	"My Uncle Looked Me in the Eye"
relationship with a caring "other" person	"My Brother Is as Generous as Anyone Could Be"
sense of humor	"I Want a Pet Porcupine, Mother"
sense of control over one's life	"My Family's Sleeping Late Today"

66. Rehyer, Becky. *My Mother Is the Most Beautiful Woman in the World*. Ill. by Ruth Gannett. New York: Howell, Soskin, 1945.

Trait: Relationship with a significant other.

All are preparing for a Ukrainian harvest feast and six-year-old Varya gets separated from her mother in the fields. When found by rescuers, Varya describes her mother as "the most beautiful woman in the world." Everyone searches for the mother until the child sees her rounded, "almost toothless" mother who is beautiful in the eyes of her daughter. K–2.

Target Activity: "The One Who Is Most Beautiful to Me"

Ask children to talk about who is "most beautiful" to them and to describe the person. Talk about the descriptive words. Talk about why this person is "most beautiful." What does this person do for the child?

67. Shulevitz, Uri. *The Treasure*. Ill. by the author. New York: Farrar, Straus & Giroux, 1978.

Trait: Perseverance.

In this folktale, Isaac is compelled by a dream to look for a treasure under the bridge near the Royal Palace. He makes the long journey to the capital through forests and over mountains. There, he finds no treasure but hears the words of the palace guard who says, ". . . the treasure is buried under a stove in the house of a man named Isaac." He retraces the steps of his long journey and perseveres to find the treasure buried under his own house. He uses the money to build a house of prayer with an inscription, "Sometimes one must travel far to discover what is near." 1–3.

Target Activity: "A Treasure in My House"

Discuss the meaning of treasure as more than money buried under a house. Invite the girls and boys to tell of something that is a "treasure" at their house. A treasure can be a generous brother, a caring sister, an understanding mother, a hard-working father, a musically talented relative, etc. Ask the children to complete a sentence that starts with, "The treasure in my house is . . . ." Then, ask the children to draw illustrations to show the treasure. When finished, the children get together in pairs and trade their work for discussion and feedback. Invite the children to take their work with them to show the drawing to someone in the home.

68.   Xiong, Blia, reteller. *Nine-in-One Grr! Grr!* **Ill. by Nancy Hom. Adapted by Cathy Spagnoli. Chicago: Children's Book Press, 1989.**

Traits: Problem-solving; planning ahead.

In this Hmong folktale, the world began when a lonely tiger journeyed to the great god Shao to discover if she would have cubs. Shao says that she will have nine cubs a year if she can remember his words. To remember, the tiger says a memory chant on the way home with the words, "Nine-in-one Grr! Grr!" The Eu bird (black bird) asks Shao to change what he said because if Tiger has nine cubs each year, the cubs would eat all of the birds. Shao cannot change what he has said. Planning ahead about what to do, the bird flies to the tiger (who is trying to remember the magical words of the great God Shao), and interferes with the arrangement of the words by reversing the words "nine in one" to "one in nine," altering natural history. Illustrations have intricate borders and are reminiscent of story-stitching (stories told in needlework). 1–3.

Target Activity: "Black Bird's Problem"

Invite children to discuss the problem faced by the black bird and the way it was solved. Encourage boys and girls to think of other ways the story could have solved the problem for the bird. On the chalkboard, write down the ideas dictated by the children. Ask children to draw scenes of ways the problem could have been solved.

69.   Yolen, Jane. *The Emperor and the Kite.* **Ill. by Ed Young. Cleveland, OH: World, 1967.**

Traits: Relationship with a significant other; perseverance; problem-solving.

In this fanciful folklike tale, the smallest child, Djeow Seow, rescues her father, the emperor, from his prison in a tower. Using a rope, she attaches a basket of tea, rice and poppy seed to her kite. Each day the small child flies it up to the barred window of the tower. With the supplies, the emperor returns to the palace, expels the criminals, and establishes peace in the kingdom. He places a tiny throne for Djeow Seow next to his. She learns how to rule the kingdom gently and loyally when it is time. K–2.

Target Activity: "Flying a Kite of Resiliency"

Discuss the traits of resiliency shown by Djeow Seow. Draw a visual display of a large kite with a long kite-tail. Along the trail of the kite draw lines radiating outward, and on each line, write one of the traits discussed by the children. Invite the girls and boys to make their own kites of resiliency and put in their own words.

Historical Fiction

70. Brenner, Barbara. *Wagon Wheels*. Ill. An I CAN READ history book. New York: Harper & Row, 1978.

Trait: Problem-solving.

This book is based upon a true story taken from the diaries of a family of black settlers in the pioneer days. The story takes place in Kansas in the 1870s. The Muldie boys and their father have traveled the arduous trail from the east coast to Kansas in covered wagons. The boys' mother died on the trail. Now the boys and their father face a hard winter in a primitive dugout house. Looking for a better life, the father moves on farther westward, leaving the three brothers to care for one another. When at last the father sends for his sons, they must find their way out west alone, braving the dangers of the wilderness and fighting prejudice because of their skin color. 1–2.

Target Activity: "I Think I Can"

After discussing the bravery of the Muldie boys with the children, read or retell the story of *The Little Engine That Could*. Have children volunteer some tasks they find difficult to do. Write these on the chalkboard. On construction paper, have children draw a picture of one new thing that may or may not have been suggested that (s)he would like to learn how to do. Under the picture, ask children to write "I think I can _____." (Older children can write in their own words, younger children may dictate to the teacher or classroom helper.) Save entries for a class booklet titled, "I Think I Can," with the last page ending, "I Did!"

71. Byars, Betsy. *The Golly Sisters Go West*. Ill. by Sue Truesdell. New York: Harper & Row, 1986.

Traits: Problem-solving; relationship with a caring "other."

May-May and Rose are two high-spirited singing and dancing sisters who travel out west in a covered wagon, entertaining people and getting in and out of trouble all the way. First, they can't get the horse to go to begin their journey, until May-May reveals the magic word. Next, they are preparing to give a show to a crowd of people, but take so long to argue about who goes first that the audience leaves. Then May-May loses her red hat, and in another argument about who should sing first, the hat gets squashed. May-May does a sad dance, "The Dance of the Squashed Hat." Finally, the sisters hear something outside their wagon one night. They decide that their fussing has scared the prowler away. They agree never to fuss again unless they hear something outside their wagon. Though their problem-solving skills are unorthodox, the two sisters show how, even during arguments, siblings can really care for one another and work together. K–3.

Target Activity: "Who's First?"

Discuss with children how the Golly sisters always fought about who would go first. Ask them to share some of the arbitrary ways they use to decide who goes first, e.g., flip a coin, take turns going first, the rhyme "one potato, two potato...," etc. Let two children volunteer to be the Golly sisters fighting about who would go first in the show. Ask them to provide a peaceful resolution to the conflict.

72.   Coerr, Eleanor. *Chang's Paper Pony*. Ill. by Deborah Kogan Ray. New York: Harper & Row, 1988.

Traits: Problem-solving; relationship with caring other.

Chang and his grandfather have just come to California from China during the time of the gold rush. They work in the kitchen of a mining camp where Chang is often teased by the miners. He is very lonely and asks his grandfather if he could have a pony, but they cannot afford one. A kind miner, Big Pete, offers to take Chang panning for gold if Chang will clean Pete's cabin. Maybe he can find enough gold to enable him to buy a pony. He finds no gold while panning, but while cleaning Big Pete's cabin he finds some gold nuggets in the cracks in the floorboards. He turns these over to Big Pete, reluctantly. Big Pete surprises him with a pony. Educators who are interested in this historically accurate story may want to avoid the use of the illustrations of Chinese men shown with their hair in pigtails and performing menial tasks at the mining camp. K–3.

Target Activity: "I Wish I Had..."

On the chalkboard, write a collaborative poem with the class in which each line begins, "I wish..." Stop when all who wish to have had a chance to participate, then read the poem orally. Finally, ask children to offer suggestions as to how they might obtain the items they wish for. Brainstorm some possible ways that they might earn money.

73.   Coerr, Eleanor. *The Josefina Story Quilt*. Ill. by Bruce Degen. New York: Harper & Row, 1986.

Trait: Positive vision of life.

Faith's family is traveling to California in a covered wagon in the

1850s. The little girl convinces her father to allow her to take her pet hen, Josefina, with them on the journey. Her father warns that if the hen causes any trouble, ". . . out she goes!" Josefina starts a stampede on one occasion, and another time nearly drowns in a river, forcing Faith's brother, Adam, to try to rescue her. Still, Faith talks her father into allowing the hen to stay. When Josefina's cackles warn the family of robbers in their wagon one night, Josefina becomes a heroine, but dies soon after of old age. Though devastated at the loss of her pet, Faith puts her warm feelings for Josefina into a patchwork quilt that pictorially tells the story of their good and bad times together. 1–3.

Target Activity: "Story Quilt"

Hold a general discussion about the good and bad times in Faith's life. Ask children to share some of the good and bad events in their own lives. Give each child 25 three-inch squares made from different colored construction paper. Ask them to make a small picture on each square to represent some happy or sad event in their life. Allow each child to then paste the squares together to form a story quilt on a large sheet of tag board or construction paper, using any pattern they wish. Encourage them to tell about their story quilt and what each patch reminds them of when they see it.

74. Dalgliesh, Alice. *The Courage of Sarah Noble*. Ill. by Leonard Weisgard. New York: Charles Scribner's Sons, 1954.

Trait: Positive vision of life.

Eight-year-old Sarah Noble travels from the Massachusetts Colony to the wilderness of Connecticut to cook while her father builds a new home for the family. "Keep up your courage, Sarah Noble," says mother as she wraps Sarah's cloak around her before the two begin the journey. When her father goes to bring the rest of the family, Sarah stays with Tall John, his Indian wife, and their children and the words of her mother (along with her cloak) become a comforting refrain to give her strength to face the new life in the wilderness. Based on a true incident. 2–3.

Target Activity: "Courage Pages"

Invite students to consider themselves as a band of courageous people. There are many acts of courage that each knows about that the others are not aware of in their experiences. Explain that just as Sarah had courage, others must keep searching to find what makes them courageous in special situations. Write on the chalkboard or chart the following beginning sentence starters:

Once, I had courage and I _____

Today, to show courage, I would _____

Soon, I want to be able to show courage and _____

Complete the lines with dictations from the group and encourage students to contribute ideas for the sentence endings. Encourage students to write their own sentences of courage and to illustrate them if they wish to do so. Collect the pages of courage and put them into a class Courage Book. Display the book so all students can read about what the others can do or hope to do in the future.

75.   Lawson, Robert. *They Were Strong and Good.* **Ill. by the author. New York: Viking, 1940.**

Traits: Persistence and perseverance.

The author uses relatives in this biography to show ancestors who had to be strong and build the beginnings of our nation. This is the story of a mother and a father and their mothers and fathers and the country that they helped build. A Scotch sea captain, a little Dutch girl, a Minnesota girl, and an Englishman who was a preacher in Alabama are all presented as ancestors of the author. Brief text. Lawson uses the pictures to show the persistence and perseverance of his ancestors. Details in the illustrations show "wholesomeness" of the ancestors in scenes of the Civil War, a grandmother at sea, and caring for one another. 1–2.

Target Activity: "My Ancestors"

With some of the interested girls and boys, discuss the backgrounds of adult relatives in their homes (i.e., aunts, uncles, grandmothers, mothers and fathers and their mothers and fathers). Invite interested children to make a visual display of family trees of the adults in their homes.

Their mothers and fathers
(or adults in the home)

_____   _____
(name)   (name)

Mother and Father
(adults in the home)

_____   _____
(name)   (name)

Me

_____
(name)

76.   Monjo, Ferdinand. *The Drinking Gourd.* **Ill. by Fred Brenner. New York: Harper, 1970.**

Traits: Courage; problem-solving.

Tommy is a little boy growing up in New England in the decade before the Civil War. In his barn, he is surprised to find a family of escaping slaves that has been hidden there by his father. His father explains that he is a "conductor" on the Underground Railroad and that, although he doesn't like to break the law, he feels he must, because he feels it is wrong to own people. Together Tommy and his father take the family to the next station. While the family and Tommy's father lie hidden in the hay truck, Tommy drives. Tommy is stopped by a U.S. marshal and his men. They ask him if he has slaves hidden in the back of the truck. Tommy understands the importance of his mission, and shows his ability to solve his problem as he bravely thinks of a way to keep them from searching the hay truck. Quickly, Tommy says he is running away. The men laugh and tell him to go home. The family of slaves makes a safe escape. 2–3.

Target Activity: "Good and Bad"

Discuss the concept of slavery with children and make the point that it is wrong to judge people on the basis of the color of their skin. To play "Good and Bad," ask one child to leave the room. Pick a physical feature, such as eye color or hair color. Tell the students in one group, such as those with brown hair, that they are "good," while all others are bad. Have the child who has left the room return and try to figure out the basis on which children are "good" or "bad." Let each (good and bad) group share their feelings about the arbitrary labeling.

Option: "The Code in *The Drinking Gourd*"

With the children, discuss the illustration that shows the light sketches of seven runaways who carry their bundles over their shoulders superimposed over the drawing of the house and barn that gives a sense of the magnitude of cause, the task, the danger, the importance, the symbol. Discuss the danger and the excitement as Tommy goes with his father and an escaping black family to take them on the next part of the journey. Discuss the ethical considerations of knowing one must break a law. Father and son discuss the breaking of an unjust law.

The Drinking Gourd was the code song that the slaves sang. The song was used to point the direction for escape by following the North Star, using the Big Dipper as a guide. The words to the song are in the book.

77.   Parrish, Peggy. *Good Hunting Blue Sky.* **Ill. by James Watts. New York: Harper & Row, 1989.**

Traits: Feeling of autonomy; problem-solving; courage.

Blue Sky is going hunting for the first time in his young life. He tells his father, "Today I will bring home the meat." He shoots an arrow at the turkey and the turkey flees. He shoots at a deer and he, too, flees. Blue Sky decides to go after bigger quarry. When he sees a bear, he realizes it is too big, and Blue Sky climbs a tree. Feeling he has failed, Blue Sky starts toward home when suddenly he is attacked by a ferocious wild boar. Thinking quickly, Blue Sky leaps onto the boar's back and rides it all the way home, where his father shoots the boar with his bow and arrow. All the people in the village are invited to the feast. Blue Sky tells them about the hunt. They change the young boy's name to Big Hunter. K–3.

Target Activity: "Growing Up"

Explain to children that in the history of the original Native American culture, some young boys had to bring home an animal to prove they were growing up. Similarly, have children brainstorm some things that they can do now that they couldn't do, or weren't allowed to do, when they were younger. Have them draw a picture of themselves doing the activity and then share it with the rest of the class. This sharing underscores the idea that the students are growing up and capable.

78.   Provensen, Alice and Martin Provensen. *The Glorious Flight: Across the Channel with Louis Bleriot, July 25, 1909.* **New York: Viking, 1983.**

Traits: Persistence and perseverance; problem-solving.

In 1901, in Cambrai, France, Louis Bleriot has one wish—to build a flying machine. He builds a machine with wings that flap like a chicken, turned by a small motor; a gliding machine that is towed into the air by a motorboat; a machine that has two motors and two propellers but will only go in circles on the water; and finally, a machine with a powerful motor and propeller that takes him across the English Channel. 3.

Target Activity: "A Pioneer of Aviation"

The teacher asks the students to listen to the story again for information about Who, What, and Where. Then the information is reviewed again to be put together to make a sentence that sums up what was read. In other words, the students will connect the informational items in a way that summarizes information from the story.

A Pioneer of Aviation:
Who, What, and Where

Who:

Louis Bleriot _____
(resiliency traits: perseverance, problem-solving)

What:

the aeroplane, Bleriot XI   _____

Where:

Cambrai, France _____

Summary Sentence:

_____

_____

79. Rappaport, Doreen. *The Boston Coffee Party.* **Ill. by Emily Arnold McCully. New York: Harper & Row, 1988.**

Traits: Feeling of autonomy; problem-solving.

Sarah and her sister, Emma, are growing up in wartime colonial Boston. Sarah is outraged when she is sent to get sugar and the evil Merchant Thomas overcharges her for it. Then when another customer comes in, he takes the sugar from Sarah and sells it at an even higher price. When Aunt Harriet announces that Merchant Thomas has locked up 40 barrels of coffee in his warehouse so that Boston will run out of coffee and he can overcharge, the women want to do something. Instead of allowing themselves to be victimized by Merchant Thomas' greed and overcharges on food, the women and children devise a plan to solve the problem and fight back. Sarah comes up with the idea of having a "coffee party," like the men had when they threw the English tea into the harbor. The women and young children capture Merchant Thomas and force him to give them the key to the warehouse. They take all the coffee and bring it home in containers that they have brought. K–3.

Target Activity: "Coffee Party"

After reading the story aloud to children, reread just the dialogue to them, telling them that they are going to act out the "coffee party." Select children to play the roles of Sarah, Emma, their mother, Aunt Harriet, and Merchant Thomas. Let others be women and children who help to capture Merchant Thomas and fill the containers with coffee.

80. Rylant, Cynthia. *When I Was Young in the Mountains.* **Ill. by Diane Goode. New York: Dutton, 1984.**

Trait: Significant relationship with others.

In this historical fiction tale, there are memories of a girl's happy years of growing up in the mountains of Virginia. She recalls her grandmother's kisses, her cornbread, and going to the swimming hole. There is a repetitive phrase of "when I was young in the mountains...." 3.

Target Activity: "When I Was Young"

Invite the students to tell about some of their early life experiences and then turn the experiences into a brief story with the title, "When I Was Young." When the stories are drafted, the students should team up with partners and read their stories to one another. While listening to the feedback from their partner, students should use a colored pencil to write down the comments and suggestions on the draft. In a rewriting, students may choose to use any of these suggestions. The students return to their desks to rewrite the stories. If desired, the stories may be illustrated, the pages stapled together, covers designed, and the finished product displayed in the classroom book corner.

81. St. George, Judith. *By George, Bloomers!* **Ill. by Margot Tomes. New York: Coward, McCann & Geoghegan, 1974.**
   Traits: Feeling of autonomy; relationship with a caring "other."
   Hannah is an eight-year-old tomboy growing up in the year 1852. Her Aunt Lucy, one of the first women to wear bloomers, is coming to visit. While Hannah's mother thinks Aunt Lucy and her bloomers are foolish and unlady-like, Hannah thinks the bloomers would allow her to play more freely like the boys, and she adores Aunt Lucy. When Hannah accidentally rips her flowing skirt and is sent to her room, Aunt Lucy helps her to turn her torn skirt into bloomers. This turns out to be just in time, for Hannah's little brother is stranded out on the roof trying to rescue his kite. Aunt Lucy ties a rope around Hannah and Hannah bravely rescues the little boy. After the heroic rescue, Hannah's mother relents and buys her some bloomers. 1–3.
   Target Activity: "Who Are the Jobs For?"
   Read children the brief summary of the women's movement provided on page 48 of the text. On the chalkboard, make a grid to be filled in orally with the whole class:

Profession	Men	Women	Both
doctor			x
teacher			x
engineer			x
chef			x
farmer			x
lawyer			x
fire fighter			x
police officer			x
nurse			x

Ask children to think of jobs that they know. Then have them discuss whether such occupations can be undertaken by men only, women only, or both.

82.   Shub, Elizabeth. *The White Stallion*. Ill. by Rachal Isadora. New York: Greenwillow, 1982.
   Traits: Courage; problem-solving.
   Little Gretchen is carried away from her wagon train by Anna, the old mare, to which her parents have strapped her. She is befriended by a wild white stallion who gently bites off the straps and sets her down. Scared and hungry, Gretchen cries herself to sleep. The next morning she drinks from a nearby stream and nibbles on grass. Remembering that her mother has told her to always stay where you are if you are lost, the child sits down to wait. The white stallion returns and tells Anna that he will return her to the wagon train—or so Gretchen believes. K–3.
   Target Activity: "Surviving the Wilderness"
   Ask children to imagine that they are lost in the woods with nothing to eat or drink. Encourage them to consider what Gretchen did to survive. Discuss her actions. Ask children to offer other suggestions as to what she might have done. To augment the discussion, ask children what three items they might bring on a hike to be on the safe side in case they were to get lost.

83.   Wetterer, Margaret K. *Kate Shelley and the Midnight Express*. Ill. by Karen Ritz. Minneapolis: Carolrhoda, 1990.
   Traits: Persistence; problem-solving.
   In this true story from the history of the 1880s, Kate Shelley, a young girl, shows her courage when she saves the lives of hundreds of people on a train racing toward a railroad bridge, that unknown to them, has been washed away during a dangerous storm. 1–3.
   Target Activity: "When I Helped Someone Else"
   Invite the students to tell about some of their experiences where they helped others and then turn the experiences into a brief story with the title, "When I Helped Someone Else." When the stories are written as first drafts, girls and boys should divide into pairs, read their stories to one another, and offer suggestions. After rewriting the stories, students may illustrate the pages, design covers, and place their stories in the classroom reading corner.

Biographies

84. Adler, David A. *A Picture Book of Abraham Lincoln.* Ill. by **John Wallner and Alexandra Wallner. New York: Holiday House, 1989.**

Traits: Problem-solving; positive vision of life.

Lincoln's election is mentioned along with a discussion of the cause of the Civil War. Facts about Lincoln's personality are mixed in text. There are traits, family members, and events. Lincoln had a positive vision of life expressed in his desire for knowledge and his directness in solving problems. Color paintings add interest. 1–3.

Target Activity: "In-depth Study of Lincoln"

Display biographies with information on traits, facts, and personalities of Lincoln and ask students to divide into in-depth study groups where each group will research one part of the president's life: childhood, education, marriage and family, early politics, Civil War years. Consider Carol Greene's *Abraham Lincoln: President of a Divided Country* (Children's Press, 1989) for its full-color and black-and-white illustrations of battlefield scenes, portraits, the buildings and the events; or Barbara Cary's *Meet Abraham Lincoln* (Random House, 1989). To emphasize the point to third grade students of the value of authentic conversations in writing to make scenes and actions more effective, read the foreword in *Abraham Lincoln, Friend of the People* (Follett, 1950) by Clara Ingram Judson. Judson says that the conversations are the "talk" of the story. 2–3.

85. Blegvad, Erik. *Self Portrait: Eric Blegvad.* **Menlo Park, CA: Addison-Wesley, 1979.**

Trait: Developing a hobby or talent.

In this autobiography, Blegvad tells the story of his writing experiences in a careful, reflective manner. He explains his process in writing books and gives advice for those who are interested in writing for publication. 3.

Target Activity: "Self-Portraits"

Show and discuss some of the books from the "Self-Portrait" series

(Addison-Wesley) where illustrators of children's books tell their own stories and show their works of art. Titles to consider include *Self-Portrait: Margot Zemach* (1978), *Self-Portrait: Trina Schart Hyman* (1981) and Bill Peet's *Bill Peet: An Autobiography* (Houghton, 1989), a picture book with text and illustrations from Peet's early memories up to the present. Encourage children to write and illustrate their own self-portraits for their family book collection.

86. Brandenburg, Aliki. *A Weed Is a Flower*. Ill. New York: Simon and Schuster, 1965, 1968.

Traits: Persistence in the face of failure; problem-solving.

This biography of George Washington Carver gives information about his birth, early childhood and adult life. His story tells of slavery, freedom, poverty and success. Born of slave parents on a farm near Diamond Grove, Missouri, Carver worked his way through school and was graduated from Iowa State College of Agriculture and Mechanical Arts. He joined the staff of Tuskegee Normal and Industrial Institute in Alabama and contributed his life savings to the George Washington Carver Foundation for Agricultural Research, a museum of his discoveries. Today, the George Washington Carver National Monument is on 210 acres of the farm where he was born. Working as an agricultural chemist, Carver convinced farmers to grow peanuts as a crop, and in his laboratory, made approximately 300 products such as soap and ink from peanuts. Additionally, he gained recognition as a painter and was elected a Fellow in the Royal Society of Arts in London, an honor given to few Americans. 3–5.

Target Activity: "Discoveries and Inventions"

Engage children in talking about discoveries and inventions that they wish were available (i.e., what is needed in their lives or in the lives of others). What are some of the steps that would be needed to complete the suggested discovery/invention? Who is interested in making cardboard/paper models of proposed inventions to show to others in the class? Who are the students who want to join together and initiate an "Inventors' Gang" to meet weekly after school to work on their proposed inventions? Who will contact a local business to support the needs (resources) of the Inventors' Gang? At a meeting, discuss the idea of patents and what a person would do to apply for a patent for an invention/discovery. A patent is a document protecting the inventor by giving control of the manufacture and use of the invention for a certain number of years. For those interested in letter writing, information for securing a patent can be obtained from the Commissioner of Patents, Washington, D.C.

Additionally, review some of the contributions of Carver in agriculture, ideas which may turn the students' attention to the use of other plants. Carver explored the uses of the peanut plant for eating, for seed, and for animal feed which led to such products as salad oil, cosmetics, glycerin, insulation, paper board, feed meal, food flour, and fertilizer.

87.   Duvak, Mary. *Red Jack*. Ill. by Michael Wilson. Cleveland: Modern Curriculum Press, 1988.

Trait: Problem-solving.

This is a story of a mysterious woman who rode the range and became a legend in the outback of Australia. Red Jack had a mysterious lifestyle as did some of the other women who became legends. This is available with a teacher's guide that contains activities for integrating the curricula. It has math, science, social studies, and art activities. 2–3.

Target Activity: "Women Who Became Legends"

With the school librarian or children's librarian at a nearby branch, plan a field trip to the library. Ask the librarian to discuss the topic, "Women Who Became Legends," and to show the children some of the biographies available on the shelves. During the visit, the children should tour the library, fill out forms for a library card (or receive forms to take home for this), listen to the librarian discuss the books, and browse and read the one they select.

In a listening center, invite children to choose an audiotape about women of resiliency (Dog Days Records, Aegus, Ltd., 1623 Berkeley Avenue, Saint Paul, Minnesota 55105) and listen for examples of the women's resiliency, and report back to the group. Each tape also includes information about the woman, her times, dictionary words, and activity suggestions. Tapes are available about athletes, social activists, historical figures, present-day female achievers:

Social activists: Susan B. Anthony and her work in women's suffrage; Eleanor Roosevelt who was recognized for her work for world peace; Rosa Parks and her bus ride of 1955 that marked the beginning of the modern Civil Rights Movement; Lois Stelle and her struggle to become a doctor and her dedication to the Indian people; Queen Kaahumanu and her work to bring literacy to the Hawaiian Islands; Fannie Lou Hamer, contributed to the Civil Rights Movement; and Samantha Smith, worker for world peace.

Historical figures: Harriet Tubman, conductor on the Underground Railroad; Sybil Ludington, whose midnight ride warned the militia that the British were burning Danbury, Conn.; Ida Lewis, America's first lighthouse keeper, who saved the lives of 18 people; Mutsimuna, who rescued her brother during the Battle of the Rosebud; Nellie Bly, a pioneer investigative journalist; Polly Bemis, an Idaho pioneer woman.

Athletes: Gertrude Ederle, the first woman to swim the English

Channel; Wilma Rudolph, the first American woman runner to win three gold medals in a single Olympics; and Jill Kinmont Booth, a quadriplegic, world class skier, and elementary school teacher.

Other Achievers: Maria Mitchell, America's first woman astronomer; Sally Ride, America's first woman in space (this also mentions the 1986 Challenger accident); and Libby Riddles, the first woman to win the 1,100-mile Iditarod Trail sled dog race; Ellen Corby, television actress known as Grandma Walton; Kitty O'Neil, deaf stunt woman and holder of the women's land speed record; and Felisa Rincon deGautier, mayor of San Juan, Puerto Rico, for 23 years.

Back in the classroom, there should be a debriefing as the children discuss what they learned. The teacher takes their dictation and prepares an informational chart about "Women Who Became Legends." The chart is placed in the classroom book corner near the available copies of books about women and their achievements.

88.   Fritz, Jean. *Homesick: My Own Story*. Ill. by Margot Tomes. New York: Putnam, 1982.
   Trait: Persistence.
   Fritz writes about her childhood in China, the upheaval during that time, and her longed-for trip to the United States. She tells a reader that her childhood "feels like a story" and so she decided to tell it that way and let the events fall into the shape of a story. Fritz uses conversation and remembers her childhood filled with "voices." The section of family photographs shows the family's days in China in the 1920s, a time of turmoil. 3.
   Target Activity: "My Childhood Voices"
   With the children, discuss a time in childhood that is filled with conversations and the voices of others participating in those conversations. With two sheets of butcher paper on the board to be used to record a student's dictation, invite a student to tell aloud a brief event in her/his childhood that involved two people talking (e.g., talking in the kitchen, car, park, or store with a family member). As the short event is told, record the words of the two conversationalists on the butcher paper: sheet #1 is for the first speaker and sheet #2 is for the second. Introduce quotation marks to show the change in speakers. Discuss in teams of two and ask students to write their own version of an early childhood conversation with two sheets of paper, one for each speaker. When completed, students should trade conversations and listen to feedback from others.

89.   Goffstein, M. B. *A Little Shubert*. Ill. by the author. New York: Harper and Row, 1972.
   Trait: Developing a hobby or talent.

In Vienna many years ago, Schubert learned to play the piano and violin at home. Teaching to make a living, Franz Peter Schubert lived in a room with few furnishings and without heat. This story is about the life of the famous composer (1797–1828) who heard music differently from other people. It tells the ways he composed his ideas by writing down his music as quickly as he could. K–2.

Target Activity: "Listening for Moods in Music by Resilient Composer"

With the children, listen to parts of the story of Schubert's life with a recording of the operetta, *Blossom Time*, written by Sigmund Romberg. The theme song is a variation of Schubert's "Unfinished Symphony." It is referred to as "unfinished" because it has only two (not the usual three or four) movements of music expected in a classical symphony. Other versions of Schubert's melodies are heard in the operetta. After listening to parts of the operetta, discuss the melodies and the way the mood of the selections related to some (all) of the traits of resiliency (e.g., which melody makes us think of actions related to getting people's attention? of solving a problem? of feeling of autonomy? of persistence? of a positive vision of life? of a sense of humor? of a sense of control over life?) With the girls and boys, the teacher will create an informational chart for a resource in the classroom:

Resiliency Traits	*Melodies*
1.	
2.	

90.   Greene, Carol. *Robert E. Lee: Leader in War and Peace*. Ill. Chicago: Children's Press, 1989.

Traits: Persistence, perseverance; overcoming obstacles; problem-solving.

With a simple text, this story tells of family, early life and education in Virginia with some background about slavery and the Civil War years. Humility, prayer, faith and kindness were parts of Lee's daily life. His father was Henry Lee, also known as Light-Horse Harry, a Revolutionary War leader. Robert was opposed to slavery and felt it had an evil effect on all people. Tremendous difficulties faced him in his struggle against the North in the War between the States. During the War between the States, Lee accepted the leadership of the Army of Virginia, mobilized the state's volunteers, and fortified the rivers. Jefferson Davis, president of the Confederate States, named Lee as military adviser with the rank of general. Before the war was over, Lee was made general in chief of all the

Confederate armies. At war's end, Lee surrendered his armies to General Ulysses S. Grant. Full-color and black-and-white illustrations show battlefield scenes, portraits, the buildings and the events. 1–2.

Target Activity: "Leaders in Peace"

With the children, search for newspaper articles about leaders who support the idea of peace on Earth. Discuss the concept of the Nobel Peace Prize and some of its recipients in past years. As the articles are found, discuss them and the ways the leaders are talking about peace and doing something of value in their countries. Display the articles on a classroom bulletin board.

91. Meltzer, Milton. *Benjamin Franklin: The New American*. Ill. New York: Franklin Watts, 1988.

Trait: Problem-solving.

Meltzer includes numerous quotations from Franklin's writings and speeches to lend authenticity to the biography. He shows that Franklin was a multifaceted person having both strengths and weaknesses. For instance, a strong Franklin testifies in front of the English parliament and responds to 174 questions asked. His ability to solve problems as an inventor led him to prove that lightning was electrical and to invent the platform rocker, bifocal glasses, Franklin stove, and the lightning rod. 3 & up.

Target Activity: "Practicing What Franklin Says"

With the children, reread the biography and look for evidence that Franklin practiced what he wrote in his *Farmer's Almanac*.

What Franklin Wrote	*Evidence*
1. Waste not, want not.	page _____
2. Early to bed, early to rise, makes a man healthy, wealthy and wise.	page _____
3. He that goes a-borrowing goes a-sorrowing.	page _____
4. Idleness and pride tax with a heavier hand than kings and parliaments.	page _____

Option: "Biographies on Display"

Display other biographies: Maggi Scarf's *Meet Benjamin Franklin* with illustrations by Pat Fogarty; Carolyn Greene's *Benjamin Franklin: A Man with Many Jobs* with illustrations by Steven Dobson; *Meet Christopher Columbus*, written by James R. de Kay and illustrated by Victor Mays that tells of voyages, storms, Indians and the politics of the time with detailed drawings of the Santa Maria; *Meet Martin Luther King, Jr.*, written by James R. de Kay and illustrated with photographs; *Meet Thomas Jefferson* written by Marvin Barrett and illustrated by Pat Fogarty.

The teacher should plan to give brief book talks about the biographies in the display. The talks can focus on "Famous People of Long Ago and Famous People of Today." To give a book talk, introduce the book with the title, author and illustrator. Give a few salient points about the accomplishments of the person and traits of resiliency, and then focus on an interesting aspect of that person's life (solving a problem, persistence in the face of failure, perseverance, relationship with another) by reading a quote, an interesting event, or exciting dialogue between people. Close with restating the title and the author and leave the book out — perhaps standing up on the top of a bookcase — so that the children can readily find it on their own.

92. Holbrook, Stewart. *America's Ethan Allen.* **Ill. by Lynd Ward. Boston: Houghton Mifflin, 1949.**

Traits: Persistence; overcoming obstacles.

In this Caldecott biography, Ethan sacrifices his education to help take care of his family after his father's death. They have settled in the New Hampshire grants (now Vermont). He leaves the farm to fight against the French. After being taken prisoner in 1775 while trying a surprise advance toward Montreal, Canada, he was released three years later. Upon his release, he went to the Continental Congress to ask that Vermont be admitted to the Confederation. While there, the commander of the British forces in Canada suggested that Allen make Vermont a British province. Their correspondence was discovered, and Allen was accused of treason. His guilt or innocence was never proved. 2–3.

Target Activity: "Describing Ethan Allen"

After reading the story to the children, the teacher asks:

1. How many different describing words (adjectives) can you use to describe this leader of the Green Mountain Boys? List the words on the writing board and invite children to make suggestions on clustering the words to show relationships (i.e., caring for his family, fighting the French, and leader of the Green Mountain Boys in New Hampshire).

2. Why do you think some people are impressed with what Ethan Allen did?

3. What is your meaning of *being a patriot*? Name a patriotic song. What do you hear/expect to hear in a patriotic song? Tell about a patriotic demonstration. What do you expect to see in a patriotic demonstration? Tell about a patriotic speech you have heard. What feelings did you have after hearing the patriotic speech?

4. What conditions can you think of today where a soldier could be both a patriot and perhaps a traitor at the same time?

5. How do you think it is possible for Ethan Allen to be considered both guilty of treason and a patriotic soldier in the Revolutionary War by the people of his time?

93. Lasker, David. *The Boy Who Loved Music.* **Ill. by Joe Lasker. New York: Viking, 1979.**

Traits: Sense of humor; problem-solving; special skill or talent.

In eighteenth-century Austria, in the summer palace of Prince Esterhazy, Joseph Haydn, an Austrian composer, is the music director. When the Prince stays at his summer palace far into the fall and does not seem to be interested in returning to Vienna where the musicians want to be, Haydn, a great master of the symphony, composes the *Farewell* symphony. There is a surprise ending as Haydn hints that the musicians of the orchestra would like a vacation, for in the final movement, the musicians leave the stage, one by one, after blowing out the candles on their music stands. Only two musicians are left, leaving Haydn with no orchestra to conduct. The music persuades the Prince to return to Vienna with his musicians and the court. 2–3.

Target Activity: "Humor in Music"

With questions such as the ones that follow, the teacher can ask children to reveal the extent of what they know about some of the larger ideas and meanings of the book.

1. After listening to a recording, how many different describing words can you use to tell about what you hear in the *Surprise Symphony?* The *Farewall Symphony?*

2. Why do you think many people are impressed by Haydn's music?

3. What do you believe are some of the main reasons why Haydn created his surprise ending in the *Farewell* symphony? Why do you suppose he made this decision? How do you suppose the musicians might have been affected if he had not put this surprise ending in the music?

94. Norman, Gertrude. *Johnny Appleseed.* **Ill. by James Carraway. New York: Putnam, 1960.**

Trait: Positive vision of life.

With a setting in the wilderness of colonial America, this is the story of the pioneer, John Chapman (1774–1847). It relates events from his childhood as a boy seven years old, from his experiences as Johnny Appleseed (given this name because he devoted his life to planting apple trees) and from his days as an elderly man. 1–2.

Target Activity: "Describing Johnny Appleseed"

Invite children to think of a picture of Johnny Appleseed as the teacher reads this description:

Johnny Appleseed went to Ohio and wore old trousers, a coffee sack for a shirt, and a saucepan for a hat. He carried a Bible and apple seeds. He was a friend to both white settlers and to Indians, to animals and the birds.

The teacher should invite the children to use the description and to create their own original illustrations of this pioneer. After the illustrations are finished, discussed and displayed, the teacher can show the children ways that Carraway and other artists have imagined Johnny Appleseed in their books.

95.   Powers, Mary Ellen. *Our Teacher's in a Wheelchair*. Ill. Niles, Illinois: Albert Whitman, 1986.

Traits: Perseverance; problem-solving.

The subject of this biography is Brian Hanson. Hanson is partially paralyzed and uses a wheelchair as he teaches daycare classes. His story discusses the injury that caused the paralysis and his many accomplishments. K–3.

Target Activity: "Understanding and Helping Others with Disabilities"

Engage children in helping one another as they take turns being the one who "cannot get out of his/her chair" for a brief specified amount of time. The "helping" child is supportive and sharpens the pencil, picks up dropped items, gets paper and books, or assists in any way needed. Roles are reversed and the helper becomes the one sitting in the chair. Discuss: How did you feel as the helper? As the one in the chair? What can you do to help others who need assistance?

96.   Smith, Kathie Billingslea. *Harriet Tubman*. Ill. by James Seward. New York: Messner, 1989.

Traits: Perseverance; overcoming obstacles.

Born in Dorchester County, Maryland, Harriet Tubman (1821–1913) did much to help her people. As a young girl she was a field worker and then escaped to the North. There, she decided to help others escape from slavery. She took trips into slave territory and led more than 300 slaves to freedom, thus earning her the name of "Moses." Illustrations are both in full color and black and white. A read-aloud. 2–3.

Target Activity: "Moses of Her People"

Pair this story of Tubman's life as a read-aloud biography with *Runaway Slave* (Four Winds, 1968) by Ann McGovern and discuss the ways the two authors create the excitement of Tubman's life drama.

For independent reading and study:

1. Since it was neither underground nor a railroad, find out the reasons the system for moving escaped slaves to Canada in the days before

the War between the States was called "the underground railroad." What was the meaning of "stations" in this system?

2. React to the selection in a letter beginning with "Dear Journal" in your student journal.

97. Stevens, Bryna. *Deborah Sampson Goes to War*. Ill. by Florence Hill. Minneapolis: Carolrhoda, 1984.

Traits: Persistence; problem-solving.

Deborah Sampson fought as a soldier in the American Revolution and suffered many illnesses and injuries. She disguised herself as a man and no one learned of her female identity until near the end of the war. 2–3.

Target Activity: "Soldier Sampson"

With the children, the teacher encourages the girls and boys to imagine the conversation(s) that Deborah Sampson might have had with others during her enlistment as a soldier in the American Revolution. How would she keep her identity a secret? How would she talk? How would she walk? Imagine her dialogue with others as she talks about some of the major causes of the Revolutionary War.

1. Restrictive laws limited the growth of the colonies. British soldiers were quartered in the colonists' private homes.

2. The colonists objected to paying for tax stamps and said, "Taxation without representation is tyranny."

3. Restrictive navigation laws brought protest from merchants who wanted easier trade laws.

4. The ill will and friction between British soldiers and colonists led to the Boston Massacre. For example, in one event, boys pelted an English sentry with snowballs, then trouble began and men and boys of the colony threatened the British soldiers with clubs and stones. The British retaliated by killing five men and wounding six others.

5. Colonists dumped a shipload of tea into Boston Harbor to fight against the "Tea Act." This act let the British East India company sell its tea in America at prices so low that the local tea merchants could not compete.

6. The British attempt to seize the colonists' military stores at Concord led to the first battles at Lexington and Concord and then war.

Record the dialogue that might be involved in one of these situations.

98. Wilder, Laura Ingalls. *West from Home: Letters of Laura Ingalls Wilder to Almanzo Wilder, San Francisco, 1915*. Roger MacBride, ed. New York: Harper, 1974.

Trait: Developing a hobby or talent.

To get a sense of Laura's personal insights as well as what the country was like during the early 1900s, read *West from Home*. These are the letters written by Laura to Wilder's husband while she was visiting her daughter Rose and attending the 1915 Panama Pacific International Exposition. This is an example of documentary literature.

Target Activity: "Documentaries"

Point out the value in *West from Home* as well as in *The First Four Years* (Harper, 1971), a journal-like account about the first years of Laura's married life with descriptions of problems, and philosophies of the period.

Then, select Giff's new biography, *Laura Ingalls Wilder*, for its coverage, length, and tone for children who enjoy the "Little House" books. Giff sorts out some of the questions about how the books differ in detail from the author's real life, such as the age of Laura and Mary when they lived in the Big Woods. But since so many of the facts of Laura's girlhood are well known from the series, this book's chief contribution is its information about Mrs. Wilder's writing experiences and her adulthood, especially the later years. The style is reminiscent of Wilder's own, direct and simple, with many of the same devices for revealing thoughts and feelings. "Little House" fans may be able to read first the series, and then this biography, with a sense that a similar hand is writing the story. 2–3 and up.

II. Literature for Grades 4–8

Contemporary Fiction

Realistic Fiction

99. Armstrong, William. *Sounder.* **Ill. by James Barkley. New York: Harper and Row, 1969.**

Traits: Significant relationship with another; courage, human dignity, and love.

Stealing meat from a white man's smokehouse to feed his hungry family, the father, a black sharecropper, is arrested and taken away. His protective dog, Sounder, leaps at the sheriff's wagon where his master is chained. One of the men shoots the dog, leaving him disfigured and crippled, and without the spirit for barking. When the husband receives a sentence of working on a gang, his wife endures, and each year his son searches for him after the crops are in. During a search, the boy meets an old black man who becomes his friend and teacher. Six years later, the father walks home, partially paralyzed and deformed from a dynamite blast in the prison quarry. When Sounder recognizes him, the dog bays a welcome. The father and Sounder both die soon after. After seeing that his mother and the young children have wood and are prepared for the winter, the boy returns to his teacher. 5–8.

Taking place in the South with unnamed characters, *Sounder* has courage, human dignity, as well as tragedy and some cruelty. Told to the author when he was a child by a gray-haired teacher, this oral history retells part of the teacher's childhood and encourages the binding relationships with others.

Target Activity: "Two Events"

Ask students to think of two events in their lives when 1) they were happy because they had something positive happen to them and 2) when they were painfully sad and miserable because of the worst bad luck or misfortune. Discuss both situations and what they did to tell their feelings to others or to hide their feelings from others. When they felt comfortable in sharing their feelings with others, what type of person was the significant caring other?

100.   Ashabranner, Brent. *Born to the Land: An American Portrait.* **Photographs by Paul Conklin. New York: Putnam, 1989.**

Traits: Persistence; sense of humor.

People—women and men, old and young, minorities, old-timers, and newcomers—from Luna County, New Mexico, are interviewed. A reader learns about the relationship of generations, the effect of history on the present, the impact of geography on the development of the area, and the always-present threat of drought. 4 & up.

Target Activity: "They Say—We Say"

Discuss with students the real messages behind two sayings from the anecdotes: "...if you wear out a pair of boots in this country, you will never leave" and "...if you stay that long, you won't have enough money to leave." After discussion, ask students to write what their perceptions about the meanings would be:

1. "...if you wear out a pair of boots in this country, you will never leave." _____

2. "...if you stay that long, you won't have enough money to leave." _____

101.   Buff, Mary and Conrad Buff. *Magic Maize.* **Ill. by the authors. Boston: Houghton Mifflin, 1954.**

Traits: Persistence; positive vision of life.

When his brother, Quin, a peddler, visits Fabian, Quin gives him 20 kernels of corn that will (he promises) produce so much more than the old that it is really "magic" maize. Quin gets the seed from "gringos" (whom Father distrusts) and so Fabian plants the seeds in secret in an ancient Mayan ruin, the City Up Yonder. Later, when Father sees the plants, he is convinced of the superiority of the new seed and changes his opinion of the white men because of the treatment they show his sons. They convince Father that Fabian should go to school and pay Father well for the jade earplug Fabian finds in the ruins. 4–6.

Target Activity: "Up to Date"

Encourage students to look for information in recent books that bring additional information about Guatemala up to date and to add to a discussion about ways of life today.

102.   Byars, Betsy. *Summer of the Swans.* **Ill. by Ted Conis. New York: Viking, 1970.**

Traits: Problem-solving; positive vision of a new life.

As she moves into adolescence, Sara begins to see life as a series of "huge and uneven steps." She finds her mood swings overwhelming, for example, and begins to worry about her physical appearance—namely that her feet appear to be too large for her body. In the middle of Sara's struggle with her own feelings of loneliness and awkwardness, Sara's brother Charlie, who is mentally retarded, becomes lost while leaving his home to visit some swans who have settled in a nearby pond. From the beginning of the summer when the story begins, to the end of the story, at summer's end, the reader can follow Sara's growth of understanding of herself and her depth of caring for her brother. Charlie's disappearance has allowed Sara to come to terms with what is important in her life and, by facing the problem squarely, has given her newfound confidence in her own abilities.

At the beginning of the book, Sara is painfully self-absorbed. As she attempts to find Charlie she begins to have a more accepting attitude toward the things she cannot change, while beginning to appreciate the positive relationships in her life. 5–6.

Target Activity: "A Week with Charlie"

Summer of the Swans can be discussed for both content and writing style. This story of a mentally handicapped brother offers possibilities for follow-up discussion: Understanding of a handicapped youngster; grasp of attitudes toward his condition; examples of imagery can be reread; the development of plot and the growth of Sara's characterization. Students may review the story to find evidence of the family interaction; some of the sensory experiences; to look for art ideas; to discuss different points of view; to talk about the character's feelings; to relate the story to personal feelings.

Option: "We Instead of Me"

Discuss with students situations in which the idea of "We Instead of Me" helped resolve a problem. In her determination to find Charlie, Sara turns to Joe Melby, the boy she had despised the day before, to help her. Together they find Charlie. There is a serious theme that captures the conflicting feelings of a 13-year-old first reaching out to others.

103.   Capote, Truman. *A Christmas Memory.* **Photographs by Beth Peck. New York: Knopf, 1989.**

Trait: Caring relationship with another.

Set in rural Alabama in the early 1930s at Christmas time, in a parentless, poor home, seven-year-old Truman Capote and his friend, an eccentric elderly cousin, prepare several dozen fruitcakes and mail them to people they admire. They gather pecans from harvest leavings, buy illegal whiskey to soak the cakes, cut their own tree, and decorate it with homemade ornaments. 4 & up.

Target Activity: "Whom Do We Admire?"

Discuss: Almost everyone has some kind of reputation and it's possible that a person's reputation at home, school, in the neighborhood, in gangs, or with friends may be different in each situation. What kinds of reputations do some of the people you admire have? How does one get a reputation? How does one change a reputation? Encourage students to write a letter to someone they admire and tell them why they admire them.

104.   Clark, Ann Nolan. *Secret of the Andes.* **Ill. by Jean Charlot. New York: Viking, 1952.**
    Trait: Relationship with another.
    In Peru, Cusi leaves Hidden Valley up in the Andes and goes down to the lowlands in search of another way of life. When his search fails, he realizes he wants to remain with old Chuto, care for the heard of llamas, and carry on this work when Chuto is gone. Chuto tells Cusi of his heritage, that he is descended from Inca nobility and says the golden earplugs he wears are proof. 5–8.
    Target Activity: "Links to the Past"
    According to one legend told by Chuto, the llamas they tend have a special relationship, too, to the time of the Incas. The Spanish captured a "mighty Inca" and "the Indians sent ten thousand llamas, carrying bags of gold dust to ransom their king." The Spanish, however, feared the wrath of their King if they set the Inca free, and so killed him. "And the ten thousand llamas marching down the trails of the Andes vanished from the land, and with them vanished the gold dust, ransom for the King." Chuto takes Cusi to Sunrise Rock to show him a secret cave containing the bags of gold dust. It seems the llamas they tend are descended from those of long ago. Cusi vows to keep the secret of the cave forever. Encourage students to explore the links of their heritage to the past by asking adults in the family to tell them of stories from their history. Invite students to tell their stories to others in the class. If interested, students may record the stories into a class book.

105.   Conrad, Pam. *My Daniel.* **New York: Harper and Row, 1989.**
    Traits: Persistence; problem-solving.
    Julia Creath Summerwaite (80 years old) flies to New York to visit her son's family and to take her grandchildren to the Natural History Museum. Verbal flashbacks from past to present link the story together. Summerwaite tells of her love for her older brother Daniel, his love for fossils, his search for a dinosaur, and the competition among paleontologists for the fossils found in Nebraska. At the museum, the children learn of the harshness of pioneer life and the life of their Great-Uncle Daniel. A read-aloud. 5 & up.
    Target Activity: "Daniel's Pioneer Life"
    With the students, discuss some of these aspects related to the story:
    1. Search for discoveries. Go on a newspaper search and begin to collect all the articles you can find about fossil discoveries in the United

States. Allow yourself several weeks and use as many different souces (magazines, reports on television) as you can find. After you have collected and mounted your fossil articles in a scrapbook, how will you respond to the following: If you were to write a definition for the words *dinosaur hunter*, what would it be?

2. Find out all you can about one of our real-life dinosaur hunters and fossil-finders and ask, What has this scientist found? What have we learned from his/her findings? Look for resources with facts about Jim Jensen, Robert Owen and others.

3. What kinds of differences do you think there are between a person who is competitive in the search for fossils and one who is harmfully aggressive?

106. Du Bois, William Pene. *The Twenty-One Balloons*. Ill. by the author. New York: Viking, 1947.

Trait: Humor.

In 1883, retired professor William Waterman Sherman starts out over the Pacific in a huge balloon, *The Globe*, well-stocked with food. Sherman allows *The Globe* to land wherever the wind blows him. Three weeks later, Sherman is picked up by a freighter in the Atlantic. He is clinging to a wrecked platform to which 20 deflated balloons are attached. Rescued, Sherman says he will tell his unusual adventures to the Western American Explorers' Club of San Francisco and the rest of the book is the tale. It seems that on the seventh day out, a seagull punctured his balloon and he went down on a small volcanic island, Krakatoa. Sherman found the island inhabited by the richest people in the world — 20 families from San Francisco. The source of their wealth is the site of the fabulous diamond mines at the base of the volcanic mountain on the island. When the Earth trembled, the Krakatoans expected an explosion, and evacuated the island on a giant balloon raft lifted by 20 balloons. They passed over India and 19 of the families left the raft to float to Earth in parachutes. The last family dropped to Earth in Belgium and Sherman was left to land the raft over a large body of water. The inventions of the wealthy Krakatoans show the author's playfulness and humor: there is the airy-go-round, the giant balloon life raft, and a Moroccan house with electrified chairs and couches, continuous sheets, and elevator beds. 5–8.

Target Activity: "Drama with 21 Balloons"

Discuss choices for extending the book:

1. Create the scene in which a sea gull punctures his balloon and he goes down on a small volcanic island, Krakatoa.

2. Dramatize the greeting scene in which Sherman finds the island inhabited by the richest people in the world — 20 families from San Francisco.

3. Interview William Waterman Sherman. How does he describe the possessions of the Krakatoans? How can you tell he is pleased (displeased) with such things as the elevator beds, continuous sheets, and electrified chairs and couches?

107.   Estes, Eleanor. *The Hundred Dresses*. Ill. by Louis Slobodkin. Scarsdale, New York: Harcourt, Brace, 1944.

Trait: Problem-solving.

Having to wear the same faded blue dress each day to school, Wanda Petronski tells a classmate that she has 100 dresses all lined up in her closet. This starts a daily teasing by the other girls. When the Petronskis move to the city, Wanda's father writes a note to her new teacher saying, "No more holler Polack. No more asky why funny name. Plenty of funny names in big city." Wanda leaves her old school before the winner of the drawing for a coloring contest is named. Wanda is the winner with her 100 dress designs "all different and beautiful." In this Newbery book, the reader feels compassion for Wanda as Peggy picks at Wanda each day and at Maddie who just stands by. Finally, Maddie realizes her conduct is as shameful as Peggy's even though Peggy has tormented Wanda more. Maddie decides she will never again stand by and say nothing when she sees another person mistreated. 4–6.

Target Activity: "Response to One Hundred Dresses"

Invite the students to respond personally in writing to such questions as:

1. How would you have felt if you had been Wanda and been forced to wear the same dress/shirt day after day?

2. What would your reaction have been if you had to move to the big city?

3. Have you ever known anyone or read about anyone who was mistreated because that person seemed to be different from others around him? Has mistreatment happened to you? When did this happen? Who helped you when you needed help in this situation? How will you help someone when you see this happening in the future?

108.   Ferguson, Alane. *Cricket and the Crackerbox Kid*. New York: Bradbury, 1990.

Traits: Friendship; problem-solving.

Cricket is the lonely only child of yuppie parents who tries to stay on the fringes of a clique, realizing it is social suicide to be friends with the kids from a less affluent neighborhood. A new boy in class, a crackerbox kid, Dominic, is assigned to be her partner for a school project, and they become friends. They discover that family income is not a measure of friendship and happiness. Cricket rescues a dog from the animal shelter and finds that the dog is Dominic's lost dog, Coty. Cricket refuses to give up the dog. The principal settles the argument by a trial: the owner of the dog will be decided by a jury of fifth graders from another class. When a verdict is reached in the trial, the winner does some problem-solving and must decide which is more important—being legally or ethically right. 4–6.

Target Activity: "Legally or Ethically Right?"

After discussing these statements in small groups, ask students to respond (agree or disagree) to them: 1) If it's legal, it is right. 2) If it's ethical, it is right. 3) A person with ethics is easily upset by imperfect things. 4) A person who follows the legality (or the ethics) of each situation always makes the best leader. Encourage the students to give reasons for their answers.

109. Fox, Paula. *The Village by the Sea*. Ill. New York: Orchard Books/Watts, 1988.

Traits: Persistence; sense of control over one's life; the contrast of envy with love and self-esteem.

While her seriously ill father undergoes heart surgery, young Emma is sent to live by the ocean with her erratic Aunt Bea. Her aunt does nothing to make Emma feel welcome or wanted, merely tolerating her presence. Surviving in this oppressive atmosphere becomes a challenge for Emma, but is made easier with the help of a new friend, Bertie. Together the girls play on the beach and begin to create a village on the sand, using odds and ends they collect. One night, in a rage, Aunt Bea destroys the village. Emma is devastated by this irrational act. It is only later, after Emma reads what Aunt Bea has written in the girl's diary that she begins to understand the woman's actions and her hatred for her aunt dissolves.

In the beginning of the story Emma is clearly an unfortunate victim of circumstances. When she stops being angry and defensive and begins to understand her aunt's feelings, her compassion allows her to reach out and change the situation in a positive way. 4–8.

Target Activity: "Understanding the Characters"

Students will be placed in groups of six and assigned a particular character to study. Students will review the personality traits of their character. They should analyze what is told of that character's life, and try to understand the motives behind their character's behavior. Each group member will also write a question to ask of another book character (each group member will question a different character). When the groups are ready, students from different groups role-playing the same character will sit at the front of the room *and* field questions from the rest of the class. This procedure is repeated until all character groups have been questioned. The teacher then leads a "debriefing" discussion to help children see that understanding a person's behavior can help one to cope with it more effectively.

Option: "Emma's Family and Friends"

Invite students to consider that in all families, each member has certain feelings, habits, and ways of living which the others need to understand and try to adjust to. Beside each name of a member of Emma's family or friends, write some of the unique characteristics.

Aunt Bea _____

Uncle Crispin _____

Emma herself _____

Emma's new friend _____

Option: The teacher can acquire more information about the genesis of this story in "The Village by the Sea" by Paula Fox, an acceptance speech for the Boston Globe–Horn Book Award for fiction in *The Horn Book Magazine* (January/February, 1990): 22–23. With the information, the teacher can review with the students the way the author thought about the art of writing this story and its resilient character.

110.   George, Jean Craighead. *Julie of the Wolves*. Ill. New York: Harper and Row, 1972.

Traits: Persistence; positive view of life.

Thirteen-year-old Julie Miyax, an Eskimo girl, leaves her father-selected husband, Daniel, to cross the tundra toward Point Hope where she plans to leave for San Francisco to find a California pen pal, Amy. Lost, Julie survives because of her knowledge of Eskimo lore (setting her course by migrating birds and the North Star) and her friendship with Amaroq, the leader of a wolf pack. 6–8.

Target Activity: "Items for Survival"

Considering the way that students live today, they should have no use for many of the items that are listed below. The teacher should ask the girls and boys to imagine that they are caught in a snowstorm in the tundra, lose their way, and feel lost and become "marooned" on the ice and snow. There are no other human inhabitants—just Julie's wolf pack. Ask the students to rank order the items a student feels are necessary for him/her to survive in this situation.

Items for Survival

_____ a dog sled

_____ spear

_____ bow and arrow

_____ knife

_____ dishes

_____ food and water

_____ pet

_____ firewood

_____ flintstone

_____ clothes

_____ hut, cabin, other shelter

_____ fence

_____ signal device (flashlight)

_____ fishhook and line

_____ snowshoes

111. George, Jean. *Shark Beneath the Reef.* **New York: Harper and Row, 1989.**

Traits: Overcoming obstacles; perseverance.

Tomas Torres, a young Mexican Indian, loves his life as a fisherman in the waters off of Baja coast. Changing times, including government interference, are destroying the life Tomas and his family have known in the past. These changes bring choices for the family: whether to continue to fish and try to cling to the old familiar way of life or go to school and work toward a new way. There is an emotional struggle as well as the physical fight with a huge shark. The ending is a compromise. 5–6.

Target Activity: "Understanding Resiliency in Another's Life"

One of the ways for a student to experience what it is like to be resilient in times of stress is to read books about children the same age who have faced stress by being resilient. What are some stories that the students have read and can suggest for a class display?

112. George, Jean Craighead. *On the Far Side of the Mountain.* **Ill. by the author. New York: E. P. Dutton, 1990.**

Traits: Persistence; problem-solving.

Sam and his friend, Bando, search for Alice. During the search, they discover a ring of illegal falcon dealers. Told in first-person narrative with journal entries similar to those in *My Side of the Mountain* (Dutton, 1988) with personal observations and growth in Sam's character. 4–6.

Target Activity: "Sam's Needs—Sam's Curiosity"

The teacher initiates the discussion by asking students to recall the inventions Sam creates to make his rugged life in the mountains easier. With student volunteers writing on the board, the ideas are listed. The teacher invites discussion about each device with the question, "How can you argue that this device was made because of Sam's practical needs (solving a problem) or because of Sam's curiosity?"

113.   Greene, Bette. *Philip Hall Likes Me. I Reckon Maybe...* **Ill. by Charles Lilly. New York: Dial, 1974.**

Traits: Relationship with significant caring other; humor; persistence.

Eleven-year-old Elizabeth "Beth" Lorraine Lambert is liked by Philip Hall, who is best in everything at school and who lives on the Hall dairy farm adjoining the Lambert poultry and pig farm in Arkansas. Because he likes her, he lets her do his chores every evening. Beth (with Philip's help) captures thieves, pickets the local stores that sell poor merchandise, and wins the 4-H calf-raising contest. Recognizing Beth's accomplishments, Philip gets used to being second best and teams up with Elizabeth for a square-dancing contest. 4–6.

Target Activity: "I Reckon Maybe..."

With the students, the teacher discusses the ways Philip Hall shows Beth that he likes her. After discussion, the teacher invites the students to start a list of names of friends and the ways they show their friendship. The list is titled, "I Reckon Maybe..."

"I Reckon Maybe..."

Likes Me (name)	Because (ways to show friendship)
1.	
2.	

114.   Gripe, Maria. *Agnes Cecilia.* **Translated from the Swedish by Rika Lesser. New York: Harper, 1990.**

Traits: Relationship with another; positive vision of life.

Nora lives with her Aunt Karin, Uncle Andre and Cousin Dag. She constantly feels as if she has been abandoned, and she feels like an outsider. When they move to an old home to restore it, Nora feels that a spirit from another time is trying to communicate with her. Other strange things happen. In a phone call from an old woman, she is told to go to an old doll shop in Stockholm where she receives Agnes Cecilia, a lifelike doll. Through her friend's grandmother and great-grandmother, Nora learns about the house, a former ballet dancer, the name Agnes Cecilia, and other events that happened long ago. Doing this, Nora discovers her own self and her place in the family. From her cousin Dag, Nora learns that it is logical to presume that we have much more to understand in this world than has been proven. 6 & up.

Target Activity: "True Stories from Old Family Treasures"

Ask children to talk about Uncle Andre and the things he found as he began to restore the old house and uncover some high old cupboards that were boarded up. Talk about the objects found in Nora's room: ballet shoes, broken clock, dog's leash with the name *Hero*, and perfume. Invite deductions from the students: From these objects, what would their "hunches" be about the owner?

Discuss with students the question, What are some of the true stories about old family souvenirs (dolls, heirlooms, momentos, pictures, toys, and other treasures) once owned or used or played with by grandparents or great-grandparents? Invite students to interview an adult in the home to obtain information about family souvenirs. Information can be recorded on tape or written in notes.

115. Hamilton, Virginia. *M. C. Higgins, the Great*. New York: Macmillan, 1974.

Traits: Relationship with significant others; persistence; problem-solving.

Living on Sarah Mountain near the Ohio River, M. C. sees an enormous spoil heap left by stripminers. The heap is oozing slowly down the hill heading toward the house of his family. This place has been home to his family since 1854 when his great-grandmother Sarah, a runaway slave, found refuge on it. His father refuses to accept the danger of the landslide and M. C. realizes he must save his family. To divert the slide, M. C. builds a wall of earth reinforced with branches, old automobile fenders and a gravestone. He has interactions with his family; Ben Killburn, a child of a family shunned by the neighbors; Luhretta Outlaw, a strange girl; and James K. Lewis, who travels through the hills and records folksongs on his tape recorder. Advanced. 6 & up.

Target Activity: "I'm a Great One, Too"

Discuss the meaning of the word "greatness" and its meaning in the story. Does greatness mean helping prevent a danger from occurring? Being physically strong? Knowing the right thing to do? Reaching out to make friends with those shunned by others? Realizing that what is inside is more important that what is outside? The teacher invites the students to reflect upon the thought, "I'm a great one, too" and privately record reasons in their journals as to why they should be considered great.

116. Hamilton, Virginia. *The Planet of Junior Brown*. New York: Macmillan, 1971.

Trait: Persistence.

Junior Brown, an eighth grader, is a talented pianist and artist who weighs 262 pounds. His friend, big Buddy Clark, is brilliant in science and math, works part time at a newsstand, and leads a group of homeless boys who live on their own "planet" in the basement of an abandoned house. Junior and Buddy spend their time with a janitor, Mr. Poole, formerly a math and astronomy teacher, in his basement room behind a false wall in the broom closet. Mr. Poole and Buddy show Junior a ten-planet solar system, lit up and revolving, with the tenth planet named Junior Brown and shaped in the "soft, round contours of Junior Brown's own face" and "glazed in beige and black." Neither has attended classes at school for two and one-half months. Frustration after frustration affects Junior as he slips away from reality. Events during this story, which covers one week of time, include his music lessons with Miss Peebs who won't let Junior play her grand piano but makes him beat out the music on a chair, his playing at home on a piano whose wires have been removed because the sound bothers Junior's mother, his caring for his asthmatic mother, his painting of a huge figure of a Red Man with smaller figures of people living their lives inside it, and its destruction by his mother who considers the painting a "terrible sick thing." During another music lesson with Miss Peebs, Junior realizes she is crazy as she insists she has a filth-diseased relative in her apartment. Leaving, Junior tells Miss Peebs he is taking the relative with him but talks to the imaginary relative on the bus back to school. Mr. Poole takes Junior, Buddy, and the ten-planet solar system to the "Planet" of the homeless boys which Buddy renames "the planet of Junior Brown." Buddy says, "We are together . . . because we have to learn to live for each other." 5–8.

Target Activity: "Living for Each Other"

The teacher asks the students to consider the idea: *What would you have done to help the boys if you had been there with them when:*

1. the group of homeless boys went to their own "planet" in the basement of an abandoned house.

2. Mr. Poole and Buddy showed Junior a ten-planet solar system, lit up and revolving, with the tenth planet named Junior Brown and shaped in the "soft, round contours of Junior Brown's own face" and "glazed in beige and black."

3. neither of the boys went to classes at school for two and one-half months.

4. Junior began to slip away from reality.

5. Junior took his music lessons with Miss Peebs who wouldn't let him play her grand piano but made him beat out the music on a chair.

6. he cares for his asthmatic mother.

7. he painted a huge figure of a Red Man with smaller figures of people living their lives inside of it and it was destroyed by his mother who considered the painting a "terrible sick thing."

8. during the music lesson with Miss Peebs, Junior realized she is crazy as she insisted she had a filth-diseased relative in her apartment.

9. Mr. Poole took Junior, Buddy, and the ten-planet solar system to

the "planet" of the homeless boys which Buddy renamed "the planet of Junior Brown."

10. Buddy said, "We are together . . . because we have to learn to live for each other."

117.   Haven, Susan. *Is It Them or Is It Me?* **New York: Putnam, 1990.**

Traits: Humor and wit; persistence.

Resilient Molly copes with adolescence and forgives friends and enemies. There is some humor found in her first detention, her first kiss, her friendships. Molly's place in the crowd takes precedence over family and grades and her wishes range from wanting a boyfriend and a new history teacher, to wanting an invitation to join the staff of the school newspaper. 5–8.

Target Activity: "Molly's Wishes"

When the students have finished *Is It Them or Is It Me?*, they understand that Molly had wishes just as many other people do. Ask students to recall some of their wishes (Are any similar to Molly's?). Discuss Molly's wishes, write them, and then tell why they think it was or was not necessary for a particular wish to come true for Molly. Which of Molly's wishes would make her more resilient in solving her problems?

118.   Konigsburg, Elaine. *From the Mixed-up Files of Mrs. Basil E. Frankweiler.* **Ill. by the author. New York: Atheneum, 1967.**

Traits: Problem-solving; humor.

Eleven-year-old fussy and bossy Claudia Kincaid runs away from her routines of home and school in Greenwich, Connecticut. With nine-year-old Jamie (her middle brother) Claudia hides out in the Metropolitan Museum of Art in New York. To help solve the problem of who sculpted Angel, the newest statue acquired by the museum, the two travel to see Mrs. Frankweiler, the former owner of Angel. In return for taping their adventure, Mrs. Frankweiler allows them to look through her mixed-up files to find the identity of the sculptor. Using the tape, Mrs. Frankweiler writes the narrative for the story and sends it along with a letter to her lawyer, Saxonberg, who is the children's grandfather. 4–6.

Target Activity: "Secrets That Make You Different on the Inside"

Discuss the idea of "secrets" and reasons why knowing certain secrets makes you feel different. Claudia, the main character, is discussed along with the secret she finds in the files. The girls and boys are encouraged to think of "secrets" they would like to know that would be meaningful and make them feel happy on the inside. The teacher should invite the students to write privately in their journals about these secrets.

119.   L'Engle, Madeleine. *A Ring of Endless Light.* **New York: Farrar, Straus & Giroux, 1980.**

Trait: Relationship with a significant other.

Sixteen-year-old Vicky and her family move to Seven Bay Island off the coast of New England to live with her grandfather who is dying of leukemia. At the Marine Biology Station on the island, Vicky helps a friend, Adam Eddington, with his summer dolphin project. Vicky finds she has a rapport with the dolphins and communicates with them telepathically. As her grandfather's health deteriorates, there is an emphasis on death and on accepting death as a friend to affirm the cyclic wholeness of life. To emphasize this wholeness, the words of Henry Vaughn, a 17th century English poet, noted in the book's title, are quoted by Grandfather: "I saw eternity the other night/ Like a great ring of pure and endless light." Though emphasizing the naturalness (and beauty) of death, this is a story of pleasing family relationships that sustain the family in the difficult times. Vicky interacts with the dolphins, her parents and grandfather. At the station, the loving behavior of the dolphins help Vicky keep her perspective on life. At home, Mrs. Austin sings to the family and accompanies herself on the guitar. She reads aloud from Shakespeare and all spend time talking together in family conversations. At the hospital, Grandfather accepts death.

Target Activity: "Wholeness of Life"

With the students, the teacher discusses the concept of the wholeness of life including death as part of life's cycle. There is an emphasis in this story on death and on accepting death as a friend to affirm the cyclic wholeness of nature. The discussion should include some of the supporting family relationships that sustain a family in these difficult times. The teacher should ask the students to find other books that they would suggest to others to read that reflect this concept of the wholeness of life and of support from the family.

120.   Myers, Walter Dean. *The Mouse Rap.* **Ill. New York: Harper, 1990.**

Trait: Problem-solving.

Living in Harlem, fourteen-year-old quick-thinking, fast-talking Frederick Douglas is known as "The Mouse." "Ka-phoomp! Ka-phoomp! Da Doom Da Dooom!/ Ka-phoomp! Ka-phoomp! / Da Doom Da Dooom!/ You can call me Mouse, 'cause that's my tag/ I'm into it all, everything's my bag" is a sample of his fast talking. Focuses on family and peer relationships during one busy summer as Mouse, who loves basketball, sorts out his feelings for his girlfriend, her request for him to dance in a talent contest; for his friend, Styx, and his once estranged father now trying to get back into the family. He searches for a treasure hidden by

Tiger Moran, a gangster of the '30s. Through a mock bank robbery, Mouse and other teenage friends (with the help of Sheri's grandfather and Sudden Sam, a cohort of Moran's) find the money in an abandoned building. Shows independence. 6–8.

Target Activity: "Everything's My Bag: Mouse's Feelings"

Related to Mouse's feelings about his estranged father, discuss with students different reasons they can think of to explain why some teenagers are convinced that their parents don't care about them. What do you think can happen rather suddenly that would make a teenager feel unwanted by a girlfriend? boyfriend? friend? parent? To make a visual display of Mouse's feelings, draw a large "paper grocery bag" in the center of a sheet of art paper and write the name Mouse. Draw lines outward from the "bag" and at the end of each line draw smaller "bags." Inside the "bags," write these headings: Mouse felt happy when...; Mouse felt afraid when...; Mouse felt sad when ...; and Mouse felt angry when.... Now, discuss the headings with others in a talking circle group and finish the sentences on your paper. Read what you wrote to others.

121. Page, Valerie King. *Pi Gal*. Ill. by Jacques Callaert. New York: Dodd, Mead, 1970.

Traits: Persistence in the face of failure; a positive vision of life.

Prince Williams is a young boy growing up on Cat Island, an outer island in the Bahamas. Like many other children on the island, he longs for a chance to live a more exciting life in exotic places far beyond the island. While searching for his lost dog, he comes upon two divers who have come to the island to salvage a lost barge. Prince soon learns to dive and the beautiful underwater life of the reef is revealed to him for the first time. After many frustrating attempts, Prince finds the barge they have been seeking and at the same time discovers he is a talented diver and decides to pursue diving as a career. 5–6.

Target Activity: "Human Resources Book"

Invite students to consider the idea that their class is a bounty of human resources; there are many talents and abilities that each student has that perhaps the others do not know about. Explain that just as Prince Williams had to discover his talents, others must keep searching to find what makes them unique and special. Write on the chalkboard the following three sentence stems:

Once I couldn't _____

But today I can _____

Soon I may learn to _____

Fill in the lines as a group, allowing many students to contribute ideas for the blanks. Next, encourage students to write their own human resource poems, illustrating them if they so desire. Collect the poems and put them into a class "Human Resources Book." Put the book on display so that all can see what their classmates can do and someday hope to do.

122.   Paterson, Katherine. *Bridge to Terabithia.* **Ill. by Donna Diamond. New York: Harper & Row, 1977.**

Traits: Courage in the face of adversity; positive relationship with a significant other.

Jesse Aarons is a ten-year-old boy growing up in rural Virginia with what he describes as "a great piece missing" because of his fear of swinging across a high creek on a rope. He has formed an unlikely friendship with Leslie Burke, a little girl whose family has left the city for a better way of life. Leslie's life is filled with books and imagination, and together the two create Terabithia, their secret kingdom in the woods where magical, beautiful things happen routinely through the forces of their imaginations.

Jesse admires Leslie because she not only has led him to this magical world, but she seems to have no fears. When Leslie is killed crossing the creek to Terabithia, Jesse uses all that Leslie has taught him to enable him to cope with the unexpected tragedy. Jesse brings his little sister into Terabithia helping to assuage his pain. He begins to share his new values with his family. 4–6 & up.

Target Activity: "My Special Kingdom"

Ask students to describe Terabithia, the world that Leslie and Jesse had created. Ask them if they have ever made up a fictional place. Who were its citizens and what were the rules? What was it like?

Have children form small groups and create a fantasy world and have them assign themselves royal roles in their kingdoms. Ask them to make group decisions to do the following:

1. Who will be allowed to enter your kingdom?
2. What are the rules in your kingdom?
3. What other creatures live in your kingdom?
4. How do all the members of the kingdom get along?
5. What is magical and beautiful about your kingdom?

Children may want to draw a mural of their kingdoms. Additionally, encourage them to "discover" their kingdoms outside of school.

123.   Peake, Katy. *The Indian Heart of Carrie Hodges.* **Ill. by Thomas B. Allen. New York: Viking, 1972.**

Traits: Relationship with a caring "other" person; ability to plan ahead and solve problems.

Carrie Hodges is a serious and sensitive little girl who loves animals and nature. Growing up in the desert environment of Southern California, she has come to appreciate the flora and fauna around her. She is befriended by a desert-seasoned old recluse, Foster, who shares her love of nature and begins teaching her about the Indian ways and the magical relations that once existed between the Indians and the animals. Carrie is tormented when the ranchers in the valley decide to kill all the coyotes in the area because one coyote killed some sheep. She sets out on a mission to save the coyotes and learns about her own animal spirit at the same time. 5–6.

Target Activity: "Animal Research"

Tell children that they are going to do a very peculiar kind of research. They are going to research animal spirits "by finding out everything they can about five wild animals of their choice." Explain that they may use any resources available—zoologists, encyclopedias, Indian legends, video tapes, etc.—to find out what these animals' "souls" are really like. When the five animals have been researched, ask children to write an essay describing which animal is closest to them in spirit and why and how they think this is so. Finally, have pairs of children share which of the animals they feel the other child is most like and why before sharing their essay with a significant other. Provide an opportunity for children to tell about how their essay compared with their partner's feelings about which animal they are most like.

124. Pfeffer, Susan Beth. *Courage, Dana*. New York: Delacorte, 1983.

Traits: Perseverance; courage.

Dana is a self-effacing twelve-year-old who inadvertently becomes a local heroine when she rushes into traffic to save a little child's life. She becomes an instant celebrity, but doubts that she is really a brave person. Her best friend, Sharon, devises a test for Dana to prove to herself that she is not a coward: an evening in a cemetery. Dana passes this test, but on the way home observes a classmate writing graffiti on the school wall and writing someone else's initials. Dana confronts the boy, but he blackmails her by telling her that he will tell Dana's parents what *she* is doing if she tells on him. When Dana finally confesses to her parents and tells the principal who really wrote the graffiti, she realizes that it has taken more courage than anything she has ever done. Dana learns that courage can involve choosing between right and wrong as well as being physically brave. She comes to terms with her own courageousness. 5–6.

Target Activity: "Confrontation Roleplay"

Point out to the students that the entire theme of the book might have changed if Dana had been successful in her confrontation with the boy who wrote the graffiti. Explain that confrontations about unpleasant subjects are usually difficult, but that there are many in life, and our ability to handle them successfully depends on our tact, honesty, and ability not to back down in the face of unfair or untrue accusations. Have the children volunteer to be Dana and the graffiti-writing boy replaying the scene where Dana catches him in the act of writing the graffiti. Ask the children to think of an alternative way for Dana to confront the boy so that he confesses to the principal himself. Instruct the rest of the class to watch what the two characters do and say and to be thinking of an alternative dialogue. Encourage other pairs of children to roleplay alternative outcomes. Discuss the relative merits of each.

125.   Pitseolak, Peter. *Peter Pitseolak's Escape from Death.* **Introduced and edited by Dorothy Eber. New York: Delacort/Seymour Lawrence, 1977.**

Traits: Perseverance; courage; human dignity.

On a walrus hunt in his canoe with his son, Peter Pitseolak, an Eskimo artist of Baffin Island, finds himself stranded in a huge ice field that is moving swiftly out to sea. After two nights on the ice, a bluebird appears to Peter in a strange dream. The dream gives Peter courage and hope that they will find a path through the ice field and return to safety. The wind, that Peter had once feared, drives their canoe back toward Baffin Island. Peter notes in his retrospective story, "There is nothing in the world that is not good. I understood this then." The story is related as a firsthand account by the author. He poignantly portrays his fear of never seeing his family again, which is contrasted with his renewed feeling of hope and optimism after the dream. 4–6.

Target Activity: "Obstacle or Challenge?"

Write on the chalkboard the following sentence from *Peter Pitseolak's Escape from Death*: "There is nothing in the world that is not good." Ask children to share what they think Peter meant by this statement in the context of his harrowing experience. Bring out the idea that some very difficult situations that we go through seem overwhelming and unfair at the time, but they often bring us new understandings about ourselves and the world, new friends, or in some other ways turn out to have been positive challenges. Write on the chalkboard, "Obstacle or Challenge?" Invite children to share some past event they have experienced that first seemed like an obstacle, but later, in retrospect, they can view as a challenge because it turned out to have had positive benefits. After all who wish to have shared orally, ask students to select one event to describe in essay format using the title, "Obstacle or Challenge?"

126.   Radley, Gail. *The Golden Days.* **New York: Macmillan, 1991.**

Trait: Relationship with a significant caring other.

Cory, an 11-year-old foster home runaway, and elderly Carlotta, a nursing home runaway, are brought together by their need for love, acceptance and freedom. They wish to start their "golden days of freedom." Carlotta, a former circus trouper, takes charge until she is hospitalized and Cory takes over their responsibilities. Calling his social worker, Cory is reunited with his former foster parents, the Keppermans, who agree to share their home with Carlotta, too. 5–8.

Target Activity: "Golden Silence about Golden Days"

Independent silent reading by an interested older student (grades 5–8) is a "golden silence" activity and gives time for the reader to reflect about this intergenerational story that focuses on the bravado, hesitancy and near-misses of eleven-year-old Cory, a foster home runaway, and elderly Carlotta, a nursing home runaway, in their travels together which they call their "golden days." After the silent reading, the student should meet with the teacher for a literature response conference and come prepared to answer the basic questions of Who (were the main characters?), What (was the setting?), When and Where (did the story take place?), and Why (did the characters solve the problem[s] the way they did?).

127.   Roy, Ron. *Where's Buddy?* Ill. by Troy Howell. New York: Clarion, 1982.

Trait: Problem-solving.

Mike is supposed to take care of his little brother Buddy, who is a diabetic, but Mike leaves Buddy with a friend so that he can go and play football, promising his little brother that he'll pick him up in time for lunch and his insulin shot. Mike comes back ten minutes late and Buddy is gone. A frantic search ensues to make sure Buddy gets his medication before it's too late. Mike and Buddy both learn important lessons about taking responsibility in this suspense story. 4–6.

Target Activity: "Supersleuth"

Put students in the class into pairs. Explain to them that they are going to have five minutes to decide what to do if they were faced with a big problem. Tell them the following scenario:

"Your parents are on vacation. They have left you in charge of picking up your younger sister (six years old) from the babysitter when you come home from school. You are late coming home because you were talking to your friends after school. When you get to the babysitter's, she tells you that Janey started to walk home; that you had said it was all right. You must find Janey right away! Panic sets in, but you fight it."

Give children three minutes to write down what they would do. Then allow them two minutes to share ideas with their partners. Finally, allow each pair to tell the class how they would solve the problem.

128.   Sachs, Marilyn. *Underdog.* **Garden City, NY: Doubleday, 1985.**

Traits: Persistence in the face of failure; will to succeed; ability to solve problems.

Izzy's father has just died and her mother died when she was four. No one wants her. She is sent to live with an aunt and uncle who barely know her; she is clearly an intrusion in their ultra-ordered lives. Izzy tries vainly to please, hoping that her aunt and uncle will change their minds about sending her to boarding school in the fall. While looking through old photos, Izzy discovers a picture of herself, her mother and the family dog, Gus, taken the day her mother died in a freak accident. Suddenly remembering how much she loved her dog, Izzy goes on an all-out search to find Gus, who has had a series of owners. She finally finds him and convinces her aunt and uncle to accept Gus—and her. 5–6.

Target Activity: "Izzy's Diary"

Diaries can be especially cathartic activities to children who are going through difficult and confusing times, as Izzy was. Discuss with students the fact that Izzy really had no one she could talk to about her father's death and her new living situation. Explain that sometimes writing is a good way to explore one's own confused feelings and that this would have helped Izzy. Read sections of *Diary of Anne Frank* to students to demonstrate how feelings can be written down and clarified using a diary format. Ask children to write five diary entries that Izzy might have made. Using the chalkboard, brainstorm some espcially low or confusing times when Izzy might have benefited from writing down her thoughts (e.g., when her father died, when she went to live with her uncle, when she was frustrated in her attempts to find Gus, etc.).

129.   Singer, Marilyn. *It Can't Hurt Forever.* **Ill. by Leigh Grant. New York: Harper & Row, 1978.**

Traits: Positive vision of life; feeling of autonomy.

Eleven-year-old Ellie Simon has a heart defect and this book describes her experiences during twelve days of hospitalization for heart surgery. Ellie goes through the gamut of emotions about her impending operation—fear, mistrust of the doctors, anger—as well as caring relationships with Susan, a young nurse, and Sonia, a young patient who has already had heart surgery and teaches Ellie about hospital life. After the operation there is tremendous pain—more pain than Ellie had ever anticipated. Ellie struggles with overwhelming fear and helplessness during her hospitalization. She overcomes these feelings and grows as a person through the experience. She has made an important decision while in the hospital. She has decided to become a surgeon like the one who so skillfully repaired her defective heart. 5–6.

Target Activity: "Advice Column"

It Can't Hurt Forever tackles the natural fear a young girl has concerning her heart operation. Many fears, however, are irrational. Ask children to share some fears that they have that they would like to overcome. To open up this delicate subject, the teacher may first want to share her/his fears. Next, ask each child to pick a trusted friend for a partner. Each child will write a "Dear Abby" letter to her/his partner describing a fear and asking advice on how to conquer the other's fear. Because children often suffer from similar fears, yet believe they are unique in being afraid, they learn through this activity that everyone is afraid of something, and they begin to accept their own fears. Also, giving their partner advice helps them to realize they have in themselves the capacity to deal with their own fears.

130. **Slepian, Jan.** *Risk 'n' Roses*. **New York: Philomel, 1990.**

Trait: Problem-solving.

In her new neighborhood, Skip wants to be accepted into Jean Persico's gang. The girls have a secret club and each must meet a challenge stated by Persico. Persico is a pest and torments old Mr. Kaminsky (who has befriended Skip's retarded sister, Angela, but who has no use for the gang leader). Since she feels the rejection, Jean talks Angel into cutting the flowers from all of the old man's prize roses, another one of her torments. Skip stops being mesmerized by Jean and decides to go her own way. 5–7.

Target Activity: "The Secret Club"

The teacher sets the stage: Imagine that every one in your class is a member of the secret club. In the group each student prints his/her name on a paper. The paper is passed to the right (or left) to the person next to him or her. Each student in turn writes something positive about the person whose name is on the sheet. Finally each student has his or her own "good word" sheet to keep as an initiation into the secret club of the class.

131. **Snyder, Silpha Keatley.** *Libby on Wednesday*. **New York: Delacorte, 1990.**

Traits: Persistence in responding to difficulty; caring about others.

Educated at home, Libby goes to public middle school where she feels she is superior to her classmates and they feel she is socially inferior to them. Libby, one who takes refuge in writing, tells her story in journal entries and tells it as a third-person narrative. Members learn of the serious problems of others in their writers' club during Wednesday meetings. Honest characterization. Recommended. 5–7.

Target Activity: "Emergency Situations"

Invite volunteers to contribute any emergency situations they know about from their lives or the lives of others. On the chalkboard, list some of the items which could be used to help children get out of the trouble or the emergency situation. Ask children to close their eyes for mental imagery and to try to picture themselves in such a situation. Discuss the items that could be useful in the emergency. Ask children to draw sketches to show how they would use some of the items to get out of the situation.

132. Stopl, Hans. *The Golden Bird*. Ill. by Lidia Postma. New York: Dial, 1990.

Traits: Courage; positive vision of life.

Eleven-year-old Daniel is hospitalized with cancer. In a first person narrative, he sees three birds on the sill, one green, one blue and one golden. The blue bird brings messages from the golden bird daily—messages that say, "Watch the tree outside your window. It may look dead to you, but it you look more closely, you'll see buds on it." Daniel discusses death with his mother and the nurses and, lovingly and honestly, they help him face his death. Daniel comes to see death as a transformation similar to the reflowering of the cherry tree outside his window. Family love supports the story as reader sees the nature of death. Realistic scenes include the hospital, mother at the bedside, nurses caring for him, and visitors talking with Daniel. Realistic yet reassuring approach for those who face the death of a terminally ill child. 4 & up.

Target Activity: "Daniel's Opinion"

In small response groups, encourage children to consider: What opinions do you have about the situation which developed where the blue bird brings messages daily from the golden bird to Daniel? What do you think Daniel means when he says death is a transformation similar to the reflowering of the cherry tree? Each group asks a volunteer to report on the group's considerations when all the students return together as a total group.

133. Strachan, Ian. *The Flawed Glass*. New York: Little, Brown, 1990.

Trait: Persistence.

On an island off Scotland, Shona MacLeod and her family face poachers and a conflict with the new American owners of the island. Shona, physically handicapped and unable to walk or talk, easily refers to herself as a piece of "flawed glass." Shona is mentally clear but she cannot tell others her thoughts. She rescues Carl, the owner's son, from a potentially fatal accident, and they become friends. Sharing their new friendship, Carl teaches Shona to use his dad's computer and Shona shows Carl the birds—in particular, eagle hatchlings who, like Shona, also struggle for survival. Together they see other wonders of nature on the island. Shona's struggles to walk and talk are contrasted with the ways those

around her try to communicate with her. It is Carl and his knowledge of
the computer that help her use her strengths. And it is Shona who sees
and communicates the truth when the poachers try to incriminate her
father for their deeds. When Carl returns to the United States, Shona
communicates with him through a computer and a modem. 5–6.

Target Activity: "Flawed Glass and Other Comparisons"

In addition to "flawed glass," the metaphoric way Shona refers to
herself, there are other metaphors and similes in this realistic story. In
small response groups, encourage students to consider: What metaphors
(or similes) can you find about the situation which developed when Carl
came to the island and met Shona? What do you think Shona means when
she says she sees herself as a piece of flawed glass—mentally sharp and
clear but unable to communicate her thoughts? Each group asks a
volunteer to report on the group's elaborations of the metaphors and
similes they found when all the students return together as a total group.

Fanciful Fiction

134. Alexander, Lloyd. *The Book of Three.* **New York: Holt, 1964.**
Trait: Perseverance.

An assistant pig-keeper, Taran, dreams of finding his heritage and
becoming a hero. Alexander reminds a reader in the narrative that all are
assistant pig-keepers because one's capabilities seldom match one's aspi-
rations and often one is unprepared for what is to happen. In this battle
of the forces of good against evil, he becomes a hero when he goes out with
Prince Gwydion, a great warrior, the Sons of Don, and the Dallben, an
enchanter, to fight against an evil Horned King, who has sworn allegiance
to the Lord of the Land of Death, Arawn. The evil king wants to capture
Hen Wen, a pig who can foretell the future, because she knows his secret
name. This knowledge will enable Hen Wen to make the evil king power-
less and perhaps help destroy him. Also helping Taran on the quest are
Ffllewddur, the harpist, the creature Gurgi, and the Princess Eilonwy, a
descendent of enchanters. 4 & up.

Target Activity: "The Prydain Books"

Before the book: With the students, discuss heroism and in teams of
two, have students write paragraphs to show their interpretation of being
a heroine or hero. Students trade writing sheets, read and discuss and give
feedback. In a following discussion, focus on understanding the attempts
of any hero or heroine written about to become a champion (leader, de-
fender of good, avenger of wrongs). After listening to the story, the students return to their interpretative writing to further define/interpret what
it means to be a heroine/hero.

After the book: Display the other books in this series and discuss the quests in each through brief book talks to engage the interests of the students in reading about these resilient characters. Taran goes on another quest to fight cauldron-born creatures in *The Black Cauldron* (1965); he rescues Princess Eilonwy in *The Castle of Llyr* (1966) and seeks his true identity in *Taran Wanderer* (1967). In the last book in the series, Taran searches for and fights the Death Lord in *The High King* (1968). Invite the students to make a visual organizer to show this series. Drawing a large square in the center of a sheet of paper, the students write in the words, *Books by Lloyd Alexander.* Four radiating lines are drawn outward from the square in the center and smaller squares are drawn at the end of each line. Inside each small square, the students write a title of one of the books of the Prydain series. As a book is read, a student returns to this organizer and adds a few informative sentences to summarize it under (or near) the appropriate square.

135.   Banks, Lynn Reid. *The Indian in the Cupboard.* New York: Avon, 1982.

Trait: Problem-solving.

In England, nine-year-old Omri receives a magic cupboard for his birthday. It makes a small plastic toy Indian come alive. Omri, with his friend, Patrick, engages in many adventures with the Iroquois Little Bear, the transformed Indian toy. In their escapades, they meet people who lived during the French and Indian Wars, in the 1800s, and during the Civil War. On these adventures, Omri discovers the meaning of power, of responsibility, and of friendship—all of which help him solve the problems brought to him by the small toy Indian who comes to life. 4–6.

Target Activity: "Character Display for Little Bear"

As the students listen to or read the story, they should be thinking of the Indian's feelings, actions, and relationships with others. After the story, the students construct a display of these traits to show the major points they read in the story. When finished, the students should team up in twos and compare their displays and discuss the different ways they interpreted the character of Little Bear. A visual display may be a simple one with a large oval bearing Little Bear's name in the center of a sheet of paper, lines extending outward in "spider-leg" style, and small ovals at the end of each line. Students record information about the character in the smaller ovals. Students discuss their displays in pairs and listen for feedback. Suggestions may be marked on the displays with colored pencils.

136.   Banks, Lynn Reid. *The Return of the Indian.* New York: Avon, 1986.

Trait: Problem-solving.

This is a sequel to *The Indian in the Cupboard* where Omri brings the Indian toy, Little Bear, back to life with the magic in the cupboard. Omri discovers that the Indian has been injured critically in the French and Indian Wars and needs his help. 4–6.

Target Activity: "The Indian's Return"

To show the extent of Little Bear's illness, the things Omri does to help him, and the Indian's return to health, ask the students to draw a large circle on paper. Divide the circle into eight segments and write in the events on the wedges of the circle. In a review of the story, the students can fill in the important things that Omri did to help Little Bear. If the students want more information, other circles can be drawn. You might ask the students to discuss the things that motivated Omri to do the things he did.

137.   Conly, Jane I. *Rasco and the Rats of NIMH*. **Ill. by Leonard Lubin. New York: Harper & Row, 1986.**

Trait: Problem-solving.

For students who liked *Mrs. Frisby and the Rats of NIMH*, here is the sequel with Rasco, a city rat, the son of one of the rats who left the original farm, as the main character. Rasco brings new inventions and ideas to the country since Rasco can read. He tells other rats what he knows about dancing, rock songs, and programming computers. Rasco and the other rats engage in social action and stop their river valley from being developed into communities which people move in and take over. 4–6.

Target Activity: "Describing Rasco"

As the students listen to or read the story, ask them to write a list of words that describe Rasco or write sentences from the story that tell of his actions, habits, or characteristics (persevering, overcome obstacles). After the story is read, draw a visual (graphic) organizer in a circle-radiating line arrangement on the board or overhead transparency. Ask the students to contribute words to describe Rasco (different, observant, intelligent) and write the words on the radiating lines. Next, ask the students to copy the organizer and then use a dictionary or a thesaurus to find new words that mean the same thing as the words they have on the organizer. They write the words they find along with the appropriate words on the lines on the organizer. The students should trade papers with a partner for a partner-check and defend their choices if the partner questions any word.

138.   Cooper, Susan. *The Dark Is Rising*. **Ill. by Alan Cober. New York: Atheneum, 1973.**

Traits: Persistence; overcoming obstacles.

Another seventh son of a seventh son, Will Stanton, knows his responsibility and his destiny is to fight against evil until the end. He is the last born of the Old Ones whose powers can be used against the powers of darkness. He realizes what this means:

"Will realized once more, helplessly, that to be an Old One was to be old before the proper time, for the fear he began to feel now was worse than the blind terror he had known in his attic bed, worse than the fear the Dark had put into him in the great hall. This time his fear was adult, made of experience and imagination and care of others, and it was the worst of all."

Will's ancestors the guardians of the Light (and now Will), fight the forces of Darkness. Born in 20th century England, eleven-year-old Will learns about his heritage from another of the destined ones, Merriman Lyon. At first, his impatience and his ignorance cause Will to help the forces of Darkness. Then he swears that he will never again use the power unless he has a reason and knows the consequences. His knowledge increases until he finally understands the magnitude of his powers and is able to use them successfully. 4–6.

Target Activity: "Will Stanton"

Invite students to read more about Will to discover his traits of resiliency as he journeys to recover the stolen Grail in *Greenwitch* (1974), where he meets King Arthur's son, Bran, and they ride against evil in *The Grey King* (1975), and as Will defends good in a final battle against evil in *Silver on the Tree* (1977). With an outline sketch of Will in the center of a sheet of paper, the students can draw lines outward to organize information about his traits. Some of the traits may be tired, free, helpful, understanding, wise, careful, brave, afraid, fearful, and so on. Students can use the completed organizer to write a paragraph (or a poem) about Will.

139. Egielski, Richard. *Hey, Al!* Ill. by Arthur Yorinks. New York: Farrar, Straus & Giroux, 1986.

Trait: Positive vision of life.

Totally miserable in a crowded, cramped home, a nice, quiet janitor, Al, and his dog, Eddie, do everything together. A large, mystic bird offers them a trip to an island paradise in the sky filled with lush trees, rolling hills, gorgeous grass, waterfalls, and pools. Days pass and one morning, Al notices that he is turning into a bird-shape with a beak-like nose, wings sprouted out, and tail feathers. Flapping their wings, they rise into the air to return and Eddie falls into the sea. The last scene shows a refurbishing of their one room on the West side. They paint, patch the ceiling, and clean the shelves. Notice the use of ellipses, italics, and a moral: Paradise lost is sometimes Heaven found. 4–6.

Target Activity: "Author/artist Craftsmanship in *Hey, Al!*"

With the students, review the book and point out: 1) the illustrations become larger as the conflict develops; 2) the doublepage spread is at the height of interest in the story; 3) information about the setting and the resilient characters can be gained from the illustrations; 4) there is foreshadowing of their fate, e.g., the bird has human hands; 5) there is a person-versus-self conflict as both Al and Eddie overcome dissatisfaction in their lives (positive vision of life); 6) the idea that beautiful places can hide dangerous unknowns; and 7) the allure of beautiful places to not only Al and Eddie but also to other characters in other stories. What other stories (e.g., *The Adventures of Pinnochio* by Carlo Collodi) do the children know about that show this idea?

140. Howe, James. *The Celery Stalks at Midnight*. Ill. by Leslie Morill. New York: Avon, 1983.

Trait: Problem-solving with humor.

Chester the cat, Howard the dog, and Howie the dachshund puppy go on an adventure to search for Bunnicula, the vampire bunny, who is missing from his cage. The others help in the search for him. Some humor. 4–6.

Target Activity: "What Does It Mean When the Celery Stalks?"

Introduce a concept organizer with a visual diagram to the students. For instance, draw an outline of a large stalk of celery in the center of the board or the transparency and draw four radiating lines outward from the stalk. On the stalk, write the title and ask, "What do you think the title of this story might mean?" Use the radiating lines to help organize what the students predict about the story. Below each of the lines, cluster the children's related ideas. After reading the book, the students can create individual graphic organizers with their thoughts about the story and use the title of the book as the center of their organizing diagrams.

141. Langton, Jane. *The Fledgling*. Ill. by Erik Blegvad. New York: Harper & Row, 1980.

Traits: Relationship with a significant other; positive vision of life.

A magical adventure originates in an old house in Concord as Uncle Fred Hall, Georgie Dorian's stepfather, conducts the Concord College of Transcendental Knowledge in the 19th century house. A large Canada goose—a Goose Prince—hoots softly from the porch roof outside her window and Georgie climbs on his back for a flight around Walden Pond. He teaches her to fly, a wish she has always had. The nighttime flight and their talks come to an end when Georgie is shot by a hunter who mistakes her for a flying goose. When she is healed, the Goose Prince returns one more time with a present, a small rubber ball with blue and white streaks. Killed by a hunter, the Goose Prince is buried by Walden Pond. In her grief,

Georgie ponders the present and discovers that in the darkness of night, the ball becomes great and gleaming, lifts from her hand and slowly turns. It is an image of Earth and the Goose Prince tells Georgie to take good care of it. George remembers her promise with the words, "I will." 4–7.

Target Activity: "I Will"

With the students, the teacher discusses this premise: Think of a time when someone asked you to take "good care" of something and you promised. What words did you say when you made the promise? When the Goose Prince told Georgie to take good care of the gleaming turning ball, Georgie promised with the words, "I will." Write quietly and reflectively in your journals about something you promised to take good care of for someone else.

142.   Le Guin, Ursula. *A Wizard of Earthsea.* **Ill. by Ruth Robbins. Emeryville, Calif.: Parnassus, 1968.**

Traits: Perseverance; overcoming obstacles; problem-solving.

Ged, a seventh son of a seventh son, tells of his education as a wizard on the island of Gont in the land of Earthsea. The young boy discovers he has some powers—he can call animals to follow him. With training, he is strong enough to save his village from attacking enemies and summons a protective fog to cover it; he also has a dangerous pride and impatience that places him in harm's way. During his education, a master wizard tells him to be cautious about wanting to learn and use powers of enchantment. He is not yet mature enough to understand or to try to control his powers. A conflict with another apprentice leads to a duel of sorcery skills and Ged calls up a spirit of the dead. With a tearing in the darkness and a blaze of brightness followed by a hideous black shadow, he releases a nameless evil into the world and finds himself threatened by this shadow-beast. Ged realizes that he must face what he has created, follows this shadow-beast across the islands to the farthest waters of Earthsea, and fights it beast-to-wizard to rid the world of it. Finally, he develops an understanding that he is responsible for his actions. 4 & up.

Target Activity: "Earthsea Quests"

Ged travels on further quests in other Earthsea fantasies. He travels to the sacred Kargad Lands searching for a magic amulet. Here, he meets Arha, a high priestess in *The Tombs of Atuan* (1971), overcomes his personal problems and understands true freedom when he says, "Freedom is a heavy load, a great and strange burden for the spirit to undertake." Ged sets out on another quest to discover the reason why wizards have lost their powers throughout Earthsea in *The Farthest Shore* (1972). Invite the students to draw a visual organizer to graphically show the titles in this Earthsea series.

143. Lewis, C. S. *The Lion, the Witch, and the Wardrobe.* **New York: Macmillan, 1950.**

Traits: Perseverance; overcoming obstacles.

In an old mansion in England, four children go into a wardrobe and out through its back to enter the magical kingdom of Narnia. In this kingdom, it is always winter until the children break the spell of the wicked Snow Queen. The children are engaged in the battle between good and evil respectively symbolized by the Lion, Aslan, and the evil Witch. After years in Narnia, the children return. When they finally reach home, they find that the time arrangement in Narnia is different from that of England's and that they have not been missed. 5–8.

Target Activity: "More Adventures in Narnia"

Discuss the traits of resiliency of the four children in this adventure and display the other books in this series. Invite the students to engage in further reading about these autonomous children. The children return to Narnia in *Prince Caspian* (1951) and *The Voyage of the Dawn Treader* (1952), *The Silver Chair* (1953) and *The Boy and His Horse* (1954). They learn about how the Lion created Narnia in *The Magician's Nephew* (1955). Aslan sings the world into existence along with the stars in the sky and the creatures on the land. Narnia comes to an end in *The Last Battle* (1956).

144. O'Brien, Robert. *Mrs. Frisby and the Rats of NIMH.* **Ill. by Zena Bernstein. New York: Atheneum, 1971.**

Trait: Perseverance.

In an experiment at the National Institute of Mental Health, some rats receive steroid injections (which increases their intelligence and lifespan) to see how it affects their ability to learn. They escape from the laboratory. They arrive at a farm outside of Washington, D.C., where Mrs. Frisby and her children live. Mrs. Frisby, a widow, fears that her home in the garden will be discovered when the farmer plows in the spring. Her son, Timothy, is too ill with pneumonia to move and she seeks help. The owl sends Mrs. Frisby to the rats who live under the rosebush with the words, "You must go, Mrs. Frisby ... to the rats under the rosebush. They are not, I think, like other rats."

When Mrs. Frisby goes to the rats for help, she finds they are different from others. She learns that the rats had known her late husband and that they had escaped with him from a laboratory named NIMH. The rats can read, use machines, and talk about establishing a self-supporting rat community. They have been reading the books in the library of an empty house and practicing writing. After being at the Institute and studying humans, the rats are determined not to make the same mistakes that humans do but they fall into immoral behavior, too. The rats are building their own community on the farm (stealing electricity, food, and water) but finally leave to build a rat society in a valley far away from civilization and humans. Almost all the rats escape to a hidden valley where they intend to give up stealing and to farm the land. They help Mrs. Frisby move her home and she in turn helps them: she warns them of government exterminators on their way to kill the rats with poison gas. 4–6.

Target Activity: "Describing the Rats of NIMH"

With the students working together in pairs, ask them to find words that describe traits of resiliency on the part of the characters in the story:

1. positive vision of life
2. persistence in the face of failure
3. ability to plan ahead and to solve problems
4. feeling of autonomy
5. sense of humor
6. developing a hobby or talent
7. relationship with a significant "other"
8. ability to gain people's attention in a positive way
9. sense of control over life

145.   Rodda, Emily. *The Pigs Are Flying*. Ill. by Noela Young. New York: Greenwillow, 1986.

Traits: Courage; problem-solving.

Young Rachel has been ill with a cold and sore throat for several days; she is getting bored and tired of staying inside. She wishes something exciting would happen for a change. Suddenly it does. She finds herself riding on a unicorn into a land where it rains pigs and the intensity of a storm is measured in UEF's, or unexpected event factors. Rachel is taken in by an elderly couple who tell her that she is what is known as an "outsider." They reassure her that she can find her way back to her own world if she wants to badly enough. She is told of another "outsider" who once worked in the town and eventually managed to go back to his home. Rachel talks to several people and follows the young man's path until she, too, finally figures out how to get back home. While Rachel is at times bewildered by the strange world in which she finds herself, she manages to fight back her tears and painstakingly figures out how to return to her family. 4–6.

Target Activity: "The Insider Goes Out"

Tell children to imagine they are going to the land Rachel visited, where pigs fly and where they will be "outsiders." Ask them to imagine that they meet one child their own age who asks to return with them. Have children write a short story about their adventures with this "insider" child, including the following details:

1. What will you tell the child about "our land"?
2. What about our land does the child find exciting? frightening? unusual?
3. Have the child experience a thunderstorm. What will the child think?
4. Tell how the child feels about being away from her/his family.
5. What special way must the child return to her/his world?

146.   Tolkien, J. R. R. *The Hobbitt*. Boston: Houghton Mifflin, 1938.

Trait: Persistence.

Based on the Norse myths from northern Europe, this story tells of the material comforts in Middle Earth and of Bilbo Baggins, a hobbit, a neat, quiet little creature who has no desire to do great deeds. He is tricked into going on a quest to retrieve the dwarfs' treasure with others (the wizard Gandalf and twelve dwarfs) and perseveres as he overcomes great obstacles in this good-against-evil story. The narrative takes a reader right to the first obstacles with, "Far over the misty mountains cold/ To dungeons deep and caverns old/ We must away ere break of day/ To find our long-forgotten gold." Smaug, an evil red-golden dragon, guards precious jewels in his nesting place where lightning splinters the peaks of mountains and rocks shiver. When the dragon is slain, Baggins has been persistent and kept his pledge to help his friends. The ring Bilbo found on this quest becomes the center of the plots in three more fantasies: *The Lord of the Rings, Fellowship of the Ring,* and *The Return of the Ring.* The cast of characters includes elves as creatures who love beauty and music and who have an alphabet and language that contrasts with the language of the dwarfs and the Orcs. 4 & up.

Target Activity: "3-Column Analysis"

Ask students to fold a sheet of paper (the long way) into three columns. In the left-hand column, ask them to draw or write about the first problem that Bilbo had. In the middle column, they will draw or write what action Bilbo took, and in the right-hand column, they will draw or write the solution that came to Bilbo to resolve the problem. Have the students talk about what their drawings represent or what they wrote. Try to probe and ask them what the problem is (and why it is a problem to Bilbo) and the way it came to be a problem. Discussing the action, encourage the students to tell what Bilbo did to lead the story along toward the solution and relate his actions to traits of resiliency (positive vision of life, perseverance, solving problems, overcoming obstacles, etc.). When the three elements are discussed, the students may use their notes on the columns to retell the event. Other events in the story may be reviewed in this manner.

147.   Van Allsburg, Chris. *The Polar Express.* **Ill. by the author. Boston: Houghton Mifflin, 1985.**

Trait: Positive vision of life.

One Christmas Eve late at night, a boy boards a train, the Polar Express, that takes him to the North Pole. When he meets Santa, Santa offers the boy any gift he wants and the boy asks for one bell from the harness of a reindeer. Santa gives him the bell, but on the train trip home, the bell is lost. On Christmas morning, the boy unwraps a small gift and finds the bell inside. He shakes the bell and it makes a beautiful sound for him and his sister to hear. The boy's parents admire the bell but express their concern that the bell is "broken." It seems that only true believers can hear the sound of the bell. 4–6.

Target Activity: "The Bell Still Rings for Me"

Think carefully about a belief you have that makes this "bell ring for you." A symbolic bell can ring for you as it does for all who truly believe in something. Write in your journal about a belief you have.

148.   Williams, Margery. *The Velveteen Rabbit.* **Ill. by William Nicholson. New York: Doubleday, 1970.**

Trait: Relationship with a significant other.

Becoming real, a stuffed rabbit toy realizes this happens when one is loved for a long time. The rabbit and the toy horse discuss their lives and the rabbit asks the wise old Skin Horse what it means to be "real." The Skin Horse tells him, "Real isn't how you are made . . . It's a thing that happens to you. When a child loves you for a long, long time, not just to play with, but really loves you, then you become real." The horse tells the rabbit that other toys have become real when they become shabby (but this does not matter) because the toy is real to the child who loves it. Having been with his boy master in the nursery, the rabbit is thrown out after the boy recovers from scarlet fever. With the help of a fairy, the toy becomes a real rabbit in reward for his service, faithfulness, and love. 4–6.

Target Activity: "The Rabbit's Feelings"

Have the students draw an outline of a rabbit in the center of a sheet of art paper and make thought bubbles radiating in lines away from the outline. Write *The Velveteen Rabbit* on the outline of the rabbit. On each of the radiating lines, the students will write a word to represent the feelings of the rabbit (sad, scared, brave, strong, loving). At the end of each line the students will draw large dialogue (or word) bubbles, and in them write the specific thoughts or quotes from the story that support or give evidence of the feelings the students selected. Divide the class into smaller groups and ask them to make the same kind of visual organizer for another character in the story. Regroup together as a large group and ask one volunteer from each small group to tell about his or her character.

Folk Literature

149. Anderson, Joy. *Juma and the Magic Jinn.* **Ill. by Charles Mikolaycak. New York: Lothrop, Lee & Shepard, 1986.**

Traits: Feeling of autonomy; persistence; positive vision of life; sense of control over life.

In a setting in Muslim Africa, there is a motif (symbolism of three) for this tale of a boy whose three wishes show him that there is more magic at home than can be conjured from the family jinn jar. Being able to ask for three wishes gives the boy a sense of control over his life and a sense of autonomy. He is persistent as he faces his problems and seeks a positive vision of life. Full-color illustrations with map. 4 & up.

Target Activity: "About Responsibility"

Suppose you had the responsibility of looking after a friend's valuable jinn jar. Tell how you would feel if something happened to it. What would you do to try to repair the damage done? What lengths would you go to if you didn't want anyone to know? Where would you draw the line?

Invite the students to discuss what they would wish for if each had three wishes. Invite them to draw pictures of their wishes, to discuss their drawings with an art partner, and to write sentences about their wishes. Did any of them wish for a trait of resiliency? Invite them to read their sentences to their partners.

150. Bierhorst, John, reteller. *Doctor Coyote: Native American Aesop's Fables.* **Ill. by Wendy Watson. New York: Macmillan, 1987.**

Trait: Humor.

In this book, cultures take on new ideas by incorporating them into what is familiar. For instance, in the sixteenth century the Aztec Indians found a book of fables from a Spanish ship. With these trickster tales, the Aztecs retold them and they were translated into Aztec language by a scribe, who made the familiar Indian trickster figure, Coyote, the main character. This book has 20 tales retold from that Aztec manuscript. Coyote is in the stories along with Puma, Wolf, and other indigenous animals. There are native figures of speech such as "His mind was nowhere." These give the stories new flavor. 4 & up.

Target Activity: "Humorous Trickster Tales"

Prereading. Try to think back to a time when you were younger than you are now and you had a pet which you talked to and played with. What did you do together? How did your parents feel about your pretending things with your pet? When did your pet cause trouble for you? When did this pet help you the most and make you the happiest?

In front of each animal's name listed below, write numerals from 1 to 3 to identify your choices for your own personal animal friends from the fables. Add any animals that don't appear on this list.

_____ Coyote
_____ Puma
_____ Wolf

Tell someone in the class your favorite fable(s) and which fables have these animals as characters. Choose one character and discuss the character's trait(s) of resiliency.

Option: "Fable Report"

After reading one of the fables, fill out the report that follows:

Fable Report

Date _____

Name _____

1. How many animals were involved in the fable?
2. Where did the action take place?
3. From what you read, what were the animal(s) trying to do?
4. What troubles or problems did the main character seem to have?
5. How did the main character solve the problem(s)?
6. What silly mistakes did an animal make?
7. What ideas did an animal have?
8. What traits of resiliency did the main character have? (gain attention in a positive way; ability to plan ahead and solve problems; development of a talent or hobby; feeling of autonomy; persistence in the face of failure; positive vision of life; relationship with a caring person; sense of humor; sense of control over life.)

151.   Bierhorst, John, editor. *The Naked Bear: Folktales of the Iroquois.* **Ill. by Dirk Zimmer. New York: Morrow, 1987.**

Traits: Relationship with other; problem-solving; sense of humor.

This collection has an excellent introduction to the Five Nations of the Iroquois, the place storytelling has in this culture, the manner in which Iroquois folktales were collected, and the traditional characters that were in them. Don't miss the story of the Moose Wife who warned her husband with the prediction: "If you marry another woman your hunting power will vanish and your new wife will soon be sucking her moccasin from hunger." 4 & up.

Target Activity: "Motifs"

Bierhorst has included tales that are considered typical of the New York Indians. In these tales, the teacher asks the students to look for recurring motifs that they have found in other tales. For instance, one story contains the motif of the clever turtle that will remind one of stories from African folklore and Brer Rabbit fame. Start an informational chart for the classroom about motifs. Invite students to add information to the chart as they find motifs in the tales that remind them of other stories.

Motifs	*Name of Tale*	*Name of Other Story*
1. Overflowing kettle		*Strega Nona*
2. Clever turtle		

152.   Birrer, Cynthia and William Birrer. *Song to Demeter.* **New York: Lothrop, Lee & Shepard, 1987.**

Traits: Persistence; problem-solving.

This is the story of Demeter (Greek for Ceres), the goddess of agriculture including grain, harvest, fruits, flowers, and fertility of the earth. She was greatly grieved when her daughter Persephone was abducted by Pluto. The story tells of seasonal changes. Hades, god of the underworld in this Greek myth, carries Persephone off to his land to be his bride. Her mother, Demeter, mourns for her daughter and asks Zeus to do something. She is told Persephone can return if she has eaten nothing in Hades. However, since she ate pomegranate seeds, she has to return for four months every year. 4–6.

Target Activity: "Resiliency in Illustrations"

With the students, the teacher discusses the way that an artist can show that characters are resilient with the manner in which the scenes are illustrated. For instance, the students will see there are lines of stitching on the gods' white robes giving the appearance of marble statues— showing sturdiness, strength, and perhaps, the gods' immortality. With the girls and boys, the teacher discusses other illustrations in this book and points out that the originals were machine-stitched applique and had embroidery on fabric. After the students contribute their comments about the illustrations, the teacher should return to selected pages and elicit more information. Looking closely at the pictures, the students may comment on the embroidery that adds color, depth, and details to the scenes. As part of the details, the teacher may mention that the rams have a nubby fleece emphasized by the stitching, the grapes seem to be real and project from a vine, and the jewels of the god Zeus appear to glitter in the light.

Introduce students to other versions of this story for a "What's similar?/what's different?" discussion: Margaret Hodges' *Persephone and the Springtime: A Greek Myth* (Little, Brown, 1973); Gerald McDermott's *Daughter of Earth: A Roman Myth* (Delacorte, 1984); Penelope Proddow's *Demeter and Persephone* (Doubleday, 1972); Sarah Tomaino's *Persephone, Bringer of Spring* (Crowell, 1971).

153.   Climo, Shirley. *The Egyptian Cinderella*. Ill. by Ruth Heller. New York: Thomas Y. Crowell, 1989.

Traits: Overcoming obstacles; positive vision of life.

Recorded by the Roman historian Strabo (first century, B.C.) this is an old (yet factual) story about a Greek slave girl, Rhodopis, who married the Pharaoh Amasis (*ah-may-ses*) and became his queen. Some if it is partly fable, for it is believed that one of her fellow slaves was a man named Aesop who told her fables about animals. Because she is a Greek slave in Egypt, Rhodopis (*ra-doh-pes* meaning Rosy Cheeks) washes clothes in the Nile, tends the geese, mends clothing, bakes bread, and gathers reeds along the bank. Scorned by the Egyptian girls, her friends are the animals and she dances for them. Her master, seeing her dance, gives her a pair of dainty leather slippers with the toes gilded with rose-red gold. When the pharaoh and his entourage are nearby, the Egyptian girls row away to Memphis to visit the pharaoh's court. Rhodopis polishes her shoes and puts them on the bank. A great falcon soars away with one of her slippers in his talons. The falcon flies to Memphis where Amasis, the pharaoh, is holding court and drops the slipper into his lap.

Amasis, thinking it is a sign to find the maiden whose foot fits the shoe, announces it is the will of the gods that the maiden should be the queen. During his long search, Amasis visits every place along the Nile and the Egyptian girls try to cramp and curl their feet into the slipper. When he discovers Rhodopis and commands her to try on the slipper, Rhodopis puts her foot into the slipper with ease and shows him the other shoe. Saying that she is not fit to be queen, the girls protest and say that she is a slave and not even Egyptian. "She is the most Egyptian of all," says the pharaoh, "for her eyes are as green as the Nile, her hair is as feathery as papyrus, and her skin the pink of a lotus flower."

Target Activity: "Something Positive"

The teacher encourages all in the group to be friends with one another. In the group each student prints his/her name on a paper that is passed to the right (or left) to the person next to him or her. Each student in turn writes something positive about the person whose name is on the sheet. Finally each student has his or her own "good word" sheet to keep.

This is a list of written compliments for the student to take home, show to others, and keep as a souvenir of the lesson.

154. Curry, Jane Louise, reteller. *Back in the Beforetime: Tales of the California Indians.* **Ill. by James Watts. New York: Macmillan, 1987.**

Trait: Problem-solving.

Curry tells of the beforetime, when the world was newly made by Old Man Above and when animals lived together as people. The stories are told as a chronology and trace the world from its creation, to Coyote stealing the sun, to his first making of man, and then to the awakening of the first man. When man awoke, great changes came to the world, as well as a warning to the animals. The Old Man Above warned:

> For in the aftertime to come, no longer will any of you be shape-shifters and workers of magic. You will be animals only, and only Man will have the powers of speech and spirit. Coyote has made Man worthy to rule, so rule he will.

Grades 4–6.

Target Activity: "Changes Came to the World"

The teacher encourages all in the group to think of some "changes that could come to the world." Each student prints his/her thoughts on a paper and passes it to the next student. Each student in turn writes something more about "changes that could come." Finally each student has his or her own "changes" sheet to keep. This is a list of written ideas for the student to use as a resource during the class discussion.

155. Demi. *Chen Ping and His Magic Axe.* **Ill. New York: Dodd, Mead, 1987.**

Trait: Ability to gain the attention of others in a positive way.

This retelling of an ancient Chinese folktale concerns the value of truth and the rewards that virtue will bring. Chen Ping is a poor peasant who works for a rich man, Wing Fat. One day Chen Ping sets out to cut firewood and accidentally drops his axe into the river. An old man appears and offers help. Jumping into the river, he attempts to return a silver and then a golden axe to the boy. Chen Ping replies that these fine axes are not his. When his own axe is returned to him it now possesses magical powers to reward the boy's honesty. Each time the old man appears, fantastic animals follow him: a dragon, a phoenix, and a variety of others. Upon hearing of Chen Ping's adventure, his greedy master attempts to repeat the boy's experience and claim the gold axe for his own. But Wing Fat's ill-gotten treasure leads to disaster and he is never seen again. 4–8.

Target Activity: "If I Had Chen Ping's Magic Axe, I Would . . ."
Discuss this folktale and the concept of honesty gaining the positive attention of others and being rewarded in time. The teacher should invite the students to draw an outline of a large axe (the shape should fill the page) and inside the outline write the thoughts they have about using the magic of the axe for positive accomplishments in life.

156. Dewey, Ariane. *The Thunder God's Son: A Peruvian Folktale.* **New York: Greenwillow, 1981.**
Traits: Ability to gain people's attention in a positive way; feeling of autonomy; positive vision of life; sense of control over life.
Thirteen-year-old Acuri, son of the thunder god, is disguised as a beggar and sent down to earth to learn about the people. Acuri learns the meaning of dishonesty in the thefts of golden rings, vanity in the contests of drinking chicha, dancing, house building, and stone throwing, and recognizes greed in the house with the feathered roof. Under the powerful eye of his father, who is never far away from Acuri, he learns to punish and to reward. With this education over, he returns to the heavens as a much wiser young god. 5.
Target Activity: "Time to Brag"
Write down sentences from the story from which one can infer traits of resiliency.

Traits of Resiliency	*Sentences Found*
1. Gaining people's attention in a positive way.	
2. Ability to solve problems.	
3. Feeling of autonomy.	
4. Persistence.	
5. Positive vision of life.	
6. Sense of control over life.	

Option: "Time to Brag"
Ask students to write wonderful and exaggerated statements about themselves to emphasize their positive attributes.

157. Goble, Paul, reteller. *Beyond the Ridge.* **Ill. by the reteller. New York: Bradbury, 1989.**
Trait: Positive vision of life.
An old woman goes from her deathbed to the world beyond the ridge, pulls back to the world where her family mourns her, and then goes forward to where she is reunited with all of her loved ones who have gone before her. Includes native chants and prayers in this living-dying story.

In the illustrations, notice the contrast of the sorrow and pain of the griev-
ing family and the joy of the elderly grandmother as she travels beyond
the ridge. The Plains Indians' perception of passing from life to death—
only a change of worlds—presents a positive vision of life's cycle. 4 & up.

Target Activity: "Beyond the Ridge"

Compare this selection of folk literature with realistic fiction, *A Ring
of Endless Light* by Madeleine L'Engle. Goble refers to a change of worlds
(from life to death) and L'Engle refers to the wholeness of life as including
death. What similarities could the phrases "beyond the ridge" and "a ring
of endless light" have in common? How do these two phrases portray a
positive vision of life from the author's point of view?

Compare the two selections on the story elements of: setting, characters, plot, goal, resolution.

**158.   Goble, Paul, reteller. *The Girl Who Loved Wild Horses*. Ill.
by the reteller. New York: Bradbury, 1978.**

Trait: Relationship with a significant other.

A girl goes down to the river at sunrise to watch the wild horses, rests
in the meadow, and then sleeps. A thunderstorm rumbles and the girl
joins the horses running away from a lightning flash and a gathering
storm; she finally goes to live with them.

Once students understand the point of view that many Indian tales
are handed down from a time when the distinctions between animals and
humans are blurred, they realize that in the early beginnings of these tales,
animals and humans could understand one another or "speak the same
language." Thus, there is no distinction between animals and humans interacting in some of the ancient original Native American tales, or in this
one, a story of an Indian girl's attachment to horses. 5–6.

Target Activity: "Animals and Humans Were as One People"

Before reading the story to the students or before their independent
reading, the teacher should remind students that in many of the Indian
tales the distinctions between animals and humans were not differentiated
and that in some tales, the animals and humans were as one people and
could speak the same language and understand one another. Thus, it is
no surprise when a human goes to live with or marries an animal in some
of the ancient Indian tales. Remind the students of the Indians' belief in
the beforetime, when the world was newly made by Old Man Above and
when animals lived together as people. Discuss the point of view shown
by this story and the ways it may differ in the points of view held by some
children in the class.

Next, read another story to show that distinctions between animals
and humans were not made in these early tales; read *Buffalo Woman*
(Macmillan, 1984) by Paul Goble. In this tale, a young hunter marries a

female buffalo in the form of a beautiful maiden. When his people reject her, he must pass several tests before he is allowed to join the Buffalo nation so that he can be with her. Discuss the vocabulary of buffalo, Calfboy (a character), Chief of the Buffalo Nation, tipi, and Straight-up-person (character).

159.   Grifalconi, Ann. *The Village of Round and Square Houses.* Ill. by the author. Boston: Little, Brown, 1986.

Traits: Problem-solving; persistence; sense of control over life.

Tells why the men in a Cameroon village, Tos, in central Africa, live in square houses while the women live in round houses. One night long ago, the old Naka mountain volcano erupted and left only two houses standing in the village—one round and one square. To take care of the people while the village was being rebuilt, the village chief sent the tall men to live in the square house and the women to live in the round house. The teller of this tale says that this arrangement is peaceful and continues to this day because people need a time to be apart as much as a time to be together. The women decided they enjoyed being together to talk, laugh, and sing in the round houses and the men became used to relaxing in their own place in the square houses. A read-aloud. 4–6.

Target Activity: "Storytelling"

Introduce the storytelling beginning of "In the days of long, long ago," and storytelling ending with "And that is how our way came about and why it will continue...." Ask the students to retell the story to one another in pairs. Each one takes the turn of beginning the story with the beginning words, "In the days of long, long ago," and then ending the story with, "And that is how our way came about and why it will continue." Have the student switch roles so all have a turn to say the storytelling beginnings and endings.

160.   Grimm Brothers. *Hansel and Gretel.* Retold by Rita Lesser. Ill. by Paul O. Zelinsky. New York: Dodd, 1984.

Traits: Perseverance; problem-solving.

Near a large forest, a poor woodcutter lives with his wife and two children by a former marriage. He listens to his wife who wants to take the children to the thickest part of the woods and leave them. Despite attempts to leave the children in the woods, the children manage to find their way home. Left once again, the children wander three days and arrive at a cottage made of bread and cakes. The window panes are of clear sugar. An old woman, really a witch who waylays children, fattens them up with milk, pancakes, sugar, apples, and nuts. Her plan is to eat the children, but Gretel foils her plan.

This classic tale of an evil witch, a selfish mother, a weak father and two resourceful children tells of the problem-solving done by the two children. Faced with the prospect of seeing if the oven was "hot enough," Gretel tricks the witch into showing her how to do it and Gretel gives her a push into the oven, shuts the iron door, and bolts it. She releases Hansel from his cage, and they collect the witch's pearls and precious stones. They return to their father who has not had one happy hour since he left the children in the forest. 4–6.

Target Activity: "There Runs a Mouse"

Engage children in selecting another tale from folk literature that features the resourcefulness of the characters. Encourage the children to use an old folk tale beginning or ending to open or close their story:

Openings:

"Once upon a time..."
"I will tell you the story I heard when I was little."
"Many years ago..."
"There was once..."
"There lived in ancient times..."
"This is the story that was told..."
"Know, O my brothers and sisters..."

Endings:

"There, that is a real story!"
"There runs a mouse! Whoever catches her may make a great, great
   cap of her fur."
"You see, that's my story. I heard it when I was a child, and now
   you've heard it too, and know the tale of _____."

161. Harris, Joel Chandler. *Jump! The Adventures of Brer Rabbit.* **Adapted by Van Dyke Parks and Malcolm Jones. Ill. by Barry Moser. New York: Harcourt Brace Jovanovich, 1986.**

Traits: Problem-solving; sense of control over life; persistence.

Five traditional black American slave tales set in Hominy Grove, where Brer Rabbit's mischievous wit outsmarts more powerful animals. Universal themes are portrayed in diluted Gullah dialect and masterful watercolor and ink illustrations. Music and lyrics from "Hominy Grove" and a storyteller's historical note are included. 4 & up.

Target Activity: "Match Traits of Resiliency to Story Action"

Invite students to match the titles of the tales and Brer Rabbit's traits of resiliency in each. Traits of resiliency to match up with the titles are: problem-solving; persistence; positive vision of life; sense of humor; and sense of control over life. The teacher should inform the students that more than one trait of resiliency can be identified and written down for the stories. Discuss what was identified and ask children to give reasons for their choices.

Traits	Titles
_____	The Comeuppance of Brer Wolf
_____	Brer Fox Goes Hunting But Brer Rabbit Bags the Game
_____	Brer Rabbit Finds His Match
_____	Brer Rabbit Grossly Deceives Brer Fox
_____	The Moon in the Millpond

Option: "Don't Skip the Storyteller's Note"

Discuss what can be learned from the author's note in the book: Malcolm Jones and Van Dyke Parks tell about the history of the tales as told by black slaves in the southern United States who had come to America against their will. The stories are examples of the pluckiness and cleverness of the small winning out over those with brute strength. In the late 1800s, a newspaperman in Georgia by the name of Joel Chandler Harris collected the tales. He presented the stories in the Gullah dialect of the nineteenth-century black storytellers and created an elderly black plantation slave, Uncle Remus, to tell the stories about Brer Rabbit and his friends to a little white boy. Through the years, Harris has been deeply criticized for this portrayal; however, the lessons in the stories have universal themes that send the message: no one can be totally owned who does not wish to be.

162. Heyer, Marilee. *The Weaving of a Dream: A Chinese Folktale.* **Ill. by the author. New York: Viking, 1986.**

Trait: Problem-solving.

A poor widow weaves her dreams into a beautiful brocade and will die of grief if her three sons are unable to recover her treasure from the fairies who stole it. A magical Chinese legend retold with rich, full-page, full-color illustrations. 4–6.

Target Activity: "My Dreams"

Discuss with the students the idea of thinking of all of their dreams and concentrating on having their dreams all in one place. Since their dreams will include beautiful settings, ideas, and objects, the teacher could suggest a beautiful arrangement be made in the form of material (cloth) and invite the students to design their dream cloths with paper, crayons, paints, and colored pencils. To accompany their cloths of dreams, the students could write a narrative to explain the meaning of their designs and read aloud some of their thoughts to others.

163. Highwater, Jamake. *Anpao: An American Indian Odyssey.*
Ill. by Fritz Scholder. Philadelphia: J. B. Lippincott, 1977.

Traits: Persistence; problem-solving.

In this Blackfeet legend of Scarface, scarred Anpao (whose name means Dawn) goes on a Ulysses-type quest to obtain the permission of the sun to marry beautiful Ko-ko-mik-e-is. Befriending Morning Star on his trip through a terrible desert, Anpao saves Morning Star (whose parents are the Sun and the Moon) from monster birds. In return, the Sun removes the scars from Anpao and recognizes Anpao as a long-lost son of the mighty sun and an earth woman. On his return trip, Anpao meets Smallpox who tells Anpao that sooner or later everyone will come to know Smallpox and that all the people he visits will die (a reflection on the Blackfeet's experience with the white man). Carrying beautiful gifts from the Sun, Moon, and Morning Star, Anpao returns to Ko-ko-mik-e-is, marries her, and they live happily in a village below a great water. Bibliography. 6 & up.

Target Activity: "Making a Mural of the Quest"

After discussing the events in the story and recording them in sequence with the students, the teacher should invite the students to make a picture of the long quest and to draw the events in order on butcher paper. The paper will make a mural for the classroom. Two students are assigned to each event and to a section of the paper. The students are encouraged to consult the story as needed to get information for their drawings. After the mural is completed, the two students will write a narrative to explain their event and place the paragraph(s) beneath their section of the mural for others to read.

164. Hodges, Margaret, adapter. *Saint George and the Dragon.*
Ill. by Trina Schart Hyman. Boston: Little, Brown, 1984.

Traits: Courage; problem-solving.

An English legend adapted from *The Faerie Queene*, a 12-book poem by Edmund Spenser, includes this episode about a noble hero who is brave and wants to avenge a wrong. Saint George, the Red Cross Knight, engages a dragon, who holds a kingdom in fear, in battle. St. George is wounded and falls. He recovers his strength by the river. In a second encounter, he faces the dragon again. Overcoming the dragon, George is offered the hand of the King's daughter, Una, in marriage. Each page of text has drawings of plants found in the British Isles. 4–6.

Target Activity: "Righting a Wrong"

After discussing the events in the story and listing them in sequence with the students, the teacher invites students to make a picture of this episode and to draw the events in order on art paper. Two students are assigned to each event. The students are encouraged to consult the story as needed to get information for their drawings. After the work is completed, the two students will write a narrative to explain their event and place the paragraph(s) with their art work for others to read.

165.   Huck, Charlotte. *Princess Furball*. Ill. by Anita Lobel. New York: Greenwillow, 1989.

   Trait: Problem-solving.

   When a beautiful motherless princess grows up, her father, the king, promises to marry her to an ogre in return for a fortune. To avoid the detested idea of marrying the ogre, the princess asks for a dowry that no one can fulfill: a coat made of the skins of a thousand different kinds of wild animals, and three dresses. One dress was to be as "golden as the sun," the second as "silvery as the moon," and the third as "glittering as the stars." However, the king brings her the dresses and coat and the princess runs away. Wrapped in her fur coat to warm her in the snow and carrying her three dresses, her mother's golden treasures (a tiny spinning wheel and a ring), and seasoning for soup, she goes into the forest and falls asleep in a hollow tree where she is found by the king's hunters and their white dogs. Taken back to the castle, she works as a servant to the servants. When the king gives three gala affairs, the princess wears her three dresses and a handsome prince says, "I cannot live without you." They are married and live happily ever after. 4–5.

   Target Activity: "Descriptive Language"

   After reading the story, the teacher discusses the descriptive language of the tale with the students. The words that describe the gowns of Princess Furball, the golden treasures, and her coat of wild animals are reviewed. The students are invited to think of their own words to describe the full-page illustrations that lead into the first page of the story. Crucial to setting the background of the story before the words start the telling, the scenes are discussed by the students. The illustrations show:

   1) that the baby princess, dressed in a white gown, is held by her nurse dressed in red, and taken to the funeral of her mother;

   2) that a slightly older princess stands sadly under a portrait of her mother;

   3) that the princess is affectionate; the princess embraces her kind nurse;

   4) and that the princess has friends; she plays with other children while her nurse watches over her.

166.   Hutton, Warwick, reteller. *Theseus and the Minotaur*. Ill. by the reteller. New York: McElderly Books/Macmilllan, 1989.

   Trait: Problem-solving.

   This book takes the reader to the somber and human world of the myth and introduces Theseus, one of the early Athenian kings who was the son of Aegeus. This is one of his exploits that shows him as a flawed hero and it includes the death of Aegeus, his father, who kills himself when he believes Theseus has lost his life on the mission to kill the Minotaur. It includes the abandonment of Ariadne, daughter of King Minos of Crete. Ariadne, with a ball of thread, helps him find his way from the labyrinth where he has been confined to be devoured by the minotaur. She falls in love with him, marries him, but is deserted by him on the Aegean island of Naxos. 4–5.

Target Activity: "Theseus and His Quest"

The teacher should ask the students to locate the setting of this Greek myth on a world map. The events in the story are reviewed and the students trace the travels of Theseus on the map. A wipe-off marker allows a student volunteer to draw lines to indicate his journeys. Talk about the details in the illustrations that give more information about his ship and his weapons. Then, with the teacher serving as a facilitator, the students should review the events in this tale and select events they want to dramatize in brief scenes for others to see.

Following a review of the reading related to their assigned events, the students roleplay one or two scenes related to their events. Then, they can divide into study groups and identify another monster against which the hero, Theseus, can test his resiliency. With a new monster as the villain in the story, the group members can create an original myth about Theseus and his traits of resiliency.

167. Lattimore, Deborah Nourse. *The Flame of Peace: A Tale of the Aztecs.* Ill. New York: Harper and Row, 1987.

Traits: Persistence; problem-solving.

In a story that borrows from and extends Aztec mythology, young Two Flint honors his father's death by going on a quest to bring a new flame of peace from the hill of Lord Morning Star. Along the way he outwits nine demons including Lord Smoking Mirror, with his cloak of forgetfulness, and the chattering bones of Lord and Lady Death. He is rewarded by Lord Morning Star with a "feathery touch" of New Fire, which he delivers to the temple in Tenochtitlan. There he glows "bright and true" to mark an end to war and fighting. 5–8.

Target Activity: "Read the Illustrations with the Picture Glossary"

The teacher shows the illustrations and comments on their color and energy. The teacher shows the stylized forms from Aztec arts that are arranged to make busy patterns of angles and curves. The pages are colored like parchment and decorated with narrow red borders that can't quite contain the action. The teacher points out that the Aztec-based system of visual symbols includes roses, foxes, rabbits, and many other representations not immediately identifiable to the eyes of children today. Select some students to puzzle out these symbols by using the attractive picture glossary on the endpapers. Ask the students to work together or in groups and report what they find to the class. Encourage them to find any information related to traits of resiliency:

1. ability to gain people's attention in a positive way
2. ability to plan ahead and solve problems
3. development of a talent or hobby
4. feeling of autonomy
5. persistence in the face of failure
6. positive vision of life
7. relationship with a caring "other" person
8. sense of humor
9. sense of control over life

168.   Lester, Julius. *The Tales of Uncle Remus: The Adventures of Brer Rabbit*. Ill. by Jerry Pinkney. Foreword by reteller. Introduction by Augusta Baker. New York: Dial, 1987.
   Trait: Problem-solving.
   Lester arranges 48 adventurous stories by themes (how the animals came to earth) and links them in opening paragraphs. In the tales, Brer Rabbit shows different facets of his character: helplessness in "Brer Rabbit Goes Back to Mr. Man's Garden"; playing tricks in "Brer Rabbit and Brer Lion"; and being gullible in "Brer Rabbit and the Tar Baby"—a tale which tells of his temper rising when one hand gets stuck to the silent tar baby. Each of the adventures is a complete story in itself. Interacting in different problematic situations, Brer Rabbit reveals aspects of the complex structure of character. Included in the author's notes is a rationale about why these basic tales are part of the foundation of African-American culture. Background information about language and images of folklore and the origins of the figure of Uncle Remus, a controversial figure, is given. 4–6.
   Target Activity: "Getting Close to the Feelings of Others"
   Encourage children to talk about experiences from their background that help them relate to the feelings of Brer Rabbit during his different adventures. Questions for discussion:
   1. Brer Rabbit felt helpless in the garden. As you think about this situation, what might convince you that Brer Rabbit's feeling of helplessness could be just about the same as a feeling of helplessness you have had?
   2. Why do you suppose that Brer Rabbit felt he had to play tricks in "Brer Rabbit and Brer Lion?" Do you think the tricks were justified or unjustified?

3. Brer Rabbit was gullible in "Brer Rabbit and the Tar Baby." What situations can you think of where someone else was gullible? What example can you give that clearly tells us what being gullible is? being helpless? playing a trick?

169.   Lester, Julius, reteller. *The Tales of Uncle Remus: Further Adventures of Brer Rabbit, His Friends, Enemies, and Others.* **Ill. by Jerry Pinkney. New York: Dial, 1988.**
   Traits: Sense of humor; problem-solving.
   This, the second part of a two-part retelling of the African-American folk tales collected by Joel Chandler Harris in the late 19th century, includes 37 more folktales that did not appear in the earlier volume, the *Tales of Uncle Remus: The Adventures of Brer Rabbit* (Dial, 1987). As with the first volume, the retellings remain faithful to the spirit of the originals, but without the drawbacks of heavy dialect and a stereotypical narrator. 6.
   Target Activity: "Read Other Versions of Brer Rabbit"
   Select *Bo Rabbit Smart for True: Folktales from the Gullah* (Philomel, 1982) retold by Priscilla Jaquith and illustrated by Ed Young. In this collection, there are four tales from the islands off the Georgia coast.

170.   Levitt, Paul M., and Elissa S. Guralnick. *The Stolen Appaloosa and Other Indian Stories.* **Ill. by Carolynn Roche. New York: Bookmasters Guild, 1988.**
   Traits: Perseverance; problem-solving.
   This book has five tales from the Pacific Northwest Indian tribes. In "The Story of Hot and Cold," mythic characters tell the story of how seasons come to change, one to compare with the story of Demeter and Persephone. In another, a woman prefers a dog to a human suitor (there is no clear distinction between animals and humans in the ancient tales) and is reunited with her people only when her offspring prove to be the hunters that save the village during a difficult winter. In the *Stolen Appaloosa*, two magicians battle over the beautiful horse in a contest of will and power. Traits of resiliency are found in such tales as the one about how the Indians used their magic to defeat an attempt to steal their home by the white "face." Still another tells of the ability of the people to outwit the evil bush-tailed rat man and win back their families, their livelihood, and their dignity. A read-aloud. 4–6.
   Target Activity: "How Seasons Came to Change"
   Bring children together to discuss "The Story of Hot and Cold" and ask them if they know of similar stories about the reasons seasons change. Read the story of *Demeter and Persephone* and discuss the similarities between the two stories. Build a chart of information that compares points in the two stories and display it so that children can add information to

it as they find additional stories. Review the stories again to look for evidence of traits of resiliency in the main characters. Add the information to the chart.

Demeter and Persephone	*The Story of Hot and Cold*
1.	
2.	
3.	
4.	
5.	

171.   Monroe, Jean Guard and Ray A. Williamson. *They Dance in the Sky: Native American Star Myths.* **Ill. by Edgar Stewart. Boston: Houghton Mifflin, 1987.**

   Trait: Problem-solving.

   This volume of Native American star legends, reflecting a tribe's interest in explaining nature, is told in language that lends itself well to reading aloud. The first two groups of stories deal with the Pleiades and the Big Dipper; thereafter, they are organized by geographic area. Each group has introductory notes about the tribes of the area and their general beliefs (that reflect their versions of trait of resiliency) providing a context for the legends that follow. Notes at the end of each section correlate Indian and Western names for constellations and stars whenever possible. In addition to tales from well-known tribes such as Navajo and Mohawk, there are selections from the Tlingit, Wasco, Picuris, and other small groups. The coyote appears in many of the tales, causing trouble (and problem-solving) whenever he appears. Wolves, bears, eagles, and other animals also inhabit the stories—and the constellations in the night sky. 4–8.

   Target Activity: "Reading Aloud"

   With the students, the teacher discusses the tellings and the style of the oral tradition in which these stories were originally passed along to others. The teacher may decide to save this one for the end of the school year as students begin to talk about going to day camp in town or away to camp in the country. After reading some of the selections, the teacher can encourage the students to take it along (checked out from the library) with a chart of the skies.

172.   Lewis, Naomi, reteller. *Stories from the Arabian Nights.* **Ill. by Anton Pieck. New York: Henry Holt, 1987.**

   Trait: Problem-solving.

   This is a long novel of tales, some with humor. It is Shaharazade's scheme to keep her head on her shoulders and to please a mad king. At first her stories focus on "rare and curious" objects (and the characters are objects, too) that can be desired or destroyed. Later, some of the stories are about real devotion and lasting love. Sometimes with the help of magic and sometimes without it, the characters solve their problems. Consider some of the characters: 1) A young merchant "as beautiful as a moonlit night" who rescues a buried alive, bejeweled maiden; 2) a flying ebony horse; 3) a tortoise who is a gourmet chef; 4) a Magnetic Mountain that smashes ships; 5) and a Jinni who becomes a flea in order to wake a sleeping princess. 4 & up.

Target Activity: "Cinderella's Cousins"

The teacher discusses some of the versions of Cinderella to compare with one story in this book. Use Lewis's version in a brief story talk: a poor youngest sister puts on borrowed finery and visits the royal harem. When she slips away, her diamond anklet falls into the water trough to be discovered the next day by the prince. The students will guess the rest. Some other versions are:

Cole, Babette. *Prince Cinders*. New York: Putnam, 1988. (male Cinderella)

d'Aulaire, Ingri and Edgar. "Karl Woodenskirt" in *East of the Sun and West of the Moon*. New York: Macmillan, 1938. (male Cinderella)

Huck, Charlotte. *Princess Furball*. Ill. by Anita Lobel. New York: Greenwillow, 1989.

Sans Souci, Robert D. *The Talking Eggs*. Ill. by Jerry Pinkney. New York: Dial, 1989. (elements of Cinderella story with cross, mean elder sister, Rose, and sweet, kind younger sister, Blanche)

173. McCurdy, Michael, reteller. *The Devils Who Learned to Be Good*. Ill. Boston: Little, Brown, 1987.

Trait: Problem-solving.

In this Russian folktale, an old soldier on a pension gives all of his bread to two beggars he meets and says, "God will provide." In return, one of the beggars rewards him with a magical deck of cards and tells him that he can never lose a game with the cards; the other beggar gives him a magical sack which will climb anything the old soldier commands.

Returning to his village, the old soldier discovers an abandoned palace and is told that the Tsar built it but cannot live there because of the band of devils who inhabit it. The soldier goes to the Tsar and asks permission to spend one night in the palace and rid it of the devils. Using the magical deck of cards and his sack, the old Russian soldier rids the palace of the devils and convinces them to be good and improve the lives of others. 4–5.

Target Activity: "Improving Lives of Others"

With the students, the teacher discusses the objects (the magical deck of cards and the magical sack) and invites the students to think of ways they would use the objects if they took the place of the old soldier in this Russian tale. Without the use of these objects, in what ways could they convince others to be good and to improve the lives of others less fortunate?

174.   Price, Susan. *The Ghost Drum: A Cat's Tale*. Ill. New York: Farrar, Straus & Giroux, 1987.
   Trait: Problem-solving.
   In a magical place there is a cat, and this is the tale she tells:

> In a northern land where winter is a cold half-year of darkness, Chingis, a Woman of Power, is a most gifted shaman who lives in a house which runs on the legs of a chicken. Safa, the Czar's son, has spend his entire life in a windowless room (imprisoned by his father) and knows nothing of sky or trees or even the world of humans.

In one of the emotional scenes in the book, Chingis leads Safa, the adult, from his windowless prison out into the sunlit world. A read-aloud. 4–8.
   Target Activity: "Common Folklore Themes"
   The teacher points out the work of the author. In this novel the author puts together many common folklore themes into an original story that is both new and yet old. Price has a strong understanding of folklore and has previously collected some unusual and lesser-known European tales (see *Ghost at Large*, Faber, 1984).
   The teacher engages the students in discussing some of the common folklore themes they know about: motifs of magic (fairy folk, shape-changing, wise women, wizards, giants, fairy animals); magical objects; enchanted people. They discuss some universal ethics from the tales: the humble and good shall be exalted; love suffers long and is kind; and that which you have promised you must perform.

175.   Shute, Linda, reteller. *Momotaro, the Peach Boy: A Traditional Japanese Tale*. Ill. by the author. New York: Lothrop, Lee and Shepard, 1986.
   Trait: Problem-solving.
   Momotaro, born to a good old couple from the inside of a peach, is accompanied by three animal friends on a quest to punish wicked demons and restore peace to the land. Kindness and courage triumph in a traditional Japanese tale with authentic, full-color background illustrations. Includes excellent source notes and a glossary of Japanese words. 4–6.
   Target Activity: "Listening to the Story"
   Through the CMS (14 Warren Street, New York, NY 10007) recording

by Christine Price, invite students to listen to the story again before using the story as material for story theater. In story theater, the teacher will identify the characters (everyone gets to participate), list names on the board, and have a discussion of character movements when the story is reread. The plot is reviewed and the characters take their places in the room. The student leader reads the story and gives time for the pantomimes. All students participate in self-evaluation after the performance, and if the students request it, they perform it again to make the changes they want.

176. Steptoe, John. *Mufaro's Beautiful Daughters: An African Tale.* Ill. by the author. New York: Lothrop, Lee and Shepard, 1987.

Trait: Positive vision of life.

From G. M. Theal's *Kaffir Folktales* (1895), comes this tale told by people living near Zimbabwe ruins, a former site of a great trade city of Africa. The father, Mufaro, was happy, for all agreed that his two daughters were beautiful. Nyahsa was beautiful and kind, and Manyara was beautiful but had a bad temper and was selfish and somewhat spoiled. When the king decided to take a wife all the most "worthy and beautiful daughters in the land" were called to appear before him. To make certain that she is chosen, Manyara leaves before the others to get to the king. Along the way, she has three challenges, to feed a hungry boy (she tells him to get out of the way); to listen to the old woman in the woods (she tells her to stand aside); not to laugh at the grove of laughing trees (she laughs out loud at them). When Nyasha meets the same three challenges, she feeds the boy her lunch, she gives the woman sunflower seeds, and does not laugh at the trees. Nyasha's positive vision of life shows in her attitude and in her interactions with others. She is pleasant, kind, sings to her crops which makes them plentiful, and welcomes a small garden snake in her garden. She views the small garden snake in a positive way and says, "You will keep away any creatures who might spoil my vegetables." At the king's city, she finds her sobbing sister who says the king is a "great monster, a snake with five heads." When Nyasha sees the king, she sees only the little garden snake, her friend. The snake transforms into the king, Nyoka, who asks her to be his wife, the queen. Manyara becomes a servant in the queen's household. 4–6.

Target Activity: "A Modern Fable."

Draw two outlined profiles (one each to represent the two daughters) on the board or on overhead transparencies. Ask the students to dictate words or phrases that tell the characteristics of the sisters. After discussing the traits of the two, use the visual display of the profiles to write paragraphs about the two girls with the main idea that "pride goes before a fall."

Information for Profile #1: Discuss Nyasha: What are some examples of the positive vision of life held by Nyasha? When told by Manyara she will be her servant, she replies, "I will be pleased to serve you." She ignores her sister's words and goes about her chores where she sings as she works. When ready to leave to see the king, she says, "I'd much prefer to live here . . . I'd hate to leave this village and never see my father or sing to little Nyoka (snake) again." At her first sign of the city, she calls, "A great spirit must stand guard here! Just look at what lies before us. I never in all my life dreamed there could be anything so beautiful!"

Information for Profile #2: Discuss Manyara: With the moral of pride going before a fall, talk about this folktale (a modern fable) with the students. What are some of the behaviors of Manyara that show she has too much pride? Manyara proclaims that "Someday, Nyasha, I will be a queen and you will be a servant in my household." When the call comes from the king, Manyara says to her father, "I am strong. Send me to the city, and let poor Nyasha be happy here with you." Manyara steals quietly out of the village because of "her greed to be the first to appear before the king. . . ." Meeting the hungry boy, she replies, "Out of my way, boy! Tomorrow I will become your queen. How dare you stand in my path!" Meeting the old woman in the woods, she scolds with, "How dare you advise your future queen! Stand aside, you ugly old woman!" Meeting the grove of laughing trees, she shouts back, "I laugh at you, trees!" Meeting the king transformed into a snake with five heads, she sobs, "He would have swallowed me alive if I had not run."

177.   Vernon, Adele, reteller. *The Riddle*. Ill. by Robert Rayevsky and Vladimir Rayevsky. New York: Dodd, Mead, 1987.

Trait: Ability to gain attention of others in a positive way.

In this Catalan tale, when the king asks a poor charcoal maker how he manages on so small a wage, the poor peasant answers with a conundrum. The riddle is this:

> How is it possible for a peasant who earns only ten cents a day to take care of his family, pay back a debt, save for the future, and still have something to throw out the window?

The king wants the courtiers in his court to solve the riddle and tells the peasant not to reveal the answer to the riddle until the peasant has seen the king's face one hundred times. Later at court, believing that the peasant has told the answer to one of the members of court, the king brings the peasant to court to be punished for his disobedience. The peasant protests his innocence and maintains that he has seen the king's face one hundred times. The peasant explains: he saw the king's face printed on each one of the one hundred gold coins that the courtier gave him for telling the answer to the riddle. Upon hearing this cleverness, the king rewards the peasant with three bags of gold. One bag is for his debts, one is for his old age, and the last one for him to throw out of his window. 4–6.

Target Activity: "Predicting Solutions in the Story"

When reading the story for the first time, the teacher stops after the page where the peasant's riddle is presented to the king. The teacher allows the students time to think of solutions to the riddle. Their ideas are listed on the board. Continuing the reading, the teacher stops again at the point in the story where the king discovers that the peasant has disobeyed him and wants the peasant brought to court. The teacher encourages the students to talk together to try to explain what they think happened. Reading on, the teacher reads the peasant's explanation to the king for his behavior. The teacher stops again and lets the students talk among themselves about the explanation the peasant gives for his behavior in telling the secret of the riddle to the courtier; and they talk further about their reasons for justifying/not justifying the behavior of the peasant.

178. Yep, Laurence. *The Rainbow People*. Ill. by David Wiesner. New York: Harper & Row, 1989.

Trait: Ability to get people's attention in a positive way.

The story of "The Rainbow People" is a tale of a wanderer who plays his flute and walks up the path of a magical mountain ruled by a powerful wizard. Along the way, the wanderer meets some farmers—one is a young girl who has a round birthmark on her forehead—who all agree to feed him if he matches the work they do. The farmers work long into the evening and the wanderer finds that he cannot keep up with them. When twilight finally comes, the wanderer sees that the faces of the farmers begin to shine with "soft, colored lights—as if they were wearing rainbows." The farmers feed him a supper of watery soup made of weeds and rice. In explanation, the farmers say that the landlord takes everything else.

With determination to right this wrong to the farmers, the wanderer locates the powerful wizard and steals his golden flute which is the source of his power. The wizard warns the wanderer and tells him that the flute will bring him more trouble than joy, and that the wanderer could lose something in the very act of saving it. Returning to the farmers, the wanderer finds the oppressed farmers have been replaced with golden dragons leaping into the sea. In return for breaking the spell of the wizard and thinking he was saving the girl from an oppressed life, the wanderer loses the girl with the round birthmark on her forehead. In these tales, a reader finds several characters that attract attention in a positive way: there is a superior mouse, a wise woman, and a snake, colorful as jewels.

This book has a total of 20 tales collected from the people in the Oakland Chinatown during the '30s as part of a WPA project. A read-aloud. 4 & up.

Target Activity: "First Work, Then the Story"

With the students, the teacher points out the background for the tales. Yep takes the reader back to the time when Yep's father and the old-timers picking fruit in the Chinese orchards near Sacramento would gather at the end of a hard day and tell the folktales from their Chinese American heritage. The teacher may invite the students to form small groups. He may ask each group to select a tale to learn and tell to others. Returning to the total group, the students may gather together in a scene reminiscent of workers who gather around to tell and listen to stories. Taking turns, the members of the groups tell their selected story to others.

Historical Fiction

179. Bergman, Tamar. *The Boy from Over There.* **Translated from Hebrew by Hillel Halkin. Boston: Houghton Mifflin, 1988.**

Trait: Perseverance.

On a kibbutz in a children's house in 1947, several wait for their families. Rami's father returns with Avramik, the boy from over there, but Rina's father is never among the returnees. Other children misunderstand Avramik and make fun of him. When Avramik becomes a hero during the first Arab-Israeli War, the others begin to accept him. 4–6.

Target Activity: "Avramik's Feelings"

After this book is read, help the students develop a visual organizer with the title of the book in the middle of a page and then space for the boy's feelings at the end of lines radiating outward from the title. In a circle at the end of each line, write a starter for the students to complete orally or in writing. Starters include 1) When he returned with Rami's father, Avramik felt.... 2) When the children misunderstand him, Avramik felt.... 3) When the others make fun of him, Avramik felt.... 4) When he became a hero, Avramik felt.... Discuss each particular feeling. Invite the students to make a four-page minibooklet (one sheet folded into quarters) called "Feelings" in which the students write and draw about their feelings and give reasons why they felt that way at that particular time.

180. Blos, Joan. *A Gathering of Days: A New England Girl's Journal, 1830–1832.* **New York: Charles Scribner's Sons, 1979.**

Trait: Positive vision of life.

Beginning her diary, thirteen-year-old Catherine Cabot Hall tells about things that touch her life. Since the death of her mother four years earlier, Catherine has been in charge of the household and caring for her eight-year-old sister, Mattie, and her father. Catherine writes about the meals she cooks, her recipes, what she learns at school, what stories she hears from other family members, and what games they play. When her father marries a widow from Boston, Ann Higham, Catherine meets her new stepbrother. After reading news advocating the abolition of slavery, Catherine and her friend Cassie Shipman provide food and a quilt for a runaway slave. Her last entry is on March 8, 1832, when she leaves her farm in New Hampshire to help friends after the birth of their child. As a note of authenticity, two letters written by Catherine to her great-granddaughter (1899) are included. 6 & up.

Target Activity: "Catherine's Daily Writing"

Encourage students to record events from their lives in a daily writing journal. Just as Catherine did, students may write about the meals they cook or eat, the recipes, what is learned at school, what stories are heard from other family members, and what games are played.

181.   Coblentz, Catherine Gate. *The Blue Cat of Castle Town.* **Ill. by Janice Holland. New York: Longmans, Green, 1949.**

Trait: Developing a hobby or talent.

This legend is based on a true event in Castle Town, Vermont, where all the craftsmen of early Vermont who sang their own song created beauty in their work and gained contentment. Thomas Royal Dake, the carpenter, created a pulpit that was known as the most beautiful in the state of Vermont. Another, a young girl named Zeruah Guernsey, made a carpet so beautiful and unusual that it now is displayed in the Metropolitan Museum of Art. Among the many designs in the carpet is one blue cat. According to this Vermont legend, the blue cat of Castle Town enables the town to sing its own song of beauty in work and contentment. Others found contentment in their work, too: John Gilroy, the weaver, made twin white linen tablecloths and Ebenezer Southmayd created his pewter work. 4–8.

Target Activity: "Beauty and Contentment in Work"

Encourage the students to discuss their interpretation of this trait of resiliency: developing a hobby or talent. To them, what is the meaning of the legend where the blue cat of Castle Town enables the town to sing its own song of beauty in work? Perhaps students can respond to a sentence starter (e.g., What "singing a song of beauty in work" means to me: _____).

182.   De Angeli, Marguerite. *The Door in the Wall.* **New York: Doubleday, 1949.**

Trait: Perseverance.

Robin, a young boy, is crippled by a strange disease and he goes to live with some monks when the Black Plague hits London. With perseverance and the help of the monks, he learns to become independent and develops his abilities and is able to save the town where his parents live. 4–6.

Target Activity: "Understanding Robin"

To identify and understand Robin and his traits, present a character display to the students with the name of Robin displayed. To draw the character display on the board, draw a large circle and print the name *Robin* in the center. Draw lines outward from the circle and at the end of each line draw smaller circles. Write the words the students contribute in the smaller circles and add more as needed. Through discussion with the students, create the display with adjectives and descriptive words that the students have contributed. Then focus the discussion on the way the author has developed the character of Robin to show his perseverance. Reread the parts that show Robin's actions to help the listeners gain a better understanding of perseverance.

183. De Jong, Meindert. *The House of Sixty Fathers*. Ill. by Maurice Sendak. New York: Harper, 1956.

Traits: Perseverance; problem-solving.

This historical fiction tells of Small Tien Pao, swept in the family's sampan by a storm into Japanese-occupied territory. Walking back home through the mountains toward Hengyang, he helps a wounded American airman. Both are found by Chinese guerrillas who care for the airman and take Tien back to Hengyang—where the Japanese are fighting in the city. Leaving the city hidden in a deep basket with his pig, Glory of the Republic, Tien and the basket roll out the open door of the train. Unhurt, Tien is found sleeping by American soldiers who take him to the barracks where 60 men belong to a bomber squadron. This is the base of Lieutenant Hamsun, the airman he helped. The 60 men help him look for his family. 4–8.

Target Activity: "What Would You Have Done?"

With the students, the teacher may review the story and discuss the traits of resiliency that Tien Pao needed to survive the problems that he faced. The teacher invites the recall of the sequence of events. Review the events again and engage the students in contributing their ideas to the question, "What would you have done if you had been in this situation?"

184. De Trevino, Elizabeth Borton. *I, Juan de Pareja*. New York: Farrar, Straus & Giroux, 1965.

Trait: Developing a hobby or talent.

Pareja tells his own story. Early in the 17th century, Juan de Pareja was born, the son of a black slave and a Spaniard. At twelve, Juan became the property of the painter, Don Diego Rodrequez de Silva y Velasquez of Madrid, later the court painter to King Philip IV. Juan was instructed in the grinding and mixing of colors and in all matters related to painting. Juan was not permitted to practice painting. Juan taught himself to paint and Velasquez learned of his skill, gave Juan his freedom, and made him his assistant. 5–8.

Target Activity: "Teaching Yourself"

With the students, the teacher discusses the idea of teaching oneself to do something—to develop a hobby or talent. The teacher engages the students in discussion to identify which hobby or talent each is interested in accomplishing and to determine their ability to plan ahead as each thinks of ways to teach themselves to accomplish a goal.

185.   Eckert, Allan W. *Incident at Hawk's Hill.* **Ill. by John Schoenherr. Boston: Little, Brown, 1971.**

Trait: Persistence.

The story is based on a true event at Hawk's Hill, Manitoba, in 1870. Six-year-old Ben, a small shy boy, watches, follows, and mimics the movements and sounds of the animals and birds on the Canadian farm home of his parents, the MacDonalds. Following a prairie chicken on the prairie, Ben becomes lost and finds shelter in a badger burrow. The returning badger sees Ben act and talk as she does and she adopts him. The badger brings him eggs and small animals which he eats raw. Ben begins to adopt badger behavior and hunts with her. Two months later, Ben is found by his brother, 16-year-old John. 4–8.

Target Activity: "Being Helped by an Animal"

Ask the students to think of situations when a human was helped by an animal. The students should divide into small discussion groups and talk about the information they have. Each group selects/elects/accepts a volunteer to talk about their responses when they regroup into a total class.

186.   Estes, Eleanor. *Rufus M.* **Ill. by Louis Slobodkin. Scarsdale, New York: Harcourt, Brace, 1944.**

Traits: Persistence; developing a hobby or talent.

Seven-year-old Rufus lives with his mother, brother Joey, and sisters Sylvie and Jane in Connecticut during World War I. Rufus helps the war effort by knitting washcloths for soldiers. He raises a crop of vegetables in a Victory garden, and with a popcorn partnership with his sister earns enough money to become a Victory boy. In this Newbery book, Rufus is a dynamo of energy, a believable character. He pedals his tricycle to the park to ride his favorite horse on the merry-go-round, takes up magic, and practices ventriloquism at school which earns him time in the class "cloakroom." The story ends with World War I coming to an end on Armistice Day. 4–6.

Target Activity: "Helping the War Effort"

With the students in small groups, the teacher invites them to discuss what they would do to help their nation if the nation were at war as it was during World War I. The students consider such things as: ways to provide clothing and other supplies for the nation's soldiers; ways to provide food for the family; ways they could earn money at their ages; and ways to transport themselves around town without cars and gasoline. Vocabulary unique to the setting should be discussed: cloakroom, Victory boy, Victory garden.

Option: "Window on War: Similar Problems of People During Different Times"

Several books show similar problems in various settings of war in different time periods. To show the problems occurring during war (including the personal problems of people), give brief book talks about these titles to encourage independent reading by older students who can gain a perspective through a "Window on the World of War: Similar Problems in Different Times":

Revolutionary Times: *I'm Deborah Sampson* by Patricia Clapp (Lothrop, 1977);

After the Revolutionary War: *Jump Ship to Freedom* by James and Christopher Collier (Delacorte, 1981);

Russia Under the Czar: *The Night Journey* by Kathryn Lasky (Warne, 1981);

1800s in South America: *Bolivar the Liberator* by Ronald Syme (Morrow, 1968);

Civil War in England: *Cromwell's Boy* by Erik Christian Haugaard (Houghton, 1978);

Wars During Westward Expansion: *Crazy Horse* by Doris Shannon Garst (Houghton Mifflin, 1950); *Battle of Little Big Horn: Red Hawk's Account of Custer's Last Battle* by Paul and Dorothy Goble (Pantheon, 1970);

War Between the States: *Zoar Blue* by Janet Hickman (Macmillan, 1978);

Prewar German Occupation of Greece: *Wildcat Under Glass* by Aliki Zei (Holt, 1968);

World War II: *Snow Treasure* by Maire McSwigan (Dutton, 1942).

When students locate current titles, add them for:

Vietnam action: _____

Persian Gulf War: _____

187. Felton, Harold W. *Mumbet*. Ill. by Donn Albright. New York: Dodd, Mead & Co., 1970.

Traits: Positive vision of life; overcoming obstacles; problem-solving.

This is the true story of a courageous black woman in the late 1700s. As a slave, she had a comfortable life with the Ashley family. But because she valued freedom she approached a young lawyer, Theodore Sedgwick, and asked him to help her become free. In 1781, Elizabeth Freeman won her freedom in the courts of the state of Massachusetts. It was the first time anyone of her race had dared try to achieve freedom that way, but Elizabeth had been told that the Constitution said that all were "born free and equal" and she knew that included her. After the successful trial, she joined the Sedgwick household, where her talents with the children and in the kitchen earned her the affectionate nickname Mumbet. Elizabeth Freeman never wavered in her belief that she should be free. Her courage in the face of fear continued when the house was raided and Elizabeth cleverly and courageously talked the ruffians out of taking anything. 4–6.

Target Activity: "Why I Should Be Free"

After reading *Mumbet* with the class, using the chalkboard or overhead projector, cluster the ideas children have about the word "freedom." Ask them if they are free to do anything they wish to. Ask them to select one thing that they would like to do that they are not allowed to do because they are too young, or because their parents cannot afford it, etc. Have them select a partner to be their "lawyer." With their lawyer, have them build a case for why they should be allowed to do their selected activity. Allow each pair to "present their case" to the rest of the class, who will offer arguments against the presented case.

Option: A jury, consisting of nine class members, may decide whose arguments are stronger, while a judge selected by the teacher presides.

Variations: Consider the following: 1) Give students reasonable cases in a set of six or so; 2) Explain the terms associated with the legal profession (i.e., client); 3) Emphasize the reasonableness of arguments; 4) Focus on order; 5) Consider three in a group roleplaying a client, a defense attorney and a prosecuting attorney; 6) Use graphics on board with headings of argument and counter argument, and write down their arguments with students also recording the information; and 7) Exchange papers among groups and then ask groups to try to counterargue the arguments on the paper.

188.   Forbes, Esther. *Johnny Tremain.* **Ill. by Lynd Ward. Boston: Houghton Mifflin, 1943.**

Traits: Persistence; problem-solving.

In this historical fiction, Johnny is an apprentice to Paul Revere and in this setting he becomes involved with the Revolutionary War effort, the activities for the Committee for Public Safety, the first battle of the Revolution at Lexington and Concord. Starting out as a cocky young apprentice, Johnny suffers an accident that disables his arm and hand and he turns into an embittered young man. It takes the war and its events to turn Johnny into a man with courage and ideals. Well-known figures related to the American Revolution are mentioned. Advanced 6 & up.

Target Activity: "Point of View"

With this Newbery book, a reader gets the point of view (Whig) that the American Revolution was a just revolution against a tyrant king, King George III of England. To present older students with data from the other side of the conflict that may change their opinions—consider a book written from the English (Tory) point of view, *My Brother Sam Is Dead* (Four Winds, 1974) by Christopher and James Collier.

Ask students to identify one or two of the well-known figures (Paul Revere, Sybil Ludington, and others) related to the American Revolution or found in *Johnny Tremaine*. Discuss the different periods of their lives—early childhood, marriage and family life, life during the American Revolution, and later years, and then divide students into research groups which will research one of the periods of time. Encourage students to collect as many materials for reference as they can. Mention that in references, there may be copies of the figure's speeches, copies of letters and other writing, reproductions of newspapers of the times, materials such as *Farmer's Almanac* will tell the weather conditions and other books will describe the figure's actions, beliefs, and points of view. The goal for each group is to develop the fullest picture possible with materials to show what the figure did during the period of time. Research groups report back to the total group after specified days of study to tell what has been found.

189.   Fox, Paula. *The Slave Dancer*. Ill. by Eros Keith. Scarsdale, New York: Bradbury, 1973.

Trait: Persistence.

Abducted in New Orleans in 1840, 13-year-old Jesse Bollier is taken to the *Moonlight*, a slave ship headed for West Africa. He is to play his fife for captured Africans so they will dance and exercise. Through the words and actions of Jesse and the others, the readers vicariously experience life on a slave ship. The slave trade in Africa and the United States were grim and become quite real to the reader. The sailing nightmare includes a tightly packed ship, shackled slaves with the "bloody flux," slaves thrown over the side of the ship, and the vessel, damaged in a terrible storm, sinking off the coast of Mississippi. One of the slave boys, Ras, and Jesse are the survivors. After being cared for by an old black man, Ras is sent north on the underground railroad and Jesse walks home to New Orleans. With a grim tone, the story narrated by Jesse is preceded by a history that lists the ship's name, its officers, crew, cargo, date of the wreck, and the survivors. Advanced 6–8.

Target Activity: "Discussing Values"

Suitable for one-to-one discussion, *The Slave Dancer* provides background information to talk about: 1) Why is Jesse Bollier on board the

Moonlight, a slave ship? Do you believe the reason was a good one? Why or why not? 2) Why do you believe that Ras had to be sent north on the underground railroad? Why was Jesse sent to New Orleans?

190.   Goldin, Barbara Diamond. *Cakes and Miracles: A Purim Tale.* **Ill. by Erika Weihs. New York: Viking, 1991.**

Traits: Persistence; problem-solving; relationship with significant caring other person.

In this original story set in the late 1900s, Hershel, blinded by illness, is bored and misbehaves at school. Most of all, Hershel likes to mold riverbank mud into shapes and landscapes. After dreaming that an angel tells him to make what he sees in his imagination, Herschel uses his mother's dough to sculpt unusual cookies in shapes of the images he sees in his mind and helps his mother sell them for Purim. Includes recipe for *hamantashen*, the three-cornered pastries.

Text shows the love between mother and son as well as Herschel's persistence in not being confined by his blindness. Story shows his strength of spirit in overcoming his disability. 4–8.

Target Activity: "Sculpting Cookies"

Students read the recipe for *hamantashen* three times, once silently as teacher reads it aloud, next in choral reading with the total group, and third, in a student-a-line arrangement. For those interested in this project as a homework activity, ingredients may be collected and cookies made at home. Invite students to bring one (or more) of their sculpted cookies to class to show and to discuss with a focus on, like Herschel, how does your cookie shape show something you saw in your imagination? Each cookie may be displayed along with student's writing on an index card telling something about the shape chosen for the cookie.

191.   Greenfield, Eloise and Lessie Jones Little. *Childtimes: A Three-Generation Memoir.* **New York: Crowell, 1979.**

Trait: Perseverance.

From the late 1800s to the 1940s, three generations of black Americans tell their early life experiences. Each of the book's three parts "catches up to the past" and each is focused on the "threads of strength" of one generation: a grandmother, mother, and daughter.

Target Activity: "Stop and Tell Your Story: A Childtime Is a Mighty Thing"

Share with children the hope of the authors, Greenfield and Little, and their words about other children stopping and telling the story of their time and place with: "Maybe years from now, our descendants will want to stop and tell the story of their time and their place in this procession of children. A childtime is a mighty thing." (p. 175).

Invite children to write about a time and place in their "childtime" and early life experience that they judge was a "mighty thing" (made an impression, changed their views, solved a problem, established an important friendship or relationship, created a better aspect of life).

192. Hunt, Irene. *Across Five Aprils*. Chicago: Follett, 1964.
Traits: Persistence; positive vision of life.
At the time of the Civil War, nine-year-old Jethro Creighton, a southern Illinois farm boy, sees his brothers divided on the issue of freeing the slaves. From Kentucky, Mrs. Creighton's nephew visits the family and relates the Southern point of view of the war. Brothers John and Tom and Cousin Eb fight in the west and brother Bill fights for the Confederacy. After the war begins, young but resilient Jethro is overworked and anxious and discovers cousin Eb has deserted and returned home. Jethro writes to President Lincoln to tell him about Eb. 6–8.
Target Activity: "Time Line of Five Aprils"
After discussing events in this Newbery story, students can contribute information to a visual graphic, a time line of the five Aprils. Once events are dictated, students use the visual graphic to write brief paragraphs about happenings during each of the five Aprils. For a follow-up writing activity, students may write from Jethro's point of view and tell President Lincoln about cousin Eb.

One April	Two Aprils	Three Aprils	Four Aprils	Five Aprils
What Happens	What Happens	What Happens	What Happens	What Happens

193. Hunt, Irene. *Up a Road Slowly*. Chicago: Follett, 1966.
Trait: Relationship with a significant other.
After the death of her mother, 10-year-old Julie Trelling goes to live with her strict Aunt Cordelia, a teacher in a one-room country school. Years later, when her father marries attractive Alicia, a high school teacher, Julie refuses to move into town with them and commutes to high school with a neighbor boy, Dan Trevort. Told in first person by Julie, the reader discovers that Julie matures through the 10-year period of the narrative; that she wants to be a writer, admires poems by Edna St. Vincent Millay and Sara Teasdale, has personal reactions and feelings about a classmate—mentally retarded Aggie Kilpin, and agrees to marry Dan Trevort after they both finish college. 5–8.
Target Activity: "What Poetry Do You Admire?"
Just as Julie wants to be a writer and admires poems written by Edna

St. Vincent Millay and Sara Teasdale in this Newbery book, some of the students may want to be writers and will admire poets, too. Which poets/poetry do they admire? Engage students in making poetry books shaped like large pockets to relate to the phrase "put a poem in your pocket," and invite them to write the poems they admire on the pages. The left-hand page can be reserved for an illustration that relates to the poem and on the right-hand one, a written copy of the poem.

194. Hurwitz, Johanna. *Anne Frank: Life in Hiding.* **Ill. by Vera Rosenberry. Philadelphia: Jewish Publication Society, 1989.**

Trait: Perseverance.

Tells of her life before Anne goes into hiding as well as her days in hiding. With Anne, seven other people hid for two years in a secret annex of an office building in Amsterdam but were eventually found and imprisoned by the Nazis. The book ends with an explanation of her death, for none who lived in the annex survived the war except Anne's father. Appropriate for students who are not yet able to read Anne's diary found by her father on his return to their hidden annex after the war. Includes a time line, map and list of related books. 6 & up.

Target Activity: "Anne Frank Remembered"

After the students listen to or read this book (less difficult than the diary), engage them in listening to another point of view, that of the Dutch woman who helped hide the Frank family. To supplement the Anne Frank story, read selections from Miep Gies' book, *Anne Frank Remembered* (Simon & Schuster, 1987) to show life in Amsterdam during the Nazi occupation and to present more characterizations. Advanced 6 & up.

195. Kherdian, David. *The Road from Home: The Story of an Armenian Girl.* **New York: Morrow, 1979.**

Trait: Positive vision of life.

Veron Dumehjian, the author's mother, is the center of this life story told in first person. Author's note, a map showing Veron's travels, and two quotations open the book. In one opening quotation dated September 16, 1916, the reader finds that the Turkish government has decided to destroy completely all of the Armenians living in Turkey. "An end must be put to their existence, however criminal the measures taken may be, and no regard must be paid to either age or sex nor to conscientious scruples." In a second quotation, the reader finds an order given by Hitler in 1939 which orders the extermination "without mercy or pity, men, women, and children belonging to the Polish-speaking race...."

While Veron's first seven years were happy ones, it was in the eighth year that there was an order of deportation of Armenians living in Turkey

(1919). Within three days, Veron and her family (her parents, sister, brothers, grandfather, and uncles) left their home in western Turkey in a horse-drawn wagon. By 1919, Veron's family was dead and she returned from her four year exile. During a Greek attack on Turkey, Veron was injured and hospitalized. Recovering, she traveled to her Aunt Lousapere in the city of Smyrna. In 1922, the Greeks evacuated the city, taking Armenians considered enemies of the Turks. In Greece, Veron lived with other Armenian refugees until the announcement of her engagement by her fiance's family in 1924. She traveled with his family to America and married Melkon Kherdian. Hardships, sorrow, frightening experiences. 6 & up.

Target Activity: "Early Life Stories Can Be Happy Ones"

Veron's first seven years were happy ones and could be recorded as a brief early life story. Engage students in thinking/reflecting on pleasant early life experiences for a writing experience for their journals.

196. Lester, Julius. *To Be a Slave.* Ill. by Tom Feelings. New York: Dial, 1988.

Trait: Persistence; perseverance; problem-solving.

Historical narratives from slaves, beginning in the first half of the nineteenth century, and quotations, rewritten to conform to the literary standards of the time, were taken down from the American Antislavery Society and other abolition groups. The second half, recorded in the speech patterns and language of the ex-slaves, comes from the 1930s from a Federal Writers' Project. The interviews are from ex-slaves. The quotations are organized into chapters related to life as a slave in North America, abduction from Africa, labor on the plantations, experiences with the Ku Klux Klan, and segregation in the post–Civil War years. In these two narratives, the author presents ways ex-slaves showed their persistence, perseverance, and problem-solving abilities and states that this is "a vivid picture of how the slaves felt about slavery." 5 & up.

Target Activity: "The People Could Fly, Too"

It is enlightening to some students to read some of the traditional tales of American blacks that come to us from Africans who became slaves in North America. From their experiences told in these tales, students begin to realize the impact of slavery that is present in the stories. Virginia Hamilton, in her book of folktales, *The People Could Fly* (Knopf, 1985), states that the slaves created tales in which various animals . . . took on the characteristics of the people found in the new environment of the plantation (page x). For example, Brer Rabbit, a trickster character found in *Jump Again! More Adventures of Brer Rabbit* (Harcourt, Brace, Jovanovich, 1987), is from Joel Chandler Harris' tales adapted by Van Dyke Parks. Brer Rabbit, small and helpless, usually wins out over larger, more powerful animals—bear, wolf, and fox. Slaves, who identified with Brer Rabbit, the one who survived against cunning beasts, told many stories about his experiences and achievements, for slaves saw themselves as Brer Rabbit and the slaveholders as Brer Wolf and Brer Fox. Indeed, the best way to win over all of their power and force was to be more clever—like Brer Rabbit who used his head to outdo and outwit other animals and even used trickery if he had to.

With the idea that various animals took on the characteristics of the people found in the new environment of the plantation, invite interested students to read and discuss some of the tales.

**197.	Lowry, Lois. *Number the Stars*. Boston: Houghton Mifflin, 1989.**

Trait: Perseverance.

By 1943, 10-year-old Annemarie Johansen was accustomed to the Nazi soldiers who had been on every corner of Copenhagen for three years as she walked to school with her little sister and her best friend, Ellen Rosen. Like the lack of meat and butter, the soldiers were a nuisance of the war. However, that all changed when Annemarie's Lutheran family learned the Nazis were about to relocate Denmark's 7,000 Jews, including the Rosens, who lived in the same apartment building. Annemarie discovers what courage is and that she has it. Suddenly one night Ellen comes to live with her as a sister and the older Rosens are hidden by the Resistance.

Late that night, Nazi soldiers awaken them and demand to know where their friends the Rosens are. Before the girls get out of bed, Annemarie breaks Ellen's gold chain and hides her Star of David. After searching the apartment, the Nazis ask why one daughter has dark hair. Quickly the father goes to the family picture album and rips out three baby pictures, carefully obscuring the dates of birth. Annemarie's older sister, who is dead, was born with dark hair. With this invasion into their home, the girls realize the Nazis are no longer just a nuisance.

The next morning, Annemarie's mother takes the three girls on the train to her brother's house at the sea. Uncle Henrik, a bachelor fisherman, is a member of the Resistance. After they spend a carefree day at the beach, a hearse arrives with a casket and strangers come to mourn a dead great aunt. Annemarie suspects there was no such aunt and questions her uncle privately in the barn.

That night, the Nazis show up and demand they open the casket. Annemarie's mother quickly agrees, saying she had wanted to see her aunt one last time, but the doctor told her to leave it shut because of the typhus germs. The Nazis leave. That night, the Resistance slips the mourners out to Sweden.

Annemarie perseveres as she helps the resistance slip people out to Sweden. She has to make a dash through a dark forest to deliver a critical parcel to her uncle at the boat. The parcel is hidden in a basket under a fruit and cheese lunch. Within sight of the boat, the Nazis and their dogs stop her, search her basket, and find the parcel with an embroidered handkerchief.

Not until later does the reader learn that the fabric had been impregnated with a formula of dried blood and cocaine that attracted the dogs and then killed their sense of smell for a while. The Swedes developed it when the Nazis started using dogs to sniff out people escaping from Denmark. 4–6.

Target Activity: "Destructive Force of War and Human Perseverance"

Point out to students that the destructive force of war has been with humans in all time periods where there has been war(s) and that humans have persevered. To emphasize this idea with books showing similar situations but in different time periods, a teacher takes students back in time to discover the destructive force of war and its effect of people from other time periods.

198. Matas, Carol. *Lisa's War*. New York: Scribner's, 1987.

Trait: Perseverance.

This is based on true experiences with a setting in Copenhagen. Lisa and her brother, Stefan, Jewish teenagers, fought against Jews being sent to camps with the organized Resistance movement. Lisa and Stefan warned friends to flee to coastal towns to escape to neutral Sweden in the fall of 1943 before a roundup of Danish Jews by the Nazis. 6 & up.

Target Activity: "Saving Others from Danger"

With this book, a reader needs maturity to understand that sometimes acts of violence are needed to save oneself or others from danger. The story emphasizes heroics of battling against enemies, the tragedy of war, life-threatening situations, and severe problems people have during wartime. Since these acts are not unique to any one war but to all wars, other books discuss these happenings in other time periods. Related to saving others from danger, consider reading short excerpts aloud from *Across Five Aprils* by Irene Hunt (Follett, 1964; Civil War era) or from *Johnny Tremain* by Esther Forbes (Houghton Mifflin, 1943; Revolutionary War days). With information from the excerpts, students can record the happenings during times of war.

199. Meltzer, Milton. *Rescue: The Story of How Gentiles Saved Jews in the Holocaust*. New York: Harper & Row, 1988.

Trait: Perseverance; problem-solving.

Gentiles risked their lives to save Jews in Europe from death. From archives of the Yad Vashem and other libraries in New York, Meltzer gathers his facts about the humanitarian acts by individuals and Gentiles in different countries. Exciting and true stories of the heroic and compassionate people who sought to rescue Jews from the Nazi Captors create a tribute to their courage. 6 & up.

Target Activity: "Compassionate Heroes/Heroines"

With the students, the teacher discusses the meaning of compassion and heroes (heroines). Students dictate words related to compassion and heroes/heroines and teacher lists words on the board. With discussion, words are grouped into categories to show relationships. Words in the categories are then rewritten in a word web with "Compassionate Heroes/Heroines" as the center of the diagramming.

200.   Moore, Robin. *The Bread Sister of Sinking Creek*. Ill. New York: Lippincott, 1990.

Traits: Overcoming obstacles; problem-solving.

Maggie Callahan, a 14-year-old, travels with a packtrain from Philadelphia into the Pennsylvania mountains in 1776. Finding her aunt gone, Maggie becomes a hired girl for the McGrew family and helps Mrs. McGrew with the chores, the baby, and with 12-year-old Anna who is deaf. Maggie has a family legacy—sourdough starter—which she calls spook yeast. The people of Sinking Creek trade for Maggie's bread. The book has a history of sourdough bread and recipes for starter and simple, as well as complicated, bread recipes. Don't miss the tall tales told during a Christmas party. 5–8.

Target Activity: "Maggie's Way to Solve Problems"

Hand to the students duplicated sheets that show a visual display for "Maggie's Ways to Solve Problems." In the center of the sheet is a large circle with the heading "Solving Problems," and lines radiate outward from the circle. At the end of each line is a smaller rectangle in which the students will write information as they hear it again or reread the story. The students fill in the rectangle with information about the ways that Maggie solved her different problems. They write about one problem in each rectangle. Invite the students to trade papers for a partner-check of the information. Return the sheets to the original owners and use them as a basis for a discussion of the story.

201.   Morrow, Barbara. *Help for Mr. Peale*. Ill. by the author. New York: Macmillan, 1990.

Trait: Problem-solving.

In the late 1700s, in Philadelphia, Mr. Charles Wilson Peale and his family are moving and have artifacts of natural history to contribute to a new museum home, the first American natural-history museum in the area. Faced with the problem of how to move such unusual things as exotic plants, large prehistoric bones, and stuffed animals, Peale's son Ruben organizes the children in the neighborhood to form a parade with its members carrying the items to their new home six block away. 4–6

Target Activity: "Cross Checking the Facts"

Before discussing the story with the students, discuss the concept of natural history museums. When the problem of moving items to the new museum is discussed, add information from the students' discussion about the characters, setting, problem, and the way it was solved. For those students interested in further information about this subject, suggest that they use other sources and document the establishment of the first American natural history museum in Philadelphia, 1794. Students report back to the total group to tell what they found when they cross-checked the facts in the book.

202. Reit, Seymour. *Behind Rebel Lines: The Incredible Story of Emma Edmonds, Civil War Spy.* **New York: Harcourt, 1988.**

Traits: Perseverance; overcoming obstacles; problem-solving.

Emma posed as a man (one of 400 women) to fight in the Civil War. She enlisted and was a nurse in field hospitals under General George McClellan. She served as a spy for the Union forces, and changed her appearance and personality several times to preserve her anonymity. Pair with *The Secret Soldier* by Ann McGovern or *I'm Deborah Sampson* by Patricia Clapp. Both are about the Revolutionary War heroine Deborah Sampson. Wisely included, there is a bibliography for those interested in finding out more about women and their part in the Civil War. 4–6.

Target Activity: "Emma Edmonds"

To show the changes in appearance and personality of Emma Edmonds, duplicate two outlined profiles on a sheet of paper. Show the students the profiles that have no describing words. Tell the students that Edmonds had to change her appearance and personality several times to keep her anonymity. Ask the students to generate a list of words from what they read to describe Emma and then one for her personalities. They may add some of their own descriptive adjectives to the list. Compare the lists in the group discussion. Engage students in giving reasons for some of their word choices as you emphasize the traits of resiliency. A book talk about another book telling of Edmonds' life could include some clothing similar to that used as part of Emma's disguises as she tells the class of some of her adventures, her agitations, and her cool-headed actions.

203. Sevela, Ephraim. *We Were Not Like Other People.* **New York: Harper & Row, 1989.**

Traits: Perseverance; overcoming obstacles.

In 1937, a nine-year-old boy loses his Red Army Commander father to Stalin's purge. The following six years are retold in vignettes that begin and end abruptly. The boy is resilient and at the end of the war is reunited with his family. Told in first person. Advanced 6 & up.

Target Activity: "Survivors"

Before discussing the story with the students, discuss the concept of vignettes or episodes. To show these visually on a graphic organizer, draw four rectangles side by side on the board and label them vignette 1, vignette 2, vignette 3, and vignette 4. As each episode is discussed, add information from the discussion about characters, setting, and the problem under the appropriate vignette heading. If space and class time allows, add information about the action taken to solve the problem and the final resolution. For those students interested further in this subject, suggest that they compare this story with *The Wild Children* (Scribner's, 1983) by Felice Holman.

What	*What*
We Were Not Like Other People	*The Wild Children*
Says	*Says*

204.   Turner, Ann. *Grasshopper Summer*. New York: Macmillan, 1989.

Traits: Overcoming obstacles; problem-solving.

In this story, the short chapters have historically accurate details (post-war attitudes), descriptions, and real characters with personalities. When his father decides to move the family to Kentucky, Sam feels the pain of leaving and going to Dakota territory. They plant their first crop, fight the invasion of grasshoppers, and make their dugout. 4–6.

Target Activity: "Survival in a Grasshopper Summer"

After the story is read and discussed, invite the students to help you construct a visual display (graphic organizer) about the important events in the story. With a large circle in the center of the board or transparency that is labeled "Grasshopper Summer" draw outward lines. At the end of each line write the events the students dictate in any order on the writing board or transparency and then ask the students to order them aloud in sequence. As they do this, number the events as they happened. For each event dictated, discuss the way Sam acted and reacted and discuss his traits of resiliency in this story of survival.

205.   Yolen, Jane. *The Devil's Arithmetic*. New York: Viking/Kestrel, 1988.

Traits: Perseverance; problem-solving.

In a story of transformation, Hannah, weary of hearing her Jewish relatives tell of the Holocaust, wishes to be somewhere else. Her wish is granted when she steps out into the building hallway and into a small village in Nazi-occupied Poland—she has become the villager, Chaya, whose name means "life." Chaya experiences the Holocaust. On a cattle car with her family and friends, she is branded, stripped, and shaved at the concentration camp. When Hannah finds herself again at her family's apartment, she appreciates her relatives for who they are and what they know. Advanced 6 & up.

Target Activity: "Appreciating My Family"

With students in small groups, the teacher asks them to think of their family members, what they do, and what they know. The information—contributions made by the family members to the community—is discussed in the small groups. Next, the students discuss the ways they can show their appreciation for their family members for who they are and what they know.

Biographies

206. Adler, David A. *Martin Luther King, Jr.: Free at Last.* Ill. by Robert Casilla. **New York: Holiday House, 1986.**

Trait: Overcoming obstacles.

Key events and anecdotes show the goals of the works and life of Martin Luther King, Jr. King attended Morehouse College in Atlanta and was the class valedictorian at the Crozer Theological Seminary in Pennsylvania when he graduated (1951). He received a scholarship to Boston University where he studied for his doctor's degree in theology. He was the pastor of the Dexter Avenue Baptist Church in Montgomery, Alabama. After taking part in the bus boycott initiated by Rosa Park's refusal to give up her seat on a Montgomery bus, King was instrumental in the events that led to the ruling of the United States Supreme Court that segregation on buses was against the law. He traveled, gave speeches, and urged nonviolent ways of gaining civil rights. King organized the Southern Christian Leadership Conference to fight laws that discriminate against blacks. King and his wife studied Gandhi's nonviolent ways of fighting for freedom in India. During an historic protest march on Washington, D.C. (August 1963), King spoke to protesters on the steps of the Lincoln Memorial with his "I Have a Dream" speech and was awarded the Nobel Peace Prize in 1964. With black-and-white illustrations and a list of important dates. Index. 4–6.

Target Activity: "In King's Footsteps"

The teacher discusses this thought with the students who then move into smaller groups to talk about it further: Based on some of King's problems and struggles to have people look upon blacks as equals and as human beings, what suggestions would you put into a booklet for someone who is prejudiced by color but doesn't know that he/she is?

In the groups, the students draw the outline of their feet on sheets of paper and write in their suggestions within the outlines. The suggestions are read to their reading partners. Feedback is made to each writer from the partner and the writer can choose the extent to which he/she wants to make the changes mentioned in the feedback. Revisions are made.

Returning to the total group, volunteers read some of their suggestions to the whole class. When completed, the pages are stapled together with a cover titled "In His Footsteps," and placed in the classroom book corner.

Option: "Dr. King's Birthday"

When a group of students receive their role playing cards, they work together in pairs to perform a brief skit:

Card #1: Two boys are in front of the television on the birthday of Martin Luther King. They are talking about what they know about Martin Luther King, Jr.

Card #2. In December of 1955, Mrs. Rosa Parks refused to give up her seat on a Montgomery bus and a bus boycott was planned. Dr. King was asked to help.

Option: "A Book Display of the History of Black Americans"

With the students, plan a book display of the history of black Americans. Solicit favorite titles from the students and schedule a trip to the school library or to a nearby public branch to search for more.

207. Blackwood, Alan. *Beethoven*. New York: Bookwright, 1987.

Traits: Problem-solving; developing a hobby or talent.

Ludwig van Beethoven's life was one of struggle and disappointment. He began composing music at 11 and was an assistant court organist in Bonn at 14. When his mother died (1787), Beethoven supported his brothers and sisters by giving music lessons. With the support of Count Ferdinand von Waldstein, Beethoven studied with Haydn. In Vienna, he won recognition as a great pianist playing his "Concerto in C Major." At age 28, he discovered his hearing was defective. Later in life, his total deafness kept him from hearing the melodies that he wrote for others to enjoy. This book not only includes the accomplishments of this great composer, but there is mention of his laboring over his manuscripts, his numerous passionate love affairs, his temper, and his untidiness. 5–8.

Target Activity: "What Do You Want to Know?"

Engage interested students in locating other resources and finding other facts about this musical talent. What more can be discovered about his hard work developing his musical scores and manuscripts? his temper? and his untidiness?

208. Collier, James Lincoln. *Louis Armstrong*. New York: Macmillan, 1987.

Traits: Problem-solving; positive vision of life.

In a resilient story of personal triumph, Collier tells the story of Armstrong, moving from poverty to jazz expert. As an example of his adversity, Louis was so poor as a kid growing up in New Orleans, he did not even have his own horn until he was 17. The gifted musician struggled against inconceivable odds to become one of the greatest jazz trumpeters of all time.

Target Activity: "Design a Monument to Armstrong"

With the students, the teacher integrates art into the discussion and encourages interested students to design a monument that could be built in honor of Louis Armstrong. Then, the students are asked to prepare a speech for someone to give at the dedication. The draft of the speech is shown to others for reading and suggestions for changes and improvements.

209.   Collins, David R. *Tales for Hard Times: A Story About Charles Dickens*. Ill. by David Mataya. New York: Carolrhoda, 1990.

Trait: Perseverance.

This describes how Dickens managed to leave his impoverished past behind him. He chose not to forget his past but made references to it in some of his stories. For example, he had an unhappy childhood living with a father deeply in debt (who was sent to debtor's prison in London). Dickens was put to work in a warehouse, pasting labels on bottles, an unhappy experience which later surfaced in *David Copperfield*, a telling of his own experiences during the warehouse days through the suffering of little David. For another example, his father's experience with debtors' prison was made famous in *Little Dorrit*. In *Oliver Twist*, Dickens exposed the abuses of children in the workhouse system. *Nicolas Nickleby* told of the severe punishment which children received in schools at the time and *Dombey and Son* told of unmeaningful "cramming" required in the schools. Includes list of Dickens' works with *Hard Times* (a criticism of adults for preventing the development of the imagination of each individual child) and *A Christmas Carol* in a broad overview. In spite of his unhappy childhood, Dickens persevered and showed his love for others through his humor and his exposure of social wrongs of the time (1800s). 4–8.

Target Activity: "Tales for Hard Times"

After discussion of Dickens, his perseverance, the pen-and-ink drawings in the book, and perhaps *A Christmas Carol*, students discuss ways to do the following before writing:

Describe how you managed to leave a "hard time" in your past behind you and make a reference to it as you write a brief nonfiction biographical sketch about the "hard times."

210.   Crofford, Emily. *Frontier Surgeons: A Story About the Mayo Brothers*. Ill. by Karen Ritz. Minneapolis: Carolrhoda, 1989.

Trait: Overcoming obstacles.

William and Charles, with their father, started a center at St. Mary's Hospital, Rochester, Minnesota with 13 patients and a staff made up of only the family. William got his degree in medicine at the University of Michigan and was famous for his skills in cases of gallstones, cancer, and stomach operations. Charles received his degree in medicine from Northwestern University and was recognized for reducing the death rate in goiter and thyroid gland surgery. In World War I, William served as a colonel, and like Charles, was a brigadier general in the medical reserve corps. 4–5.

Target Activity: "Letter to the Brothers"

With the students, the teacher facilitates the discussion so that each student identifies one of the anecdotes from the biography to write about in a letter to the Mayo brothers. For instance, if writing about their impressions of Will's episode of having to finish an autopsy at night without his surgeon father with him, the student can tell of his/her feelings, what he/she would have done, and express his/her thoughts about respect/admiration for the feat of this 16-year-old boy.

211. Crofford, Emily. *Healing Warrior: A Story About Sister Elizabeth Kenny*. Ill. by Steve Michaels. Minneapolis: Carolrhoda, 1989.

Trait: Problem-solving.

Kenny was an Australian nurse who developed the "Sister Kenny" method of treatment for infantile paralysis (polio). During World War I, Kenny was in the Australian Army and set up a clinic in Townsville, Queensland. Receiving funds, she set up the Elizabeth Kenny Institute in Minneapolis, Minnesota. Kenny's adventures in the Australian outback are mentioned along with her exaggerated qualifications and some of her medical successes. Concerned with the treatment of children who had polio, Sister Kenny found that the immediate application of hot packs to relieve the muscle spasms, and then gentle massage and exercise, usually kept the child from becoming crippled. Personal interviews are sources for some of the information. The bibliography clearly labels primary and secondary sources. 4–5.

Target Activity: "And They Shall Walk"

For those interested further in this subject, Kenny wrote her autobiography, *And They Shall Walk* (Prior, 1952). Invite a librarian in to talk to the students about ways to locate a book that was published long ago. If available in one of the collections of a state's library, read some of the excerpts from Kenny's own words.

212. Fisher, Leonard Everett. *Prince Henry the Navigator*. Ill. by the author. New York: Macmillan, 1990.

Trait: Positive vision of life.

Beginning with a map of the Iberian peninsula and the African continent, the book shows the expeditions organized and financed from Prince Henry's library and school of navigation at Sagres on the Portuguese shore. Includes pictures of navigational tools such as the astrolabe and compass and the first carabel. Impressive illustrations, careful research, and informational introduction with list of dates. 4–7.

Target Activity: "Navigator Project"

To determine some of the reasons why people are interested in becoming navigators, the teacher discusses this with the students and encourages them to conduct a navigator research project. Devise a questionnaire and give it to others who are willing to help with your research. Give them an envelope with your name on it. Ask them to seal the questionnaire in the envelope and give it to you (or keep it until you come back for it). Sample questions for your questionnaire: 1) What words best describe a navigator to you? 2) What do you think causes a person to become a navigator?

213. Foster, Genevieve. *Abraham Lincoln's World*. Ill. by the author. Scarsdale, New York: Charles Scribner's Sons, 1944.

Trait: Problem-solving.

In this informational biography (out-of-print but available in some library collections), the author used information from hundreds of books (diaries, letters, autobiographies). She combines history and biography to show what was happening to people around the world during the life of Abraham Lincoln. One was Napoleon (who had been born when George Washington was farming); Victoria was born in England when Lincoln was a boy in Indiana. Daniel Boone, now old, is remembered for leading pioneers into Kentucky when Washington was a farmer (late 1700s). Two indexes, one of events, nations, places, and the other of characters, are included. 5–8.

Target Activity: "Tribute to Lincoln"

Suggest to students that they write "The Lincoln Tribute." Suppose you have been asked to write an obituary for Lincoln to be printed in the local paper. What will you call your tribute? What would you write about this man?

214. Freedman, Russell. *Franklin Delano Roosevelt*. Ill. New York: Clarion, 1990.

Trait: Positive vision of life.

Young Franklin had private tutors, attended Groton School and was graduated from Harvard University (1904). He attended Columbia University Law School, and then accepted the Democratic nomination for the state senate from a New York district. When Wilson became president, Roosevelt was made assistant secretary of the Navy, and his political career after that included governor of New York and then president of the United States, when he stated in his inaugural address, "All we have to fear is fear itself." During the Depression, he ended the banking crisis and held one hundred days of legislative reforms in Congress which resulted in his "New Deal." His "brain trust" (all college and university presidents) worked ideas into bills to be presented to Congress. The bills helped the farmers, the industrial workers and businessmen. During World War II, the U.S. adopted its first draft law and wrote the Atlantic Charter, with Churchill, with its four freedoms (speech, worship, from want, from fear) which became the principles for which the free nations were fighting. Roosevelt was elected to four terms as president and died in April 1945.

With Roosevelt's own diary entries, the author tells a story of a complex individual with shortcomings who was a successful politician during the Depression and the war years during his presidency. This shows Roosevelt's dedication, initiative and the energy he brought to the Presidency as he sought to institute programs and policies. 5–8.

Target Activity: "Describe the President"

With the students as a total group, the teacher presents the thought: Many people think that someone who is the president is different from "ordinary" people like you and me. After discussion, the students work in small groups and discuss, "What would be your list of the ten most descriptive adjectives you could use to describe the behavior and traits of the current President of the United States?" First, each group member prepares a list of ten adjectives. Then the members work in pairs, read their lists to one another, change adjectives if they wish. At the end of their work, they agree to change at least three adjectives from their list. Together with another pair (four working together) they discuss their lists with the idea that each pair must add to their list three items from the other pair's list (and delete three of their own); they generate a list of adjectives. Working with another group of four students, four girls and boys, read their lists and change and delete their adjectives with the idea that each group of four must delete three of their words and add three from the other group's list. Returning to the large group, each group of eight students selects someone to read a list of adjectives from the group for all to hear. Value voting is done (e.g., students raise their hands three times to show which of the adjectives they most prefer to keep on the list).

215. Friese, Kai. *Tenzin Gyatso, the Dalai Lama.* Ill. Boston: Chelsea, 1989.
   Trait: Perseverance.

A two-year-old peasant boy was named the 14th reincarnation of the Dalai Lama, the head of Tibet. The Dalai Lama, chosen by religious and political leaders, was always the supreme ruler of Tibet until the Chinese Communists invaded the country. The Chinese Communists now rule the nation. The Dalai Lama is thought to be the reborn soul of the man who ruled before him and was born at exactly the moment the former Dalai Lama died. The wise men of the country look for his appearance on the surface of the holy lake and then search among the children born at the right moment for a face to match the one in the lake. He comes to the throne very young in a colorful ceremony. This book describes his unique education, his efforts to keep the culture alive, his life in exile, and his Nobel Peace Prize. Useful reference tools include photographs with captions, quotes, bibliography, chronology, and index. 5 & up.

Target Activity: "Keeping the Culture Alive"

With the students, discuss the idea of "keeping the culture alive" and its meaning for those in the classroom. In what ways could a group's culture die? What meaning does this have for you if your group's culture dies? Stays alive?

216.   Fritz, Jean. *The Great Little Madison.* **Ill. New York: Putnam, 1989.**

Trait: Problem-solving.

This is the biography of James Madison, the fourth president of the United States, with historical facts about his life and his wife, Dolly Payne Todd Madison. Madison was known as the "Father of the United States Constitution" for he was the one who planned the checks and balances among the legislative, executive and judicial branches. A close friend of Thomas Jefferson, he carried on Jefferson's policies as president. This book traces events related to the building of the United States as a new nation, its leaders of the time, and ways their lives were connected. Some of the events include the Americans in West Florida breaking away from Spain (1810); the starting of the Cumberland Road (1811); the joining of Louisiana to the Union (1812); "Old Ironsides" sinking the British ship *Guerriere* (1812); the burning of Washington by the British; and the writing of "The Star-Spangled Banner" (1814).

The author describes scenes where great decisions were made and shows readers ways data are used to describe what must have been Madison's thoughts and feelings related to the time. Notes, bibliography, illustrations. 5–8.

Target Activity: "Great Little Madison Roleplaying"

Distribute roleplaying cards that describe vignettes from Madison's life to children and ask them to research the information they need in related books and then to act out the parts. Events to consider: 1) two or three citizens of the times talking to each other about the most successful and least successful parts of Madison's career; 2) Madison telling how he served his own state, Virginia, before he became president; 3) two newspaper editors of the time telling some of the things that Madison stood for in the Continental Congress; 4) two military officers of the time telling some of the reasons that Madison recommended war against the British in the War of 1812; and 5) two or three members of the Federalist Party telling why the Hartford Convention was called and the reason they think this convention harmed the Federalist Party.

217. Geary, Robert. *The Elephant Man*. London: Allison & Busby Ltd., 1983.

Trait: Positive vision of life.

This is the true story of Joseph Merrick, a boy who managed to triumph over the worst fate could do to him. He grew up so facially distorted and physically ugly that he was known as the "Elephant Man." Everyone ran away from him or laughed at him until by accident he was rescued from his torments and it was revealed that inside his disfigured body was a brave and gentle human being. Even though Joseph Merrick had to live with the cruel ravages of a disfiguring disease and the taunts of unkind strangers, he was courageous enough to win many friends with his sensitivity to nature and his gentle ways. He triumphed over his disease by showing others how the person he really happened to be was more important than his crippled body and distorted face.

Target Activity: "If We All Looked Alike"

Ask children to consider how life would be difficult if everyone looked exactly alike. Make two columns on the chalkboard, one labeled "advantages" and the other "disadvantages." Solicit some ideas from the children about the positive ramifications. Then ask children to decide for themselves which of the two columns provide stronger arguments. Finally, ask them to write a position paper on the advantages and disadvantages of everyone looking alike, as Joseph Merrick might have written it.

218. Ghermann, Beverly. *Sandra Day O'Connor: Justice for All*. Ill. by Robert Masheris. New York: Viking, 1991.

Traits: Positive vision of life; problem-solving.

Tells of an influential, controversial woman who was the first female Supreme Court justice. Tells of her stands on important and controversial issues. Compare this one with other biographies such as *Justice Sandra Day O'Connor* (Messner, 1985) by Judith Bentley or *Equal Justice* (Dillon, 1985) by Harold and Geraldine Woods. Younger readers will want to find Carol Greene's *Sandra Day O'Connor: First Woman on the Supreme Court* (Children's, 1982).

Target Activity: "Comparing Biographies"

In a small group with a discussion facilitator, the students discuss the various ways in which the authors of different biographies of O'Connor gave the idea that she overcame obstacles caused by the fact that she was a female. What traits of resiliency do you think are needed by a justice of the Supreme Court? By a female justice of the Supreme Court?

Option: Find out all you can about how a person goes about being appointed a justice of the Supreme Court of the United States. In addition to using the encyclopedia, you might write to the clerk of the Supreme Court. What does the title "justice" mean? How long does a justice hold office on the Court? What kinds of cases do the justices make judgments about?

219.   Goodall, Jane. *My Life with the Chimpanzees.* **New York: Minstrel, 1988.**

Trait: Overcoming obstacles.

Jane Goodall grew up in a well-to-do English family and could have lived an easy, privileged life. Instead, her dream was to spend her life in Africa studying animals. At 26 she first entered the forests of Africa to study chimpanzees in the wild. On her expedition, she braved the dangers of the jungle and survived encounters with wild animals in the African bush. She documented her adventures with chimpanzees and the discoveries she has made about them and their relationships to us have gained her worldwide recognition.

Jane Goodall's autobiography gives an amazing account of a person pursuing a dream and not giving up. She attributes the positive happenings in her life to "good fortune," but also she says that ". . . the other kinds of good things are those you *make* happen through your own efforts . . . I refused to give up, even when it seemed very difficult."

Target Activity: "Letter to Jane"

Ask children to share what they would choose to be if they could be anything they wanted to. Discuss the improbability of Jane Goodall's dream. Ask the students why they think she succeeded in realizing her dream against impossible odds. Ask students if they can think of other famous people who succeeded against great odds, e.g., George Washington Carver, Maria Tallchief, Helen Keller, Greg LeMonde, etc. Tell children they are going to write a letter to Jane Goodall, or another famous person who was mentioned. Have them include the following in the letter:

1. Why they admire the person.

2. How the world is a better place because the person succeeded.

3. Their own ambitions in life.

4. Questions they would like to ask the famous person about succeeding.

220. Greene, Carol. *Simon Bolivar: South American Liberator.*
Ill. Chicago: Children's Press, 1989.
    Trait: Perseverance.
    Bolivar is regarded as "the George Washington of South America"
since he fought on behalf of the independence of the South American
republics from Spanish colonialism and earned the name of "the Liberator." He was head of the patriot forces and when Venezuela and New
Granada united with Colombia, he became its president, and later, the
dictator of Peru. The southern provinces of Peru formed a separate state
in 1825 and called themselves Bolivia, in his honor. Bolivar retired in the
1800s, and died in exile and poverty, having spent his fortune in the cause
of liberty and on his idea to bring all the republics of the American
hemisphere into a sort of League of Nations. Black and white photographs. 4–6
    Target Activity: "The George Washington of South America and
the Simon Bolivar of North America"
    With the students, the teacher leads the discussion to compare the
lives of these two men who are both noted and remembered in their countries for their greatness. After reading this biography, the students will
record the information about Bolivar and Washington that relates to each
event. After responding to the events, the students should work in pairs
and compile a summary statement 1) first, about Bolivar and 2) second,
about Washington. When completed, the students should read their
statements aloud to others.

Event	*Bolivar*	*Washington*
devoted himself to freeing his native land		
head of the patriot forces		
fought with great courage		
became president		
gained independence for the country		
state/city named in his honor		
tried to bring all countries together		
reelected president		

forced to retire, died in exile and in pov-
    erty, having spent his fortune for the
    cause of liberty		

Summary statement: _____

221. Greenfield, Eloise. *Nathaniel Talking.* **Ill. by Jan Spivey**
Gilchrist. New York: Writers & Readers, 1989.
    Trait: Positive vision of life.

Biographical information is found in first-person poems of a nine-year-old black child. They are about himself and his world, his memories, and his future. As part of his memories, Nathaniel pays tribute to each generation of his family through a musical form associated with their time period. For example, in "Grandfather Bones," the rhythm and words remind one of African folk instruments, in "My Daddy," the words and rhythm remind one of the blues, and in his own "Nathaniel's Rap," the rhythm is, of course, a rap rhythm with the words, "I can rap/I can rap/I can rap rap rap/ Till your earflaps flap." Confident Nathaniel tells the reader "It's Nathaniel talking/and Nathaniel's me/I'm talking about/ My philosophy." 4–5.

Target Activity: "Tribute to Someone in the Family"

Invite the students to think about the things they have done during the week to pay tribute to someone in their family. What events can they recall where they paid tribute to someone in the family? Discuss what situations children were in that now causes them to say: 1) I should have...; 2) If only I had not.... Begin "Reflection Pages" for writing these thoughts and others.

222.   Howe, James. *Carol Burnett: The Sound of Laughter*. Ill. by Robert Masheris. New York: Viking/Kestrel, 1987.

Traits: Sense of humor; ability to gain people's attention in a positive way.

Carol Burnett grew up shuttled between her grandmother (who was on welfare and lived in a one-room apartment) and her parents (both alcoholics), who divorced when she was very young. Though she felt she was far from beautiful, she longed to become a great actress and spent much of her time at the movies or putting on plays. She learned that by laughing at herself she could help others to laugh at themselves and eventually became one of America's favorite comediennes. The book recounts her determination to succeed, her rise as a comedienne, and her struggle to like and accept herself. 4–6.

Target Activity: "Making a Good Situation Out of a Bad One"

Discuss how Carol Burnett used laughter to make unhappy situations into positive ones. Read to students *Alexander and the Terrible, Horrible, No Good, Very Bad Day*. Taking the events one at a time, brainstorm some ways Burnett might have made these bad situations into hilarious comedy routines. Divide students into groups of three or four and allow them to pick favorite events from the book for humorous sketches.

223.   Levinson, Nancy Smiler. *Christopher Columbus: Voyage to the Unknown*. Ill. by Stephen Gammell. New York: Lodestar, 1990.

Trait: Persistence.

With an interesting conclusion, this biography tells of books that influenced his early life (Marco Polo's *Travels*) and relates some of the cultural and political times. It tells the danger of the voyages, the Spaniards' cruel treatment of the Indians, his failure to prevent this bloodshed, and his later years. Attractive; with paintings, maps, engravings, and photographs. 6–8.

Target Activity: "Voyage Plan"

Ask the students to suppose they were members of Columbus' planning team for the voyage, and knowing what they know about the problems and dangers of the voyages, how would they plan a voyage from beginning to end? Use a Voyage Plan form:

	Problem Situation	*Problem Solution*
1.		
2.		
3.		

224. McMullan, Kate. *The Story of Harriet Tubman, Conductor of the Underground Railroad.* **Ill. by Steven James Petruccio. New York: Dell, 1991.**

Trait: Overcoming obstacles.

Born in Dorchester County, Maryland, Tubman as a young girl worked as a field hand. She escaped to the North and decided to help others escape. She took trips over the Underground Railroad and led slaves back to freedom. This earned her the name of "Moses." She was one of the greatest fighters for freedom. She returned to the South again and again to rescue over 300 slaves. 4–5.

Target Activity: "The Tubman Scene"

The teacher discusses the writing of a script for a brief scene using the character of Harriet Tubman.

Working in groups, the students consider the task: Write a dramatic script for a "scene" between Harriet Tubman and one of the rescued slaves. In your script you will want to include important information about the people and events.

Option: Introduce the book, *Take a Walk in Their Shoes* (Dutton, 1989) written by Glennette Tilley Turner and illustrated by Elton C. Fax.

The skit titled "The Douglass 'Station' of the Underground Railroad" may be performed without permission if not given for profit and so is appropriate for use in the classroom. The setting is late one night in November just after the 1850 Fugitive Slave Act became law. Tubman and eight fugitive slaves have just arrived at the Douglass home in Rochester, New York. A narrator sets the scene to tell of Tubman's quiet knock at the door, the greeting by Douglass as they all enter to warm themselves at the fireplace, to eat, and to sleep. Tubman tells of their trip through the snow from Wilmington, Delaware, escaping the slave catchers' dogs by hiding in water, riding to Philadelphia in a wagon with a false bottom. Douglass and Tubman discuss the plan for getting the fugitives into Canada. Tubman (with a $40,000 reward out for her) wants to leave immediately and go across the lake to the Canadian shore. The brief skit ends with: "The coast is clear. Let's go."

225.   Mayberry, D. L. *George Lucas*. Minneapolis: Lerner Publications, 1987.

Traits: Feeling of autonomy; sense of control over one's life.

George Lucas wanted to be a race car driver when he was a little boy. But one day he was in a car accident in which he was almost killed. During the four months of his recuperation, he realized his own will to survive. He decided this energy could be channeled in a good or bad way; the choice was his. He changed his career goal to one of making movies with positive visions. The book follows his career from filmmaker to producer, director, and editor. Throughout the movie industry, George Lucas is known not only as one of Hollywood's most talented filmmakers, but as an honest and hardworking man who has never been afraid to deviate from the crowd. George Lucas' fertile imagination and his ability to go off into uncharted directions has changed the direction of movie-making. 5–7.

Target Activity: "If I Could Be Anything"

After reading this book with students, explain that filmmaking— George Lucas' career—is very difficult to break into. George himself never thought that he would be as successful as he eventually became. Ask children to think for a few minutes about the most exciting and fun career that they could possibly imagine. Then ask them to also "dream big" and write a paragraph that begins, "If I could be anything, I'd be. . ." and tell about what career they would choose and why.

226.   Meltzer, Milton. *George Washington and the Birth of Our Nation*. Ill. with prints and photographs. New York: Franklin Watts, 1986.

Trait: Perseverance.

A wealth of fascinating factual content that focuses on George Washington's adult life. This biograpy of the first president contains well-selected journal excerpts, drawings, and primary source materials that includes Washington's notes for a draft of the United States Constitution. Includes a section for further reading that suggests related avenues of research. Index. 4–6.

Target Activity: "Constitution of Our Classroom"

Engage students in discussing ways to write a constitution for their classroom. A constitution (a basic set of rules by which a group is governed) provides for the form of government, limits powers of the government, and assures the rights and liberties of its citizens.

227. Neimark, Anne E. *One Man's Valor: Leo Baeck and the Holocaust.* **Ill. with photographs. New York: Lodestar, 1986.**

Trait: Perseverance.

After Hitler's rise to power, Leo Baeck, the chief rabbi of Berlin, helped many Jews, especially the children, escape from Germany. He continued to defy Nazi tyranny while imprisoned in the Theresienstadt Concentration Camp, an ordeal he miraculously survived. This book is one of several in Lodestar's "Jewish Biography" series. Bibliography for further reading and index. Advanced 6 & up.

Target Activity: "Stuggles for Freedom"

Discuss: How can you explain the fact that Baeck helped many Jews escape from Germany even though it meant endangering his life? Struggles for freedom are continuing today and some evidence of this is found in news articles.

Engage the students on a newspaper search to find all the examples they can about people's causes and struggles for freedom. They can be stories about one individual or about a group. After many articles have been found, discuss the following: In a free country, how is it possible that so many people (from the news articles) find that they have to go to great lengths (sometimes to the Supreme Court) to get the freedom that they are after?

228. O'Connor, Karen. *Sally Ride and the New Astronauts.* **New York: Franklin Watts, 1983.**

Trait: Perseverance.

This book provides in-depth information to augment what the news magazines and television shows have given. It shows how Ride prepared herself to fulfill her dream by earning a doctorate in astrophysics and by undergoing the special training required for this job. 4 & up.

Target Activity: "Fulfilling a Dream"

The teacher discusses the book with the students and the way that

Sally Ride prepared herself to fulfill her dream of being an astronaut. Review some of the text to find traits of resiliency, such as persistence, overcoming obstacles, etc.

Discuss with the students: What are some of the "impossible things" you have thought about in your life? How does it make you feel when things look "impossible" to you? What could you do to turn the impossible into something possible? How would you try to do this?

229.   Raboff, Ernest. *Picasso*. Ill. with reproductions of paintings. New York: Harper & Row, 1987.

Trait: Developing a talent or hobby.

Pablo Picasso was a Spanish painter who was a leader in the cubism type of art which tried to reduce everything in nature to the cube, the cone, and the cylinder. His "Blue Period" showed sad clowns and circus dancers in blue colors. His "Pink" period and "Negro Period" followed. In his later years, his interest turned to realistic work, symbolism, surrealism, and ceramics. A look at the painters who lived during the times of other famous people will give students a fuller understanding of a particular time period that is studied during a social studies unit. This reissue (grade 4 & up) tells about Picasso's life and interprets some of the full-page reproductions. This biography makes his works available to students. Other titles in the series include *Rembrandt* and *Renoir*.

Target Activity: "Interviewing and Reporting"

Engage the students in being newspaper reporters with the assignment to get a personal interview with Picasso. The students should write about the things that stand out in their minds that he did to overcome some of the obstacles in his life. The students may work together in news teams and write a news article to try to tell the others in the class as much as they can about the ways Picasso resolved or overcame problems in his life.

230.   Rosenburg, Maxine B. *My Friend Leslie: The Story of a Handicapped Child*. Photographs by George Ancona. New York: Lothrop, Lee & Shepard, 1983.

Trait: Overcoming obstacles.

Leslie, a kindergarten child, has auditory and visual handicaps. There is an understanding teacher, a best friend, and some responsive classmates who encourage Leslie to do well. Leslie becomes the best reader in the class, and her interpretive skills inspire sustained applause from her appreciating classmates. 4–6.

Target Activity: Engage the students in thinking about a typical weekend day and ask them to make a list of what they do from the time they get up in the morning to the time they go to bed.

For each of these activities, the student should have two columns. In one column, the student will write all the things for which a person needs to be able to hear to do them. In the other column, the student will write all those things for which a person needs to be able to see.

When this is accomplished, invite the students to write a brief paragraph about how he would spend the time during this same day the very same place if the student had the auditory and visual handicaps that Leslie did. Discuss: How did this paragraph change any of your ideas? opinions? feelings? ways of thinking?

231. Schroeder, Alan. *Ragtime Tumpie.* **Ill. by Bernie Fuchs. New York: Joy Street/Little, 1989.**

Traits: Positive vision of life; developing a hobby or talent.

Showing an urban black community, this fictional biography tells the life of Josephine Baker, a dancer famous in Europe early in the 20th century. As a young girl, Josephine (Tumpie) picks fruit from the yards and gathers coal fallen off the hopper cars at the railroad tracks. At night, she goes with her mother to hear ragtime music and to dance to the drums in the honky-tonks. One day, she wins a dance contest sponsored by a traveling peddler and receives a shiny silver dollar. After winning the contest, Josephine Baker follows her interest and becomes a famous dancer. 4–5.

Target Activity: "Ragtime and Resiliency"

Discuss: Why do you think it was a good idea for Tumpie to enter the dance contest? Tell why you would (or would not agree) that it was a good idea for Tumpie to go with her mother at night to hear ragtime music. What are some of the things you remember from the story that would prove that Tumpie had a positive vision of life? That she could solve problems? Had a sense of humor? Overcame obstacles?

232. Schur, Maxine. *Hannah Szenes: A Song of Light.* **Ill. by Donna Ruff. New York: Jewish Publication Society, 1990.**

Trait: Perseverance in the face of failure.

As a teenager, Hannah Szenes leaves the stifling anti–Semitism of Hungary in 1939 for a new life in Palestine. In 1943, she parachutes back into Nazi-occupied Yugoslavia to save the lives of Jews. Captured and tortured, she defies the Nazis only to be executed in the closing days of the war. An inspirational story of a young woman's bravery. Advanced 6 & up.

Target Activity: "Impact of Hitler's Policies"

For those students (advanced 6 and up) interested further in the subject, there is Albert Marrin's book, *Hitler* (Viking, 1987). Hitler's life is inseparable from Hitler's war so it is not surprising that, after describing the dictator's childhood and youth in Austria, Marrin describes the campaigns of World War II. Through the history of events, however, he points to the influence of Hitler as a dictator, his irrationality about his racial policies, and his responsibility for major military decisions. The book emphasizes facts that young readers should know about the impact of Hitler's policies on the lives of people, the controls he exercised, and the horrors of World War II. In addition to its insight into the nature of totalitarianism, the book is a valuable addition to a collection on the subject since it includes maps, photographs, bibliography, and index.

233.   Sills, Leslie. *Inspirations: Stories about Women Artists.* **Ill. Chicago: Albert Whitman, 1989.**
   Trait: Developing a hobby or talent.
   These biographical stories show art works and the intensity of the vision of such artists as Georgia O'Keefe (striking flower studies), Frida Kahlo (symbolic self-portraits), Alice Neel (sad-eyed children), and Faith Ringgold (intricate cloth pictures). The colorful artwork from talented artists attracts anyone browsing through this collective biography and the narratives explain the way each talented artist was influenced in her work. 4 & up.
   Target Activity: "Portraits with Words"
   Invite children to create portraits of the artists with words. Discuss some of the details that could be used in making these pictures with language (e.g., using information about: 1) what children's reactions and feelings to a work of art are; 2) artists' likes and dislikes; 3) choices or subjects of art works; and 4) unusual behaviors, habits or artistic media techniques).

234.   Stanley, Diane. *Peter the Great.* **Ill. by the author. New York: Four Winds, 1986.**
   Trait: Problem-solving.
   This is a lively biography of the extraordinary tsar, Peter I, "the Great," who reformed and westernized Russia. He introduced European ways into Russia, enlarged the Russian territory, and made reforms in government (put the church under control of the tsar; created a new army and navy), economics (introduced communications and public works) and education (based on the European system, he changed the calendar and gave women more freedom). From the illustrations, a viewer learns of examples of some of the entertaining times in the early 18th century. The performers walk in on a narrow Russian carpet under vaulted and decorated ceilings of the palace and wait to entertain. Includes a list of source material for documenting the facts. 4–6.
   Target Activity: "Document Your Facts"

Working in pairs, students will experience the study step of documenting facts from another source that they read in a biography. In solving the problems of Russia, Peter I accomplished many things. Each student will select another biography about this great Russian tsar and locate information that documents the following topics: introduced European ways into Russia; enlarged the Russian territory; reformed the government; reformed economics; and reformed education.

Engage students in discussing what they wrote and give directions for sharing the writing: "Give your fact sheet to another learning partner to read; discuss what you wrote, and add other facts you and your partner agree upon and which are based upon your reading(s)."

235.   Trull, Patti. *On with My Life*. New York: Putnam, 1983.
Trait: Perseverance.

In Pattie Trull's autobiography, we learn that cancer and amputation of a leg are less traumatic than the unthinking reactions of those around her. Patti overcomes both types of pressure and begins working as a therapist to young cancer patients. 5 & up.

Target Activity: "On with My Life"
The teacher should invite the students to consider a time when they faced a debilitating trauma (or knew someone who did). Writing reflectively in their journals, the students are to consider their thoughts about the stress the traumas caused and what a person needs to do to overcome these stresses and pressures.

236.   White, Ryan, and Marie Cunningham. *Ryan White: My Own Story*. New York: Dial, 1991.
Trait: Positive vision of life.

White tells of his struggle, how he acquired AIDS, his legal battles, and dealing with the press, along with details about his personal life. This speaks to the strength of White's spirit and the importance of understanding one who has AIDS. 5 & up.

Target Activity: "My Own Story"
In our modern times, everyone has a story about a time when she/he had to show strength of spirit. Encourage the students to think of a struggle in their life to write about reflectively in their journals during a quiet thinking time during the school day.

237.   Wolf, Bernard. *This Proud Land: The Story of a Mexican American Family*. Photographs. New York: Lippincott, 1978.
Traits: Persistence; problem-solving.

Traveling from the Rio Grande valley to Minnesota to find work, the proud Hernandez family is shown through its relationships at work and at play as they create a better life for themselves in difficult times. Wolf, the author, focuses on the "many Americas" in this "proud" land and writes: "There is an America of inequality and racial prejudice. There is an America of grave poverty, despair, and tragic human waste. And yet because of people like the Hernandez family, there is also an America of simple courage, strength, and hope" (p. 95). 6 & up.

Target Activity: "Many Americans with Courage, Strength, and Hope"

Invite students to discuss some of the literary elements in this biography or in another of their choice:

What theme does the title of the biography reflect?

What problems were presented in the biography?

What was the biographer's purpose in writing?

Find example(s) of ways the biographer caught your interest.

What evidence can you find for the biographical character's ability to show "courage, strength and hope" and triumph over obstacles? If you were to draw an illustration of the biographical character, what information would you find to help you make a drawing?

Find the specific locations mentioned in the biography and locate these places on a map or globe. If you were to draw the setting, what information would you find to help you make the drawing?

In what ways can you check the accuracy of dates and happenings in other informational sources?

238. Zola, Meguido. *Karen Kain: Born to Dance*. New York: Franklin Watts, 1983.

Trait: Developing a hobby or talent.

This is an easy-to-read biography of Karen Kain and will appeal to the student interested in ballet. There is flowing language that follows this well-known Canadian in her career, from her first decision to become a professional to her best moments on stage. Music mentioned. 4–6.

Target Activity: "Reading Two Biographies"

When a reader is interested in a topic, the teacher should recommend several biographies about the tropic to pass along to the student. One biography always should be an easy one—a book the teacher predicts the student will read. The second biography may be more difficult; this one the teacher (or peer tutor) may read aloud to the student.

With the students, the teacher asks them to identify a person they want to know more about as they study traits of resiliency. The teacher mentions that the points of view of the authors will be different as they write biographies of the same person. Ask students to find two biographies about the person they select and to tell others which one appears to be the more difficult. The student should read both and compare them.

III. Extended Activity Units for Grades K–3

Selected Books

239. *Adoption Is for Always* **by Linda Walvoord Girard. Ill. by Judith Friedman. Niles, Ill.: Albert Whitman & Company, 1986.**

Theme: Positive vision of life; ability to solve problems; relationship with caring others.

Overview: Celia was told she was adopted when she was a tiny girl, but she is just beginning to realize what the word means; she is consequently feeling angry and insecure. Her loving adoptive parents gently deal with her anger by helping Celia understand how much they wanted her and why her birth parents gave her up. Grades 2–3.

New Vocabulary: Adoption agency, birth parents, courthouse judge, celebrate.

Materials: Poem (below), construction paper, crayons.

Motivation: Linking prior knowledge; getting "into" the reading activities.

1. Write the word "adopted" on the board. Ask if any child knows what the word means. Ask them if they or anyone they know was adopted. Share your personal anecdotes, where relevant, or tell children that Gerald Ford, past president of the United States, was adopted.

2. Read children the following poem:

Not flesh of my flesh, nor bone of my bone,
    but still miraculously my own;
Never forget for a single minute,
You weren't born under my heart
    but in it.

Anonymous

Ask children if they think they know what the mother in this poem is trying to express to her child. Explain how special this mother feels her adopted child is.

Purpose for Reading or Listening: "We are going to read (listen to) a story about a little girl named Celia who has just begun to understand that she is adopted. At first she feels very angry. Listen (read) to find out how her parents help her feel good about being adopted.

Discussion Questions (through the reading activities):

1. How old was Celia when she was adopted?

2. Why was Celia feeling angry about being adopted?

3. What did Calia's father mean when he told her, "You're ours for keeps, Pumpkin"?

4. What did the judge ask Celia's parents? Why?

5. Why did Celia's parents want to celebrate Celia's adoption day every year?

6. Why were Celia's parents grateful to her birth parents?

7. What do you think made Celia feel better about being adopted?

8. How do you know Celia's adoptive parents love her very much?

Retelling: Groups of students can roleplay the conversation between Celia and her mother; Celia and her father; Celia and Mrs. Thomas.

Extended Activities (beyond the reading activities):

1. In the book, Celia's father says to her "...there's only one Celia O'Shaunessy." Ask children what they think he meant by this remark. Then have pairs of children turn to each other and tell one special thing that makes *them* unique.

2. Have children consider what Celia might say to another child who just learns she is adopted. Allow children to share their thoughts on how the conversation might go.

3. Have each child interview a person whom they know was adopted. Questions might include: "When did you find out you were adopted? How did you feel? Are you happy to have been chosen by your adoptive parents?" Allow children to share the results of their interviews with the rest of the class.

4. Discuss with children how much Celia's adoptive parents love her and all the ways they showed that love in the story. Have children write a note to Celia telling her how lucky they think she is.

Interdisciplinary Ideas:

Social Studies: Discuss the emotions with children, paying particular attention to "anger." Ask children if they have ever been angry. Ask them to suggest ways Celia might have expressed her anger other than by saying hurtful things and disobeying her mother. Make a list of positive ways that anger can be expressed without hurting anyone.

Recreational Reading: For younger students, consider Sydney Taylor's *Ella of All of a Kind Family* (Dutton, 1978) to show warmth of a family. For older students, suggest *The Great Gilly Hopkins* or *Runaway Alice* to children. Both are books about children in foster homes who long for "forever" homes. Discuss the feelings of these children. Create a "perfect" family for these children.

Art: Have children draw a picture of Celia and her parents celebrating her adoption day. Provide construction paper and crayons. Let children discuss how each of the people in the picture is feeling.

240. *Crow Boy* **by Taro Yashima. Ill. by author. New York: Viking, 1955.**

Theme: Persistence.

Overview: A tiny boy, Chibi, feels out of place at school for five years; in sixth grade, a new friendly teacher likes Chibi's drawings and handwriting and spends time talking to him. At the talent show, Chibi imitates the voices of crows and the teacher explains how Chibi learned the calls, leaving his home for school at dawn and arriving home at sunset every day for six long years. Chibi is honored for his perfect attendance at school for six years and receives the name "Crow Boy." 2–3.

New Vocabulary: Japan, Chibi, forlorn, cross-eyed, zebra grass, imitate, perfect attendance.

Materials: Writing paper, pencils, crayons, art paper.

Motivation (linking prior knowledge; "into" the reading activities):

1. Ask students to think of ways to "kill time" and amuse themselves. Have them quickly sketch their ideas. In small groups, ask them to tell their classmates why they drew their sketches the way they did.

2. Show students the picture ways Chibi killed time—watching the ceiling, looking out the window, (p. 12–13).

3. Ask children to think if they have ever changed their minds about a tag-along after getting to know him or her. Encourage them to share incidents that made them change their minds about the person.

4. Write the words *Crow Boy* on the board. Have students turn to a partner and discuss, "One thing *Crow Boy* makes me think of is...."

Purpose for Reading or Listening: "You are going to read (hear) a story about a young boy named Chibi who was called stupid and slowpoke by the other children at school. Read (listen) to find out how others at school change their minds about Chibi after the talent show."

Discussion Questions (through the reading activities):

1. What things did Chibi do on the playground to entertain himself?

2. Describe how you think a crow must have looked to Chibi.

3. Why did Chibi learn to imitate voices of crows? How do you think he felt?

4. How do you think Chibi felt when others renamed him "Crow Boy"? What might *you* have said or done at the talent show?

5. How did the new teacher get acquainted with Chibi?

Retelling (through the reading activities):

Pairs of students roleplay the story taking turns being Chibi and the friendly new teacher.

Extended Activities (beyond the reading activities):

1. Taking the role of Chibi, invite children to tell the new teacher how he feels about school.

2. Have children retell the story, and somewhere, insert their name and personality with the words, "Suddenly, there I was. . . ." Encourage them to see how the ending to the story changes as their personality helps the tiny boy or makes choices different from Chibi's.

3. Have children rewrite the story from the teacher's point of view. Discuss and imagine the way Chibi felt during his school years.

4. Have children interview someone like Chibi with, "What was your schooling like?"

5. Invite children to write a thank-you note to Chibi for performing at the talent show.

6. Engage children in writing a letter to the author/artist and telling him what they learned about Chibi's resiliency from the story, *Crow Boy*.

Interdisciplinary Ideas:

Social Studies: Discuss some of the traits of resiliency Chibi shows in the story. Examples:

Trait: Persistence in the face of failure.

"But slowpoke or not, day after day, Chibi came trudging to school. He always carried the same lunch, a rice ball wrapped in a radish leaf. Even when it rained or stormed he still came trudging along, wrapped in a raincoat made from dried zebra grass" (pp. 16–17).

Trait: Relationship with a caring other.

"Our new teacher was Mr. Isobe. He was a friendly man with a kind smile. Mr. Isobe often took his class to the hilltop behind the school. He was pleased to learn that Chibi knew all the places where the wild grapes and wild potatoes grew. He was amazed to find how much Chibi knew about all the flowers in our class garden. He liked Chibi's black-and-white drawings and tacked them up on the wall to be admired. He liked Chibi's own handwriting, which no one but Chibi could read, and he tacked that up on the wall. And he often spent time talking with Chibi when no one was around" (pp. 19–23).

Traits: Ability to gain people's attention in a positive way and development of a hobby or talent.

"Mr. Isobe announced that Chibi was going to imitate the voices of crows. . . . Then Mr. Isobe explained how Chibi had learned those calls—leaving his home for school at dawn, and arriving home at sunset, every day for six long years" (p. 25, 30).

Trait: Sense of control over life.

"Chibi was the only one in our class honored for perfect attendance through all the six years" (p. 33).

Trait: Feeling of autonomy.

". . .nobody called him Chibi any more. We all called him Crow Boy. 'Hi, Crow Boy!' Crow Boy would nod and smile as if he liked the name. And when his work was done he would buy a few things for his family. Then he would set off on the far sides of the mountain, stretching his growing shoulders proudly like a grown-up man. And from around the turn of the mountain road would come a crow call—the happy one" (pp. 35–7).

Recreational Reading: Have children look for stories about characters and other people who change their minds about them in the plot.

Science: Investigate crows (their looks, habitat, food, and so on).

Art: Invite children to draw the scene of Chibi at the talent show.

Math: Discuss ways the author/artist, Taro Yashima, shows how time is measured with his illustrations of changing seasons (weather) and mention of sunset.

Chart the different birds in stories found by the children in the class. Discuss if there are differences between the choices of the girls and boys.

241. *Flossie and the Fox* **by Patricia McKissack. Ill. by Rachel Isadora. New York: Dial, 1986.**

Theme: Positive vision of life.

Overview: A young girl, Flossie Finley, is sent to take eggs to "Miz Viola at the McCutchin Place" and is warned about a troublesome fox; Flossie has never seen a fox and doesn't know what one looks like. Flossie meets the fox and outwits him. 2–3.

New Vocabulary: Smokehouse, Tennessee, August, slickster, critter, disremember, rascal, tucked, particular, aine, recollect, curtsy, creature, terrified, proof, generation, ceremony.

Materials: Pictures of fox; drawing paper, pencils, crayons, art paper.

Motivation (linking prior knowledge; "into" the reading activities):

1. Ask students to think of one way they would describe a fox. Have them quickly sketch their idea of a fox on paper. In small groups, ask them to tell their classmates why they drew their sketches the way they did.

2. Show students the picture of the fox. Cluster their words to describe the fox on the chalkboard or overhead.

3. Ask children if they have ever changed their minds about a person or animal after getting to know them. Encourage them to share incidents that made them change their minds.

4. Write the word *scary* on the board. Have students turn to a partner and discuss, "One thing that I thought was scary was when. . ."

Purpose for Reading or Listening: "You are going to read (hear) a story about a young girl named Flossie Finley who had never seen a fox before and she meets one when she takes eggs to Miz Viola at McCutchin's cabin. Read (listen) to find out how Flossie outwits the fox when he meets her in the woods."

Discussion Questions (through the reading activities):
1. What stories had Big Mama told Flossie about the fox?
2. Describe how you think a fox in the woods looked to Flossie.
3. Why did Flossie take the way through the woods? How do you think she was feeling?
4. How do you think Flossie felt when she saw the fox sitting beside the road "like he was expectin' somebody"? What might *you* have said or done?
5. How did Flossie introduce herself to the fox? How did the fox introduce himself to Flossie?
6. How did the fox try to prove he was a fox?
7. When Flossie said, "I don't believe you a fox, that's what," what were the fox's feelings? How do you know this?
8. What would *you* do if someone said to you, ". . . you sho' think a heap of yo'self"?
9. What do you think Flossie meant when she said to the fox, "You just an ol' confidencer"?
10. When Flossie and the fox came out of the woods, how did Flossie get him to turn back to the woods?

Retelling (through the reading activities):
Pairs of students roleplay the story taking turns being Flossie and the fox.

Extended Activities (beyond the reading activities):
1. Taking the role of Flossie, have children tell Big Mama how the fox tried to frighten her. Explain what you learned about the fox.
2. Have children retell the story with their name and personality substituted for Flossie, with the words, "Suddenly, there I was looking at the fox and. . ." Encourage them to see how the ending to the story changes as their personality makes choices different from Flossie's.
3. Have children rewrite the story from the fox's point of view. Help them to imagine that the fox is afraid of Mr. J. W. McCutchin's hound, a fast runner with sharp teeth.
4. Have children interview someone like Flossie with, "What was your day like?"
5. Have Miz Viola write a thank-you note to Flossie telling her how she needed the eggs and what she used them for at her house.

Interdisciplinary Ideas:

Social Studies: To learn more about the idea of solving a problem by yourself, children may discuss Flossie's problem in this story as an opportunity for problem solving. For example, the problem of thinking of a way to avoid the fox (or any other dangerous wild animal) may be discussed. Talk about alternatives that children in the class might have tried in facing a similar problem. Discuss how these alternative ideas might have influenced Flossie and changed her actions in the story. Discuss the relief the little girl must have felt when she reached the cabin and the frustration the fox must have felt when he failed at getting the eggs he wanted. K–2.

Discuss some of the traits of resiliency Flossie shows in the story.

Trait: Ability to plan ahead and solve problems.

"'Why come Mr. J. W. can't catch the fox with his dogs?' Flossie asked, putting a peach in her apron pocket to eat later" (p. 5 unpaged).

Trait: Positive vision of life.

"*What if I come upon a fox?* thought Flossie. *Oh well, a fox be just a fox. That aine so scary*" (p. 7 unpaged).

Traits: Ability to gain people's attention in a positive way and development of a hobby or talent.

"Flossie skipped right up to him and nodded a greeting the way she'd been taught to do. 'Top of the morning to you, Little Missy,' the critter replied, 'And what is your name?'

"'I be Flossie Finley,' she answered with a proper curtsy" (p. 9 unpaged).

Trait: Sense of control over life.

"Flossie rocked back on her heels then up on her toes, back and forward, back and forward ... carefully studying the creature who was claiming to be a fox.

"'Nope,' she said at last. 'I just purely don't believe it'" (p. 10 unpaged).

Trait: Persistence in the face of failure.

"'So, Why should I be scared of you and I don't even-now know you a real fox for a fact?' Fox pulled himself tall. He cleared his throat. 'Are you saying I must offer proof that I am a fox before you will be frightened of me?'

"'That's just what I'm saying'" (p. 11 unpaged).

Trait: Sense of humor.

"'I have the proof,' he said. 'See, I have thick, luxurious fur. See for yourself.' Fox leaned over for Flossie to rub his back. 'Ummm. Feels like rabbit fur to me,' she say to Fox. 'Shucks! You aine no fox. You a rabbit, all the time trying to fool me'" (p. 14 unpaged).

Trait: Feeling of Autonomy.

"'You know,' she finally said, smiling, 'it don't make much difference what I think anymore.'

"'What?' Fox asked. 'Why?'"

"'Cause there's one of Mr. J. W. McCutchin's hounds behind you. He's got sharp teeth and can run fast, too. And, by the way that hound's lookin', it's all over for you!'" (p. 25 unpaged).

Have children find books in the library that tell how other children have met and coped (used resiliency traits) with "slickster" animals in folk literature. For instance, introduce Wilhemina Harper's book *The Gunniwolf* (Dutton, 1987). Invite children to notice the creative use of print that looks like the running steps of the Little Girl as she runs through the jungle with:

pit-   pit-   pit-
    pat   pat   pat

Then the gunniwolf lunges after the little girl and his steps are shown with:

hunker-   hunker-   hunker-
    cha!   cha!   cha!

Recreational Reading: Invite children to look for other stories about foxes (or another wolf).

Science: Investigate foxes (i.e. their diet, looks, habitat, and so on).

Art: Have children draw the scene of Flossie's walk in the woods.

Math: Chart the number one favorite animal in stories of all the children in the class. Discuss if there are differences between the choices of the girls and boys.

Music: Refer back to Harper's *The Gunniwolf* and invite children to think of musical tones for the Little Girl's happy son as she picked flowers at the edge of the jungle. Sing the Little Girl's words using different notes (or "tunes" such as "Twinkle, Twinkle, Little Star" and others) contributed by the children:

"Kum-kwa, khi-wa,
kum-kwa, khi-wa."

242. *I Hate English!* by Ellen Levine. Ill. by Steve Bjorkman. New York: Scholastic, 1989.

Theme: Relationship with caring other person.

Overview: Mei Mei, a young girl who loved to speak Chinese, lived in Chinatown in New York and attended school where everything was done in English. Mei Mei hated English and wouldn't speak it because she thought English was a lonely language where each letter stood alone and made its own noise—different from Chinese where there were fast strokes, short strokes, long strongs in writing and Mei Mei could make the brush (or pen or pencil) fly in her hand. 2–3.

New Vocabulary: director, Hong Kong, California, covered wagon, Chinese, English, Yee Fong, Shek, char siu bao, dragon dances.

Materials: Paper, pencils, pens, illustrations from the book, chalk, chalkboard, supplementary reading books.

Motivation (linking prior knowledge; "into" the reading activities):

1. Ask the girls and boys to close their eyes and visualize one thing that they say they "dislike." Have them quickly sketch the object of their dislike on paper. In small groups, ask them to tell their classmates why they dislike this and how it makes them feel.

2. Show students some of the illustrations of Mei Mei showing her dislike of English: her stubborn look (p. 3 unpaged); her lack of participation in class (p. 8 unpaged); her thoughts about the post office in New York (p. 11 unpaged); and her thoughts about the happening of a "terrible thing," e.g., a teacher to help Mei Mei with English (p. 17 unpaged). Cluster their reactions to Mei Mei's attitude on the writing board or on transparency on the stage of the overhead. Solicit possible reasons why many students might hate English.

3. Ask the girls and boys to think if they have ever "hated" learning words in another language. Encourage them to share incidents that made them change their minds about the language.

4. Show the illustration and write the words *covered wagon* on the board. Have students turn to partners and discuss, "One thing that I know about a covered wagon is. . ."

Purpose for Reading or Listening: "You are going to read (hear) a story about a young girl from Hong Kong named Mei Mei who was determined not to speak English. Read (listen) to find out how Mei Mei became a friend of the teacher's and how the teacher, Nancy, helped her to overcome her objections to English."

Discussion Questions (through the reading activities):

1. Why did Mei Mei dislike English? Would you agree/disagree with her reasons? Why did Mei Mei call English a lonely language?

2. Describe how you think a day in Mei Mei's life must have been when most of the time she understood English and what the teacher said but she wouldn't speak English? What sort of problems, if any, could Mei Mei have had during a day at school? How could you have helped Mei Mei if you had been there?

3. Why did her cousin, Bing, take her to the Chinatown Learning Center for help? How do you think she was feeling when she wouldn't work in English?

4. Why did Mei Mei help the little ones with arithmetic? What other ways did she help at the center?

5. How did she address her letters to friends in Hong Kong? In what language?

6. What was her recurring dream?

7. What were Mei Mei's feelings about English by the end of the story?

8. Had you ever thought that the English language would have words for which Mei Mei did not know/have the Chinese counterpart? Would you guess that the reverse would be true and that the Chinese language would have words for which we would not know/have the English counterpart?

9. What would you do if you discovered someone like Mei Mei who did not want to speak the language of the country in which she was living? How could you help the person?

10. What are some ways you can become a friend to the person?

Retelling (through the reading activities):

Retell this story again using the signal words to show sequencing: first, second, third, next, last, finally.

Retell the story and mention: the name of the main character, what the character wanted, what got in the way to keep the character from getting what was wanted, and the way the problem was resolved.

Retell the story by group participation. The teacher asks the students in one group to find information that tells about the character and to write it down; a second group finds facts about what the character wanted to do and writes it; a third group finds sentences that tell what got in the way of the character's goal and writes them; a fourth group finds sentences that tell how the problem was resolved and writes them. The teacher collects the informational sheets and redistributes them to the groups. Working together and discussing the information, the members determine which of the story parts they have (character, goal, conflict, resolution) and report on the story parts in order to keep the sequence of the retelling. Of course, the members can add more information about their part.

Extended Activities (beyond the reading activities):

1. Participating as an audience, have the girls and boys give a refrain in the background during an oral rereading. As a group, the children should decide on the refrain they want to say when Mei Mei's name is heard during a read aloud (perhaps Mei Mei's feeling of "I love Chinese! I love Chinese!"); when the teacher, Nancy, is mentioned (Forever talking English! Forever talking English!).

2. Have children rewrite the story with their names substituted for Mei Mei. Encourage them to see how some of the events in the story will differ as each one's character makes choices different from Mei Mei's.

3. Have children rewrite the story from the teacher's point of view. Help them to imagine the teacher's concern for Mei Mei.

4. Have children interview a friend who has had to learn a second language in addition to their first language. Listen to them as they point out comparisons of their first language and another one. Are there any words in one language for which there are not words in the other language?

5. Have the girls and boys write a thank-you note to Nancy from Mei Mei telling the teacher at the Chinatown Learning Center how she feels two years later as she thinks back to the day when Nancy engaged her in speaking English.

Interdisciplinary Ideas:

Social Studies: Invite children to find books in the library that tell about school-age children from other cultures (e.g., Japan, China, Mexico, Original Native Americans in North America). For instance, introduce *How My Parents Learned to Eat* (Houghton Mifflin, 1984) by Ina R. Friedman and illustrated by Allen Say, a story about the girl's parents trying to please each other and learn the customs of the other's country—one trying to eat with chopsticks and the other with knives and forks. With globe or map, locate countries where the people eat with chopsticks and others where knives and forks are used. Discuss other cultural customs (favorite foods, habits) related to eating that children know about and contribute in the discussion.

Recreational Reading: Have children look for folk literature from Mei Mei's cultural group such as *The Weaver of a Dream: A Chinese Folktale* (Viking, 1986) by Marilee Heyer, a story of the Chuang Brocade.

Science: When covered wagons came to a deep river, how could the pioneers take the wagon and the oxen across? Invite children to make predictions about how well covered wagons could float. With children, discuss ways pioneers could prepare a wagon for a river crossing and use its "bed" as a raft.

Art: Ask children to make a different type of book—a "half" picture book—about the teacher and Mei Mei. To do this, the children fold two sheets of paper into quarters to make four mini-pages; each sheet with its four small pages will become half of the mini picture book. To complete the first half, the students draw illustrations to show the title page that says *Mei Mei's Story*, and on succeeding pages, the events that happened in Mei Mei's life before she met the teacher. On the last page, the children draw an illustration of Mei Mei and the teacher together as friends.

To complete the second half of the picture book, the students use a second sheet that was folded into quarters to draw the cover and title that says, *The Teacher's Story*, and then illustrations to show the events that happened in the teacher's life before she met Mei Mei. On the last page, the children draw an illustration of the teacher and Mei Mei together as friends.

To assemble the two halves to make a "half" picture book, the students assemble the first half of the book (*Mei Mei's Story*) in the usual manner. Then, the book is turned over (upside down) and *The Teacher's Story* is stapled to *Mei Mei's Story*.

With this arrangement, a student can pick up the book and look at the cover to read *Mei Mei's Story* or turn the book over to start *The Teacher's Story*. What brings the two stories together in the center is the theme of friendship and the final illustrations of the two stories—both showing Mei Mei and the teacher as friends.

Math: Tally the number of times Mei Mei expresses her dislike of a second language. In how many ways does she express her dislike?

243. *Miss Maggie* by Cynthia Rylant. Ill. by Thomas di Dirazia. New York: E. P. Dutton, 1983.

Theme: Relationship with caring other person, positive vision of life.

Overview: A young boy, Nat, had heard stories about the old lady who lives in the log hut on his family's property; a big black snake is rumored to live with her. Nat initially fears Miss Maggie but overcomes his fear when she is in trouble. He develops a special relationship with her. 2–3.

New Vocabulary: trembled, rafters, cupboards, Guernsey, wrinkled, starling.

Materials: live snake, pictures of black snake or plastic snake; drawing paper, pencils, showboxes, pipe cleaners, art paper.

Motivation (linking prior knowledge; "into" the reading activities):

1. Ask students to close their eyes and visualize one thing that makes them afraid. Have them quickly sketch the object of their fear on paper. In small groups, ask them to tell their classmates why they are afraid of the object and how it makes them feel.

2. Show students the snake. Cluster their reactions to the snake on chalkboard or overhead. Solicit possible reasons why many people fear snakes.

3. Ask children if they have ever been afraid of a person prior to getting to know them. Encourage them to share incidents that made them change their minds about the person.

4. Write the word *loneliness* on the board. Have students turn to a partner and discuss, "One thing that made me feel lonely was when..."

Purpose for Reading or Listening: "You are going to read (hear) a story about a young boy named Nat who was very afraid of an old woman named Miss Maggie who lived alone in a little hut near his house. Read (listen) to find out how Nat became Miss Maggie's friend and how Nat helped her to overcome her loneliness."

Discussion Questions (through the reading activities):

1. What stories had Nat heard about Miss Maggie and her hut? Were they true? Why did people tell these stories?

2. Describe how you think a day in Miss Maggie's life must have been before she became Nat's friend.

3. Why was Miss Maggie clutching the dead bird? How do you think she was feeling?

4. How do you think Nat felt when he saw Miss Maggie clutching the dead bird? What might *you* have said or done?

5. When was Nat no longer afraid of Miss Maggie? How did he lose his fear?

6. How did Nat and Miss Maggie become friends?

7. What were Nat's feelings about Miss Maggie by the end of the story?

8. How do you think Miss Maggie felt about Nat?

9. What would *you* do if you discovered someone like Miss Maggie living all alone without food or heat?

10. What are some ways you can become a friend to an older person?

Retelling (through the reading activities):

Pairs of students roleplay the story taking turns being Nat or Miss Maggie.

Extended Activities (beyond the reading activities):

1. Taking the role of Nat, have children write a letter to Miss Maggie telling her how she used to frighten them and why. Explain what you learned about her and how much you care about her now.

2. Have children rewrite the story with their name and personality substituted for Nat. Encourage them to see how the ending to the story differs as their character makes choices different from Nat's.

3. Have children rewrite the story from Miss Maggie's point of view. Help them to imagine that Miss Maggie is afraid of the little boy who is constantly peering in the windows.

4. Have children interview a grandparent or an elderly person living in a nearby nursing home. Questions can include, "Are you ever lonely? What is a day in your life like?" Help them to compare their lives with that of an elderly person.

5. Have children write a thank-you note to Nat from Miss Maggie telling Nat how she felt when he visited and found her alone holding the starling.

Interdisciplinary Ideas:

Social Studies: Have children find books in the library that tell how elderly people are respected and treated in other cultures (e.g., Japan, China, India, etc).

Recreational Ideas: Have children look for folklore about snakes. Discuss how snakes are considered in these legends. Why do they suppose this is so?

Science: Investigate nonpoisonous snakes (i.e., their diet, predators, habitat, etc.). Have children make a poster explaining why these creatures have been unfairly maligned.

Art: Have children construct a diorama of Miss Maggie's log house in the middle of the pasture.

Math: Chart the number one fear of all the children in the class. Discuss if there are differences between the fears of the girls and boys. Brainstorm ways to overcome these fears.

244. *Mr. Rabbit and the Lovely Present* **by Charlotte Zolotow. Ill. by Maurice Sendak. New York: Scholastic Book Services, 1962.**

Theme: Ability to solve problems and relationship with a caring other.

Overview: A little girl is trying to think of a good present to buy her mother for her birthday. She bounces ideas off her friend, Mr. Rabbit, and comes up with an appropriate gift for her mother—a basket of fruit. K–2.

New Vocabulary: cardinal, engine, taxicabs, canary, emerald, afford, sapphires, caterpillars.

Motivation (Linking prior knowledge; getting "into" the reading material):

1. Ask children who they go to if they have a problem. Have them tell how the person they choose generally helps them to solve the problem. Does (s)he tell them what to do or help them to figure it out by themselves? Discuss which approach they prefer.

2. Ask children how they would feel if they knew tomorrow were their mother's birthday and they had no present for her. What could they do if they had no money to buy a present?

3. Play a guessing game with the children. Tell them "I am thinking of a fruit that is red that will be in the story. Can anyone guess what it is?" Write the word "apple" on the board when it is guessed. Do the same guessing game with banana, pear, and grape.

Purpose for Listening: Tell children that the book they are about to listen to (read) is about a little girl who has nothing to give her mother for her birthday and is asking a rabbit for advice. Tell them to listen to find out how the little girl solves her problem.

Discussion Questions:

1. Where do you think this story takes place?
2. What season of the year do you think it is? Why?
3. What is the little girl's problem?
4. Why do you think she asks the rabbit for advice?
5. What does Mr. Rabbit mean when he says, "You can't give her red?"
6. How did the rabbit help her solve her problem?
7. What was the present?
8. Do you think the little girl's mother liked the present? Why or why not?

Retelling: This book is essentially a dialogue between a little girl and a rabbit. Have several pairs of children take the roles of the rabbit and the little girl and retell the story in front of the class.

Extended Activities (beyond the reading activities):

1. Ask children if they have ever received a gift that they did not like. What did they say? Stress the importance of not hurting someone's feelings. Have children suggest what the little girl's mother might have said when she was given the basket of fruit.

2. Write the words "red," "blue," "green," and "yellow" on the blackboard. Write the phrase "For her birthday I would give my mother a _____." Pass out lined newsprint. Put children in groups of four and assign each child a color. Invite children to each think of a present and color and complete the phrase. Children can then draw pictures of their present. Staple the paper together into a class book.

3. Discuss with children the relationship between the little girl and the rabbit. Ask them, "If you could have a friendship with an animal and could actually talk to that animal, what animal would you choose?" Ask them to give reasons for their answers.

Interdisciplinary Ideas:

Social Studies: To learn more about the idea of working together and one way this cooperation is shown in a story, children may discuss the little girl's problem in this story as an opportunity for examining problem solving. For example, the problem of thinking of a good present for Mother's birthday (or any family member's birthday) may be discussed. Talk about alternatives that children in the class might have tried in coping with the problem. Discuss how these alternative ideas might have affected the little girl and changed what she did to make the present. Discuss the appreciation the little girl must have felt toward Mr. Rabbit for helping her and the appreciation Mother must have felt when she saw the present as well as the feeling of the little girl when she saw how her present was received.

Recreational Reading: Invite children to look for stories about birthdays or making gifts for others. Read *Miss Suzy's Birthday* (Young, 1972) aloud to children. Compare the problems Miss Suzy's children had thinking of an appropriate present to buy with the little girl's problem in this story.

Science (Nutrition): Discuss the snacks children eat. Talk about which ones are healthy and which are unhealthy. Ask them if they think the fruits contained in the little girl's fruit basket would be healthy or unhealthy snacks.

Art: Bring in a fruit basket containing a banana, pear, apple, and grapes. Pass out watercolor paints and watercolor paper. Ask children to make a painting of the fruit basket.

Math: Of the four colors mentioned in this story—green, yellow, red, and blue—ask children to vote on which one they like the best. Chart the number of children who prefer each color using a simple bar graph.

III. Extended Activity Units for Grades 4–8

Selected Books

245. *Bridge to Terabithia* **by Katherine Paterson. Ill. by Donna Diamond. New York: Thomas Y. Crowell, 1978.**

Theme: Positive vision of life; relationship with caring "other" person.

Overview: Jesse and Leslie are friends and they create Terabithia, a magic kingdom in the woods where they are the lord and lady. When Leslie dies, Jesse copes through the legacy that she has left him. 4–6.

New Vocabulary: Hypocritical, proverbial, conspicuous, conceited, consolation, reassessing, siege, veiled speculation, foundling, garish, vanquished.

Materials: Songs: "Beautiful Balloon," "This Land Is Your Land," "Blowin' in the Wind," "Free to Be . . . You and Me"; newsprint; colored chalk.

Motivation (linking prior knowledge; getting "into" the reading material):

1. Write the word "kingdom" on the board. Web the concept on the blackboard or overhead, using children's free associations like so:

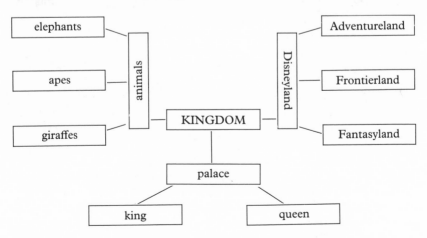

2. Discuss "fear" with children. Explain that Jesse is afraid to swing across a creek on a rope when the creek is especially high. Ask them if they find that unusual. Ask them why they think Jesse is concerned about his fear, and if any of them has ever been made fun of for being afraid of something. Discuss the positive aspects of fear. Is it "healthy" to be afraid of something?

3. Tell children that Jesse practiced all summer to become the fastest runner in his school, but then he was beaten by a girl. Ask them how they would feel about that girl. Do you think a friendship could ever develop between Jesse and the girl who beat him?

Purpose for Reading: "The book you are about to read tells about an unlikely friendship between a ten-year-old girl and boy growing up in rural Virginia. Read to find out how they become friends and why they are important to one another."

Discussion Questions:

1. Why is Jesse so fond of his sister, May Belle?
2. Why does he resent his other sister?
3. Why didn't Jesse show his drawings to his dad?
4. How did Leslie seem different from the other children Jesse knew?
5. Why had Leslie's family moved to the country?
6. How do Leslie and Jesse become friends?
7. Describe Terabithia. Why is it important to the two children?
8. Why can't Jesse accept that Leslie has died?
9. How does rescuing May Belle make Jesse feel better?
10. How had Leslie taught him to "stand up to his fear"?

Retelling: Have children pick a partner. Ask one child to tell the partner about Jesse's friendship with Leslie as Jesse might have explained it later on in life.

Extended Activities (beyond the reading activities):

1. Have children rewrite the story as if Jesse had invited Leslie with Miss Edmonds and him to the Smithsonian. Would Leslie have died? Would he have brought May Belle to Terabithia?

2. Ask children what they think Jesse will be like when he grows up. Will he be an artist? Will he still remember Leslie? Will he still have fear? Will he still be close to May Belle? Have children write a paragraph describing Jesse's life twenty years later.

3. Perhaps Jesse wishes he could have seen Leslie just one more time. Ask children to imagine what Jesse might have said to Leslie if he'd known he could have one last conversation with her.

Interdisciplinary Ideas:

Social Studies: In the story Leslie's parents would suddenly begin talking to Jesse about "how to save the timber wolves or redwoods, or singing whales," but he knew nothing about these topics. In groups of three or four, have children select one of these issues, do research, and explain why the topic might have been a concern to Leslie's parents.

Social Studies/Language Arts: Discuss the dialect of rural Virginia as presented in this story, e.g., "You shouldn't ought to beat me in the head." "You ain't got no money for school shopping!" Select some phrases from the text and have children convert them into standard English. Ask children why they think the author chose to use this nonstandard dialect in her text.

Art: Have children draw a picture of Terabithia as they imagine it using colored chalk and newsprint.

Music: Teach children the songs that Miss Edmonds taught Jesse: "This Land Is Your Land," "Blowing in the Wind," "In My Beautiful Balloon," and "Free to Be . . . You and Me."

246. *The Egyptian Cinderella* **by Shirley Climo. Ill. by Ruth Heller. New York: Thomas Y. Crowell, 1989.**

Theme: Persistence; problem-solving; sense of control over life.

Overview: A young Greek girl, a slave, is taunted and scorned by the Egyptian girls. Receiving a gift from her master for her graceful dancing, she has rose-red gold slippers that shine like the flashing of fireflies in the evening while she dances alone. The falcon delivers one of her slippers to the great Pharaoh who searches all of Egypt to find the owner of the slipper and make her his queen. 4–6.

New Vocabulary: Nile River, Rhodopis, pirates, Greece, Egypt, reeds, scoffed, nimble, papyrus, Kipa, tunic, falcon, Horus, talons, Memphis, chariot, pyramids, Amasis, lotus.

Materials: Map, writing paper, pencils, butcher paper, string and stick.

Motivation (linking prior knowledge; "into" the reading activities):

1. Ask students to look at the map of Egypt. Locate Memphis and discuss the distance and ways to travel to reach Memphis. Discuss a picture of the Egyptian girls who worked in the household to determine what we can learn from the picture about the culture of Egypt and the times.

2. Show students the picture of Rhodopis on the cover (a foreshadowing of things to come). List their responses on the writing board to: What does she appear to be—slave or queen? Where does she appear to be from? What jewelry is she wearing? Discuss head piece, eye makeup, earrings, and gold decorations. If she has these things to wear, what does this tell you about the crafts, skills, and abilities of the people of the times? What might it tell you about their ability to trade goods? How is she dressed on p. 3? How does she look different from the cover?

3. Imagine how you would feel if you found friends among the animals. How would you feel? What would you do?

4. Write the word *nimble* on the board. Have students turn to a member of the class and discuss their interpretation of *nimble*.

Purpose for Reading or Listening: "You will read (hear) a story about a slave girl Rhodopis who became the Queen of Egypt. Read (listen) to find out how Rhodopis changed from the scorn of the Egyptian girls to become a queen of the Pharaoh Amasis."

Discussion Questions (through the reading activities):

2. When her chores were done, who did Rhodopis turn to for her friends?

2. How was Rhodopis scorned by the Egyptian girls? If you had been in the story, what could you have done to help Rhodopis?

3. Seeing her nimble dancing, the master admired her and ordered a pair of dainty slippers made of real leather with the toes gilded with rose-red gold. Why do you think the Egyptian girls were jealous of her slippers?

4. Tell what happened to Rhodopis when she was left behind at the riverbank and the servant girls poled their raft toward Memphis to see the Pharaoh.

5. What did the falcon do with one of the beautiful slippers?

6. What does it mean when you read that Amasis, the Pharaoh, wore the "crown of the Two Egypts?"

7. What protests did the Egyptian girls make against Rhodopis as the queen?

8. What did the Pharaoh respond?

9. In the author's note, which part of this tale seems to be based in facts?

10. From the facts in the author's note, explain why the gold on the toes of the slippers would be of a reddish hue.

11. Why do you believe it is true/not true that a Greek slave girl, Rhodopis, married the Pharaoh Amasis and became his queen?

12. Where would you look to find more about the duties and responsibilities of a Pharaoh's queen?

Retelling (through the reading activities):

Pairs of students use signal words of first, second, third, next, and finally, to retell the main events in the story.

Reviewing the sequence of events, have the students tell what happened, and on the writing board, record key words to explain what the students learned about this tale based on facts.

Extended Activities (beyond the reading activities):

1. Take the role of Rhodopis as a child slave on the island of Samos. One of her fellow slaves is a man named Aesop who tells her stories (fables) about animals. Imagine that you are listening to one of these

fables. In cooperative discussion groups, take turns being Rhodopis and then ask a volunteer in your group to tell a fable he knows.

2. From Rhodopis' point of view, have students rewrite the event where the falcon takes her beautiful slipper; when the Pharaoh sees her hiding in the reeds near the Nile; when the Pharaoh announces that she is "the most Egyptian of all." After writing this point of view, ask the students to team up with response partners and read their writing to each other for feedback. They may rewrite if they wish.

3. Invite the students to write diary entries from the Egyptian girls' point of view when Amasis announces that "there is none so fit to be queen." Help them to imagine the first time that the girls saw the Pharaoh at the water's edge on his royal barge.

4. Suggest that the students write a diary entry from the Pharaoh's point of view when the red-gold slipper fell into his lap at court. Help them to imagine the sight of the slipper "so bright that Amasis thought it was a scrap of sun."

5. Ask the students to write their thoughts about the comment made by Kipa, the head of the servant girls: "Slaves are better off barefoot." What meaning does this have?

6. Engage the students in writing a marriage announcement to tell of the forthcoming marriage of Amasis to Rhodopis.

"You have been selected to give a brief announcement about the Pharaoh's life and accomplishments. What are you going to say? Write your thoughts out before you give the speech."

"You have been selected to give a brief announcement about the life of Queen Rhodopis and her accomplishments. What are you going to say? Write your thoughts out before you give the speech."

Interdisciplinary Ideas:

Social Studies: In a study of Egypt, students may first focus on the New Kingdom, Queen Hatshepsut, and the flourishing of Egyptian art and agriculture. Next, mention the Kingdom of Kush which established the twenty-fifth dynasty of pharaohs, and then place this story in its historical context as taking place in the twenty-sixth dynasty of pharaohs. Through the story's illustrations, introduce students to what can be observed about the culture that developed there (i.e., what evidence is there of iron agricultural tools, weapons, an alphabet, and a profitable trade system?).

Link the past to the present: Engage students in locating information about Egyptians of today to compare with the information in the book about the Pharaoh of Dynasty XXVI (570–526 B.C.).

Social Studies/Language Arts: Divide the students into study groups and assign one (or more) trait of resiliency to each group. In reviewing the assigned story (any version of Cinderella), the students will look in their individual copies for sentences in the story that document their assigned trait of resiliency. Examples of books with a version of Cinderella story: *Yeh-Shen: A Cinderella Story from China*; *Moss Gown*; and *The Egyptian Cinderella*.

Before reading the story, invite the girls and boys to write their thoughts about: *If you were to read this version of Cinderella from another culture, what would you expect to find in this tale that shows the trait of persistence in the face of failure?*

As the students read the story, they should take notes and write quotes that document something about the trait they are assigned.

After reading the story, the students go back to their notes and review what they wrote for their thoughts at the beginning of the lesson and discuss:

1. Did you change your mind about what you would expect to find in this Cinderella tale from another culture?

2. In what ways did you change your ideas about the trait of persistence in the face of failure?

3. After reading this tale, what do you know about the trait of persistence (autonomy, sense of control, developing a hobby, and so on) in the face of failure?

Recreational Reading: Invite children to find stories with Egyptian settings. They should look for *Hieroglyphs from A to Z: A Rhyming Book with Ancient Egyptian Stencils for Kids* by Peter Der Manuelian (Museum of Fine Arts, Boston, 1991). In *Hieroglyphs*, children see that people wrote with pictures and learn a few of the signs that decorate temple and tomb walls. A stencil is included so a child can trace inside a hieroglyph to write messages. Invite them to tell others what they learned about Egypt and its people from their readings. Discuss the Egyptian phrase that usually comes at the end of ancient stories written on papyrus: "Its beginning has come to its end, as it was found in writing."

Science: Conduct reading and research and find out more information about the falcon (for example, its life, behavior, food, enemies, and habitat.

Art: What did the students learn about Egyptian visual and performing arts from reading the story and looking at the illustrations? What did they observe about the artist's work found in the story?

Math: Collect information from all of the groups about all of the traits of resiliency and record/chart/graph the information gathered from versions of the Cinderella story from different cultures. As each trait of resiliency is discussed, members of groups contribute evidence from their reading and have their contributions recorded, showing information from each story. Examples:

Trait: Persistence in the face of failure

China: In *Yeh-Shen: A Cinderella Story from China:* "Time went by, and Yeh-Shen, who was often left alone, took comfort in speaking to the bones of her fish" (p. 8 unpaged).

Yeh-Shen managed to live from day to day, but lived in dread that her stepmother would discover her secret (magic fish bones) and take even that away from her.

Egypt: In *The Egyptian Cinderella:* "Although Rhodopis wore a plain tunic, on her feet were the rose-red slippers. Perhaps they will let me come along to see the Pharaoh after all, she thought. But the three servant girls poled their raft around the bend in the river without giving Rhodopis a backward glance" (p. 11 unpaged).

Southern United States: In *Moss Gown:* "Candace put on the gown and started to walk. Her feet seemed to know the way. They were fleet and sure, pulled by a force she could not control. But as the Morning Star faded, and the red sun rose, Candace saw her beautiful gown turn into rags and gray moss. She reached the end of the swamp and saw a house as fine and grand as the white-pillared mansion of her father" (p. 20).

Trait: Feeling of autonomy

China: "When she was hungry, which happened quite often, Yeh-Shen asked the [magic] bones for food" (p. 9 unpaged).

"As soon as she was alone, Yeh-Shen went to speak to the bones of her fish. 'Oh, dear friend,' she said, kneeling before the precious bones, 'I long to go to the festival, but I cannot show myself in these rags. Is there somewhere I could borrow clothes fit to wear to the feast?' At once she found herself dressed in a gown of azure blue, with a cloak of kingfisher feathers draped around her shoulders. Best of all, on her tiny feet were the most beautiful slippers she had ever seen. They were woven of golden threads, in a pattern like the scales of a fish, and the glistening soles were made of solid gold" (pp. 10–11 unpaged).

Egypt: "She [Rhodopis] slapped the wooden paddle against the cloth in time to her song" (p. 11 unpaged).

Southern United States: "She [Moss Gown] never smiled or sang, or joked with the kitchen help. She dreamed of returning home . . . She yearned to explain what she had meant when she said, 'I love you more than meat loves salt'" (p. 24).

Trait: Positive vision of life

China: "Delighted with her transformation, she bid a fond farewell to the bones of her fish as she slipped off to join in the merrymaking" (p. 11 unpaged).

Egypt: "Rhodopis found friends among the animals instead. Birds ate crumbs from her hands. She coaxed a monkey to sit upon her shoulder and charmed a hippopotamus with her songs. It would raise its huge head from the muddy water and prick its small ears to listen" (p. 7 unpaged).

Southern United States: "Moss Gown blinked her eyes and saw the gris-gris woman. Her hand was touching the gown, and it shimmered and glowed. She helped Moss Gown into the dress. 'Remember, this gown holds magic only as long as the Morning Star shines,' said the gris-gris woman" (p. 27).

Trait: Ability to plan ahead and solve problems

China: "An old man speaks to Yeh-Shen: 'The bones of your fish are filled with a powerful spirit. Whenever you are in serious need, you must kneel before them and let them know your heart's desire. But do not waste their gifts'" (p. 7 unpaged).

Egypt: "Rhodopis needs magical intervention as a great falcon, the symbol of the god, Horus, steals one of the beautiful slippers, flies to the pharaoh's court, and drops the slipper in his lap" (p. 15 unpaged).

Southern United States: "Candace needs the magical intervention of the green-eyed black woman who weaves a gossamer gown and who can be called with the words, 'gris-gris, gris-gris grine'" (pp. 16, 27).

"Day after Day, the young Master brooded ... Moss Gown found the young Master still sitting on the porch. She tapped him lightly. 'I've brought your supper,' she said. 'Go away,' said the young Master in a sad, low voice. 'Please, just take a look at what First cook has sent,' pleaded Moss Gown. The Young Master turned toward her. 'I'm dreaming,' he said. ...Moss Gown and the young Master talked on and on through the night" (p. 38).

"When her father arrives, Candace has a special dinner prepared with the salt left out of everything. This enables her to solve the problem of telling her father what she meant" (p. 42).

Trait: Sense of control over one's life

China: "Yeh-Shen went to see who it was—and found a king at her doorstep. She was very frightened at first, but the king spoke to her in a kind voice and asked her to try the golden slippers on her feet. The maiden did as she was told, and as she stood in her golden shoes, her rags were transformed once more into the feathered cloak and beautiful azure gown" (p. 24 unpaged).

Egypt: "The servant girls gawked open-mouthed as the Pharaoh knelt before Rhodopis. He slipped the tiny shoe on her foot with ease. Then Rhodopis pulled its mate from the folds of her tunic" (p. 29 unpaged).

Southern United States: "Suddenly she remembered the witch woman's words. She pulled the tattered gown from under the bed, held it in her hands and chanted, 'Gris-gris, gris-gris grine!'" (p. 27).

Trait: Ability to gain people's attention
in a positive way

China: "Her loveliness made her seem a heavenly being, and the king suddenly knew in his heart that he had found his true love" (p. 26 unpaged).

Egypt: "Rhodopis would dance for her animal friends. She twirled so lightly that her bare feet barely touched the ground. One evening, her master awakened and saw her dance" (p. 6 unpaged).

Southern United States: "Suddenly, Moss Gown's hand brushed against the rags. She trembled, afraid that the Young Master would no longer love the girl in the tattered dress. But she dared ask, 'How much do you love me now?' 'More than ever!' declared the Young Master. 'Rags and tatters could never hide your beauty!'" (p. 38).

Trait: Development of a hobby or talent

China: "With Yeh Shen's talents in cooking and cleaning and sewing [abilities] there was to be done! Yeh-Shen had hardly a moment's rest" (p. 9 unpaged).

Egypt: "Sometimes, when her chores were done and the day had cooled, Rhodopis would dance [talent] for her animal companions" (p. 6 unpaged).

Southern United States: "The handsome young Master of the house came to her with outstretched hand and swirled her away in a dance" (p. 28).

Trait: Sense of humor

China: no mention of humor in *Yeh-Shen*.

Egypt: "Rhodopis [in *The Egyptian Cinderella*] bit her tongue. One show was worse than none at all. Now she'd have to dance like a stork hopping about on one foot [p. 14 unpaged] and even the monkey would laugh" (p. 15 unpaged).

Southern United States: "Moss Gown never smiled, or sang, or joked with the kitchen help" (p. 24).

247. *Moss Gown* **by William H. Hooks. Ill. by Donald Carrick. New York: Clarion, 1987.**
Theme: Perseverance; positive vision of life.
Overview: Banished by her father, Candace falls asleep but is awakened when she hears the singing of "Gris-gris, gris-gris grine. Who'll wear my magic gown?" Candace sees that the singer is a green-eyed witch woman who leaves the gown with Candace with a promise to return to her when the girl needs her. Candace goes to work as a scullery girl in a nearby mansion and attends the Master's ball. 4–5.

New Vocabulary: Plantation, mysterious swamp, skittering wind, snickered, murky, cypress, Spanish moss, gris-gris, gossamer, white-pillared, tatters.

Materials: Paper, pencils, chalk, chalkboard, supplementary books for reading.

Motivation (linking prior knowledge; "into" the reading activities):

1. Ask students to visualize a gossamer gown, a symbol of her positive vision of life. Have them quickly sketch the object on paper. In small groups, ask them to tell their classmates why they decorated the gown the way they did.

2. Show students the gown in the illustration in the story (pp. 17, 29). Cluster their reactions to the gown in writing on the writing board or overhead. Solicit possible thoughts about why this could be a symbol of Candace's positive vision of life.

3. Ask children if they have ever been in a situation of needing new clothes. Who helped them? Encourage them to share incidents that made them appreciate the person who helped them and that made them feel "positive" about life.

4. Write the vocabulary words, *gris-gris grine*, on the board. Have students turn to a partner and discuss the meaning of the words,

> Gris-gris woman work all night,
> weave a gown so fine
> stitch in stars and pale moonlight
> Gris-gris, gris-gris, grine...

Purpose for Reading or Listening: "You are going to read (hear) a story about a young girl named Candace who was banished from her father's house (given to her sisters when her father felt she did not love him as much as the other two sisters). Read (listen) to find out how Candace was reunited with her father and how the green-eyed black witch woman (the Gris-gris woman) helped her to overcome her problems."

Discussion Questions (through the reading activities):

1. What were the author's words to call back the slender black gris-gris woman? How did it work? Hooks, the author, mentions that *Moss Gown* is based on stories he heard as a child in North Carolina. Why do you suppose people told this story?

2. Describe how you think a day in Candace's life must have been before she was banished from her father's house.

3. Why do you think Candace put on the gown to walk toward the fine grand house? How do you think she was feeling when she saw the beautiful gown had turned into rags and gray moss?

4. How do you think she felt when she was sent to the kitchen to help

with the chores? What might *you* have said or done in this situation? What name would you have given to the cook?

5. How did Moss Gown get ready for the ball?

6. How did Candace and the young Master become friends?

7. What were Candace's feelings about the young Master by the end of the story?

8. How do you think the young Master felt about Candace?

9. What would *you* do if you discovered a beautiful stranger at your dance in your mansion?

10. How was Candace reunited with her father?

Retelling (through the reading activities):
Pairs of students roleplay the story taking turns being the slender black woman in the woods or Candace.

Extended Activities (beyond the reading activities):

1. Taking the role of Candace, invite children to write a letter to the gris-gris woman telling her how she helped you and why. Explain what happened and how grateful you are for her magic.

2. Introduce another character into the story who is a friend of Candace's. Suggest that children, from Candace's point of view, write a letter to her friend and tell her what happened.

3. Have children, from the friend's point of view, write back and ask questions about the events.

4. Suggest that children design/write the invitations to the dance that were sent out inviting people to come to the young Master's house.

5. Suggest that children write a welcome-back card to the father from Candace telling him how she feels now that he is back with her.

6. Invite children to rewrite the story with themselves as the main character and substitute their names for Candace. Encourage them to see how the ending to the story differs as their characters create dialogue different from that of Candace.

7. Suggest to children that they rewrite the story from the gris-gris woman's point of view.

Interdisciplinary Ideas:

Social Studies: Have children find books in the library that tell version of "Cinderella" or stories of magic from other cultures (e.g., Japan, China, Original Americans of North America, and Russia).

Recreational Reading: Have children look for folklore about servant girls and boys who receive magical clothing. Why do they suppose this story is found in several cultures?

Other Versions of Cinderella to Compare:
Afanasyev, Alexander. *Vasilisa the Beautiful.* Translated by Thomas P. Whitney. Ill. by Nonny Hogrogian. New York: Macmillan, 1970.

Clark, Ann Nolan. *In the Land of Small Dragon.* Ill. by Tony Chen. New York: Viking, 1979.

Grimm, Jakob and Wilhelm. *Cinderella.* Ill. by Paul Galdone. New York: McGraw-Hill, 1978.

Grimm, Jakob and Wilhelm. *Cinderella.* Retold by Barbara Karlin. Ill. by James Marshall. Boston: Little, Brown, 1989.

Grimm, Jakob and Wilhelm. *Cinderella.* Ill. by Errol LeCain. New York: Puffin Books, 1976.

San Souci, Robert D. *The Talking Eggs.* Ill. by the author. New York: Dial Books, 1989.

Winthrop, Elizabeth, adapter. *Vasilissa the Beautiful: A Russian Folktale.* Ill. by Alexander Koshkin. New York: HarperCollins, 1990.

Science: In a simple, truthful way, Candace told her father how much she loved him with the words, "Father, I love you more than meat loves salt." Investigate why meat would "love salt."

Art: With resources on dance, research some of the dances that could have been performed at the young Master's house. Have children construct colorful cutouts or make a diorama of the ball reminiscent of the times.

Math: Graph the number one version of Cinderella liked by the students in the class. Discuss the differences between versions.

Music: Suggest that children contribute musical notes for the words of the gris-gris song.

248. *My Name Is Not Angelica* by Scott O'Dell. Boston: Houghton Mifflin, 1989.

Theme: Perseverance.

Overview: In Barato, Africa, Konje, Raisha and Dondo are captured at a rival king's feast and sold as slaves. They are unloaded in St. Thomas (Danish Virgin Islands), participate in the slave revolt on St. John (1733–34), see the suicide leap by slaves into the sea, and hope for a better future. 4–8.

New Vocabulary: Survivor, Barato, St. Thomas, St. John, Danish Virgin Islands, revolt, Mary Point, Martinique.

Materials: Chalk, chalkboard, paper, pencils or pens, related books for further reading, African-American folk literature, materials for constructing a diorama.

Motivation (linking prior knowledge; "into" the reading activities):

1. Ask students to imagine/sketch this scene: You have been invited to enjoy a dinner and spend the night at the home of an acquaintance in a nearby town, when suddenly, while you are sleeping, you and two of your friends are dragged from your bed and put aboard a ship bound for

another land. In small groups, ask them to tell their classmates their feelings about this scene and what they would have done in the situation.

2. Discuss the custom of each of them receiving a new name when purchased by a planter.

3. Discuss with students the ways each African responded to this captivity in the strange surroundings. Encourage them to share incidents that shows that Dondo was docile and obedient on the outside while angry inside; that Konje showed his kingly bearing and attitude and escaped to Mary Point, the gathering place for runaway slaves on the island; that Raisha hated her new name and slavery but realized that rash action was dangerous for her.

4. Write the words *rash action* on the board. Have students turn to a partner and discuss, "One thing that reminds me of *rash action* is when..."

Purpose for Reading or Listening: "You are going to read (hear) a story about a girl named Raisha who was renamed Angelica when she was sold as a slave. Raisha hates her new name and the slavery her name represents. Read (listen) to find out how Raisha changed her belief from one of despair (and jumping into the sea from Mary Point) to one of "life forever." How did Konje's love help her make this decision?

Discussion Questions (through the reading activities):

1. In Africa, what trickery was played on Raisha, her family and friends at the rival King's feast?

2. Describe how you think a day in Raisha's life must have been before she became a slave.

3. What was the cause of Dondo's death?

4. How do you think Konje felt when he escaped to Mary Point, the stronghold of the runaways on the island? What might *you* have said or done if you had been with him when he escaped?

5. When did Raisha continue to work as a personal servant for Jenna van Prok and not escape? How did she finally escape?

6. When Captain Dumont arrived with his continent of soldiers to put down the revolt of the slaves, why did Raisha decide not to join the other slaves in their mass jump into the sea?

7. What were Raisha's feelings about Konje by the end of the story?

8. How do you think Konje felt about Raisha?

9. What would you do if you faced a choice of a mass jump into the sea with other slaves or "life forever"?

10. What are some ways you can help someone who is a member of the underclass, and who, as a result, may have no hope for a better life?

Retelling (through the reading activities):

Pairs of students roleplay the story taking turns being either Raisha or Konje.

Extended Activities (beyond the reading activities):

1. Taking the role of Raisha, have children write a page in her diary telling about the day when Jost Van Prok, a planter of Hawks Nest on the island of St. John, purchased Konje, Dondo, and Raisha. Explain how Raisha felt and what actions she planned to take.

2. Have students rewrite the event when Captain Dumont arrived at Mary Point with the soldiers. Encourage them to add their name in the event as a participant and one who was there to see this.

3. Have children rewrite the story from the point of view of Captain Dumont and the planters. Help them to imagine that the planters and the soldiers were afraid of the slaves in their revolt and needed the laborers to work in the fields.

4. Have students interview a student playing the role of Raisha. Questions can include, "When are you lonely? What is a day in your life like?" Help students to compare their lives of freedom with that of another who is not free.

5. Have children write a letter to Konje from Raisha telling Nat of her plans to escape to Mary Point.

Interdisciplinary Ideas:

Social Studies: Have children find books in the library that tell how members of the underclass are treated in other cultures (e.g., India, Arabic cultures).

Recreational Reading: Have children look for folklore about the desire of people to be free. Discuss how freedom is seen in these folktales and legends. Why do they suppose this is so? Select *The People Could Fly*, a collection of African-American folktales. The title tale tells of the ability of field laborers to fly away from the harsh life as slaves.

Science: Investigate the ways that people can send secret messages. Have students write expository paragraphs explaining the use of secret writing, secret codes, secret signals.

Art: Have children construct a diorama of the capture of Raisha and her family and friends at the rival king's feast in Africa.

Math: Count the number of books the students find that tell about slavery. Graph the information in categories (e.g., informational books, historical fiction, and biographies).

249. *The Pigs Are Flying* **by Emily Rodda. Ill. by Noela Young. New York: Greenwillow, 1986.**

Theme: Courage; problem-solving.

Overview: Rachel is bored and wishes something exciting would happen. She suddenly finds herself transported to a strange land where pigs fly and storms cause the inhabitants to behave strangely. 4–6.

New Vocabulary: Succession, thunderous, hordes, nickered, dicey, documented, bilious, subsidy, scatty, reproachfully, affinity, queue.

Materials: Butcher paper, tempera paint, trade books on Australia, trade books on meteorology.

Motivation (linking prior knowledge; getting "into" the reading activities):

1. Write on the blackboard the expression, "It's raining cats and dogs." Ask children what the expression means. Have them guess where they think the expression might have come from. Ask them if they think the saying might be confusing to people who are just learning to speak English.

2. Read children the book *Cloudy with a Chance of Meatballs* by Judi Barrett. Ask them to tell how they think they would feel if, in a storm, it were suddenly raining pancakes instead of rain. What would be some advantages of this? Some disadvantages?

Purpose for Reading: "You are about to read a story about a little girl who is just recovering from the flu. She is bored and wishes something exciting would happen. Read to find out what very unusual thing happens to Rachel."

Discussion Questions (through the reading activities):

1. Why was Rachel feeling bored?
2. How did she feel when she found she was riding a unicorn?
3. What happened in a "Grunter"?
4. What was happening to Gloria?
5. How did Gloria return to Bert and Enid?
6. How had Alex returned to the outside?
7. How had Sandy caused Rachel's adventure to happen?
8. Why had they both brought UEF Force 10 back with them?
9. Do you think Rachel will ever go back to the Inside? Why or why not?
10. What would you do with the UEF Force 10?

Retelling: Have children pretend they are Rachel trying to tell her friends about her adventure as an Outsider. How would they persuade their friends that such an unlikely adventure had actually occurred?

Extended Activities (beyond the reading activities):

1. Have children write the next chapter of the book in which Rachel and Sandy return as Outsiders.

2. Ask children to write an invitation to Enid and Bert inviting them to the Outside to see what life is like.

3. Encourage children to write a diary of the strange events that occurred as Rachel or Alex would have experienced it.

4. Have children write the dialogue for a conversation among three pigs at the beginning of a storm.

Interdisciplinary Ideas:

Social Studies: The author of this book, Emily Rodda, is from Australia. Hence, many of the expressions, e.g., "scatty," "dicey," "nickered," "queue," are different. Have children make an English/Australian dictionary with their findings of differences between the two dialects.

Language Arts/Economics: Have children, in small groups, decide how they would market bottles of UEF Force 10. Encourage them to write a one-minute commercial to sell the product to the American public.

Art: Post butcher paper along the length of one wall. First using pencil sketches and then tempera paints, allow children to make a mural of pigs in a "grunter."

250.   *The Secret of Gumbo Grove* by Eleanora E. Tate. New York: Franklin Watts, 1987.

Theme: Relationship with caring other person, positive vision of life.

Overview: Raisin is interested in history and talks to Miz Effie about the New Africa No. 1 Missionary Baptist Church Cemetery. Raisin says, "We read about people doing stuff in history class, but it was always about White people when it came to Calvary County. I asked Miz Gore, my teacher, how come we never studied about anybody Black and she said nobody Black around here had ever done anything worth talking about." Raisin wants to track down the mystery of a famous person who is buried in the cemetery. She has heard stories that most people in town don't want to be reminded of their family's past; Raisin gets help from her friends, Bunny, Sin-sin, Jeff, and Junebug. 4–6.

New Vocabulary: Harriet Tubman, Sojourner Truth, research, circa, historical.

Materials: Paper, pencils or pens, chalk, chalkboard, poster board, painting materials, related books for further reading.

Motivation (linking prior knowledge; "into" the reading activities):

1. Ask students to close their eyes and think of one thing that was a mystery they wanted to solve. Have them quickly sketch the scene on paper. In small groups, ask them to tell their classmates why they selected this mystery.

2. Show students the book cover. Cluster their reactions to the picture of Raisin and Miz Effie staring at the vine-covered tombstone in the cemetery at Gumbo Grove. Solicit possible reasons why they are there.

3. Ask children whether they have ever searched for information in a

cemetery. Encourage them to share examples of information that one can collect from the cemetery.

4. Write the word *secret* on the board. Have students turn to a partner and discuss, "One secret I knew about when. . ."

Purpose for Reading or Listening: "You are going to read (hear) a story about a girl named Raisin who was interested in history and who wanted to solve a mystery about a famous person. Read (listen) to find out how Raisin and her friends discover the name of the famous person who is buried in the cemetery.

Discussion Questions (through the reading activities):

1. What stories had Raisin heard about the cemetery? Were they true? Why did people tell these stories?

2. Describe how you think a day in Raisin's life must have been *before* she started helping Miz Effie clear the weeds from the cemetery.

3. Why was Miz Effie a person Raisin liked to talk with? How do you think Miz Effie felt when she had conversations with Raisin?

4. How do you think Raisin felt when she saw the tombstone with the words *G. Dickson*? What might *you* have said or done if you had been with Raisin?

5. When did Raisin first discover the secret of the mysterious person buried in the cemetery? Where did she find the information?

6. How did Raisin and Big Head (Jeff) become friends?

7. What were Jeff's feelings about Raisin by the end of the story?

8. How do you think Raisin felt about Jeff?

9. What would you do if you discovered someone famous buried in your church's cemetery? Who would you tell?

10. What are some ways you can conduct your own historical research about a famous person who lived in your community?

Retelling (through the reading activities):

Pairs of students roleplay the story taking turns being Raisin and Miz Effie.

Extended Activities (beyond the reading activities):

1. Taking the role of Raisin, have students write an entry in Raisin's diary about missing her chance to compete in the Miss Ebony Pageant. How did she feel and why? As Raisin, explain what you learned from this experience.

2. Have students rewrite the story with their name as one of the friends that helps Raisin. Put yourself in the action when Raisin goes over to Bunny's house—her first time out after being grounded at home. What does Raisin's mother mean when she says, "Don't be gone long, else you'll be right back here, nose flat on screen, watching the world go by."

3. Have children rewrite the event where Jeff shows Raisin the book of *Great Afro-American Heroes* and they look for the man who founded

Gumbo Grove. A picture shows that Gumbo Dickson was a Black man and did "big things"—was state senator, founded Gumbo Grove, and fought as a soldier in the Chesapeake campaign. However, the townspeople thought Dickson was White until he left a will saying he was of "African descent." And now, nobody knows where he is buried. Raisin thinks this is the biggest hero she has come close to in her life and she wants to look at the record books to see if there is a map showing where Dickson is supposed to be buried.

4. Have students discuss what it was like when the Reverend Walker, Raisin's folks, friends, and others went to the cemetery to clean it up. They planned to cut, chop, "shoo" snakes, and tote trash to the trucks. After the clearing and cleaning, Miz Effie and Raisin find the tombstone with the words, *G. Dickson.*

5. Later at the pageant, the president of the Calvary County Negro Business and Professional Women's Club gives the Alfronia Meriwether Community Service Award to the recipient for the current year in recognition of hard work, determination, and her commitment to preserve the cemetery—Miss Raisin Stackhouse. Acting as Raisin, write a thank-you letter from Raisin to the president for being recognized with the award.

Interdisciplinary Ideas:

Social Studies: Invite children to find books in the library that tell ways African-Americans have positive images and are respected (i.e., *A Weed Is a Flower* by Aliki Brandenburg, *Ashanti to Zulu* by Margaret Musgrove, *Jackie Robinson and the Story of All Black Baseball* by Jim O'Connor, *Cornrows* by Camille Yarbrough, and *Cherries and Cherry Pits* by Vera B. Williams).

Language Arts: Suggest children write the acceptance speech for Raisin to read when she receives her award.

Recreational Reading: Have children look for folklore about African-Americans: for example, *Bring the Rain to Kapiti Plain* by Verna Aardema, *Akimba and the Magic Cow* by Anne Rose, and *Abiyoyo* by Pete Seeger.

Science: When the Reverend Walker, Raisin's folks, friends, and others went to the cemetery to clean it up, they planned to cut, chop, and "shoo" snakes. Do research and discover which types of snakes live in this part of the country, their markings, and what habits they have.

Art: Have children construct a large poster of Raisin accepting her community service award.

Math: Graph the number of books in each category of literature (informational, realistic, historical, biographies) with African-American characters. Discuss some of the resiliency traits of the characters.

251. *Shaka: King of the Zulus* **by Diane Stanley and Peter Vennema. Ill. by Diane Stanley. New York: Morrow, 1988.**

Theme: Persistence; solving problems; sense of control over life.

Overview: A young boy, banished from his Zulu tribe, grows into manhood and becomes the leader of a great Zulu nation. Doing this, Shaka proves his resiliency time and again. 4–6.

New Vocabulary: Drought, fragile, bellow, regiment, colony, ferociously, uncontrollably, mourning, assassins, awesome.

Materials: Spear, pictures of Shaka, writing paper, pencils, butcher paper, string and stick.

Motivation (linking prior knowledge; "into" the reading activities):

1. Ask students to look at the map of Africa and locate southern Africa. Discuss a picture of members of the Zulu tribe that lived in tandem with the South Africans. The Zulu tribe currently has six million members who live there.

2. Show students the picture of Shaka on the cover. List their responses on the writing board to: What does Shaka apear to be doing? Where does he appear to be from? What jewelry is he wearing? Discuss headband, earrings, beads, and shield. How is he dressed? In what way does he look strong? Of what use are the spear and shield?

3. Imagine how you would feel if a wild animal were to spring at you: How would you feel? What would you do? What help would you want?

4. Write the word *banishment* on the board. Have students turn to a member of the class and discuss, "How I would feel if I had to leave my home as Shaka did..." Where would I go? What would I do? In what ways would I take care of my mother?

Purpose for Reading or Listening: "You will read a story about a brave boy named Shaka who was banished from his tribe when he was young. Read (listen) to find out how Shaka survives to become a great military leader of his Zulu nation."

Discussion Questions (through the reading activities):

1. When he was young, why was Shaka banned from the village?

2. How do you feel about the village rule that banished Shaka? Do you think the rule was too harsh? Fair? Unfair? Why/Why not? What does this rule tell you about the value of cattle and sheep to the Zulus? Is a rule always meant to do the "right thing"? Discuss the difference between a rule (legality) in a situation and "what's right." Invite children to think of times when a rule (legality) seems to interfere and keep people from doing "what's right."

3. Later in his life, the other young boys admired Shaka. Why do you think they looked up to him?

4. Tell what Shaka did when he saw the leopard in the tree.

5. Why was "believing" in himself the "best" or "greatest" reward for Shaka?

6. What does it mean that Shaka, the military leader, ruled through "force and fear"?

7. Why don't we admire the idea of ruling through force and fear today?

8. Why do you think the Europeans were afraid of the Zulus?

9. Why do you think Shaka was kind and friendly to the English?

10. How did Shaka mourn Nandi's death?

11. How was the spell of Shaka's misery of his mother's death broken?

12. Have you ever heard the expression, "If a person lives by the sword, a person may die by the sword?" If so, can you tell how this saying might/might not relate to this story?

Retelling (through the reading activities):

Pairs of students use signal words of first, second, third, next, and finally to retell the main actions in the story.

Reviewing the sequence of events, have children tell what happened, and on the writing board, record key words on diamond shapes (geometric shapes found in the Zulu borders in the book) and link the shapes together closely. Explain what you learned about Shaka and his life.

Extended Activities (beyond the reading activities):

1. Take the role of a Zulu home guard and imagine that you are upset because you have just come home from a long war campaign. You expected to return for a feast and a celebration. Instead, Shaka orders you (and others) to march past your home, without rest, and head to another war, far to the north. Fortunately, you find out (that as an older boy who carried soldier's gear) you are to stay home and be a soldier in a home guard. Some of the home guard are plotting against Shaka (to kill him) and you join them in the evening when they meet at the Kraal. You are against this plot. Isn't there an alternative solution? How would you argue your point? What reasons would you have against the plot?

In cooperative discussion groups, discuss this situation and then ask a volunteer in your group to give your group's solution to the total group.

2. From Shaka's point of view, have children rewrite the event where Shaka as a herdboy let something happen to one of the sheep he was guarding. When the wild dog killed the sheep, the Chief was angry at Shaka and his mother. How did you (Shaka) feel when the sheep was killed? When your father was angry? When your mother took your side? When your father, the chief, became angry and ordered your mother to return to her family and clan? After writing this point of view, ask children to team up with response partners and read their writing to each other for feedback. The children may rewrite if they wish.

3. Suggest that children write diary entries from the European's point of view. Help them to imagine the first time that the Europeans saw Shaka and the Zulu tribe.

4. Suggest that children write diary entries from Shaka's point of view. Help them to imagine the first time that Shaka saw the Europeans.

5. Engage children in writing their thoughts about ruling through "force and fear." Realizing that Shaka led his armies through "force and fear," what would be some of the other ways he could have led his armies? What would be a way to rule where the end result would be peace?

6. Engage children in writing a eulogy for this great Zulu king through this imagined setting: Imagine you are a member of the Zulu army who loved Shaka, your king. You respected him because he was a great leader, a fighter, a builder of the Zulu nation. He was one of the finest warriors in Africa. You have been selected to give a brief speech about his life and greatness (eulogy). What are you going to say? Write your thoughts out before you give the speech.

Interdisciplinary Ideas:

Social Studies: With a map or globe, locate the historical home of the Zulus (northeast part of Natal, South Africa), brave, tall, handsome people of South Africa. According to Zulu custom, their kraals, or villages, are shelters arranged in a circle to keep the cattle inside and to protect them.

Engage students in locating information about the Zulu tribe of to-day to compare with the information in the book about the Zulu tribe in the 1800s. Refer to *The Zulus of South Africa: Cattlemen, Farmers, and Warriors* (Morrow, 1970) by Sonia Bleeker.

Select *The Diary of Henry Francis Finn* (Pietermaritzburg, South Africa: Shuter and Shooter, 1950) edited by J. Stewart and D. McMalcolm. Find the entry where Finn talks about his first impressions of the Zulus and compare this entry with the one you wrote.

Social Studies/Art: Ask the children to turn the events in the time line into scenes for a mural on the classroom wall.

Recreational Reading: Suggest that children look for more stories about Zulu kings in *The Zulu Kings* (Scribner's Sons, 1974) by Brian Roberts.

Science: Invent an assagai (spear). Imagine that you are Shaka and you determine that you hate throwing your weapon away in battle and want to keep your spear to use as a sword. However, when you use your spear as a sword, you find that the head of the spear is too light and the shaft is too long and fragile. Design a new weapon. In addition to making it useful as a sword, try to balance the spear (balance the proportion and weight of the head to the shaft so it flies straight when you throw it).

Science/Art: Have children create drawings of leopards and conduct research to find out where they live, eat and sleep.

Math: Show the children the circular shape of a Zulu home. Distribute lengths of string and sticks and ask the students to figure out how to use these objects to show (draw) a circular line in the ground and mark the location of a new Zulu home. By looking at the illustrations in the book and the size of the Zulu homes to the people themselves, the nearby trees, and other objects, how big (tall, wide) would the children estimate a Zulu home to be?

Language: Pronounce the Zulu words presented in the pronunciation guide in the front of the book. Talk about their meanings and the ways they differ from English spellings.

Index

References are to entry numbers, not pages.